Praise for *Profess*

"Bowdoin faculty members Connelly and (..... wno've strug-
gled with the challenges of research, teaching, publishing, and caring for children in defiance of the conventional wisdom that women in academia have
to choose between family and career. . . . They are frank about sacrifices and
chall_____ _____d _____ _____ _____ ___ ___ PhD disserttion, and

the   tions,
and   ic life
and   eciate
this   *oklist*

"T\   1 aca-
der   omen
see   . . . A
wel

"P1   1 aca-
der   . An
ove

seling

"With this new how-to guide for mothers in academia, Rachel Connelly
and Kristen Ghodsee invite women academics to muster their courage and
proceed despite the potential pitfalls. Their unblinking analysis of the risks
and rewards of combining academic life with motherhood is a welcome and
unique addition to the literature on the topic. . . . The book is an essential
resource for anyone considering the life of a 'professor mommy.'"

—On Campus With Women,
Association of American Colleges and Universities

"Don't believe the myths—you can conquer the academy while raising children. It isn't easy but few worthwhile things in life are. Connelly and Ghodsee show, step by step, how smart women win at work and win at home by protecting their time and focusing on what matters most (hint: it's not grading papers or ironing shirts!)."

—Laura Vanderkam, author of
168 Hours: You Have More Time Than You Think

"Rachel Connelly and Kristen Ghodsee have written a book that is not just a must-read for anyone contemplating the intricate and as-yet imperfect balance of academic life and family life but for anyone at all interested in promoting equity in the workplace and, more importantly, in the world of ideas. They show it is not easy, but it is indeed possible to be both a successful academic and a loving parent with a rich family life. More, *Professor Mommy* is a call to action: that lasting change and that longed-for balance will come only when men become aware of the stacked deck against women and when women academics make the hard decision not to opt out but to opt in, writing, publishing, thinking, promoting their ideas, and by their very presence, change the calcified system from within."

—Brigid Schulte, *Washington Post*, Pulitzer Prize co-winner

Professor Mommy

Professor Mommy

Finding Work-Family Balance in Academia

RACHEL CONNELLY AND
KRISTEN GHODSEE

ROWMAN & LITTLEFIELD PUBLISHERS, INC.
Lanham • Boulder • New York • Toronto • Plymouth, UK

Published by Rowman & Littlefield Publishers, Inc.
A wholly owned subsidiary of The Rowman & Littlefield Publishing Group, Inc.
4501 Forbes Boulevard, Suite 200, Lanham, Maryland 20706
http://www.rowmanlittlefield.com

Estover Road, Plymouth PL6 7PY, United Kingdom

British Library Cataloguing in Publication Information Available

The hardback edition of this book was previously cataloged by the Library of Congress as
follows:

Connelly, Rachel.
  Professor mommy : finding work-family balance in academia / Rachel Connelly and
  Kristen Ghodsee.
    p. cm.
  Includes index.
    1. Women college teachers—United States—Social conditions. 2. Women in higher
  education—United States—Social conditions. 3. Work and family—United States.
  4. Working mothers—United States. I. Ghodsee, Kristen Rogheh, 1970– II. Title.
  LB2332.3.C66 2011
  378.082—dc22   2011006009

ISBN 978-1-4422-0858-2 (cloth : alk. paper)
ISBN 978-1-4422-0859-9 (pbk. : alk. paper)
ISBN 978-1-4422-0860-5 (electronic)

∞™ The paper used in this publication meets the minimum requirements of
American National Standard for Information Sciences—Permanence of Paper for
Printed Library Materials, ANSI/NISO Z39.48-1992.

Printed in the United States of America

For our children

Contents

Preface to the Paperback Edition   xi

Acknowledgments   xvii

*Introduction: Why We Decided to Write This Book and
Who We Are Anyway*   1

1 A Success Story—Told with the 20/20 Vision of Hindsight   13

2 The Nefarious Nine, or The Not-So-Pretty Truth about
Motherhood and Academia   23

3 Know Thyself, Part I: On Deciding to Become an Academic   41

4 Know Thyself, Part II: Deciding Whether to Become a Mother,
How Many Children to Have, and When to Have Them   63

5 The Last Year of Graduate School: Heading for the Job Market
and Choosing the Right Institution   83

6 On the Tenure Track, Part I: Research and Networking   111

7 On the Tenure Track, Part II: Teaching, Service, and Finding
Time for Your Family   135

8 So You Made It: The Early Years after Tenure   157

9 Coming Up for Full Professor: Your Last Promotion   171

Conclusion   181

Afterword   187

Appendix 1: Association of American Universities—Members   197

Appendix 2: The Other Perspective: Words from Our Children   201

Notes   203

Suggested Reading   213

Index   215

About the Authors   227

Preface to the
Paperback Edition

When we wrote *Professor Mommy*, the term "lean in" had not yet entered popular parlance. Just a few months before *Professor Mommy* was published, Sheryl Sandberg gave her TED talk, "Why We Have Too Few Women Leaders." She offered women three pieces of advice to help them navigate the slippery rungs of the corporate ladder. While noting that employer policies such as "flextime and mentoring and programs companies should have to train women" were "really important," Sandberg chose to focus instead on things individual women could do on their own, without waiting for institutional change.

Her advice was: "One, sit at the table. Two, make your partner a real partner. And three, don't leave before you leave." It was in elaborating on that third piece of advice that she first used the term "leaning back" to describe women not pushing ahead with their careers in anticipation of childbearing (instead of at the moment of childbearing). In the Barnard College commencement address Sandberg gave six months later, she offered the women graduates of that prestigious institution almost the same advice, except she had changed the third piece of advice to the affirmative. Instead of warning the young women not to "lean back," she urged them to "lean in." It was from there that the term created a neo-feminist buzz. A quick Google search of "lean in" yields thousands of hits and almost as many meanings.

But we think it is important to focus on Sandberg's own meaning of "lean in," a personal choice women make to stay in the "game." Is the lack of women in upper management really the fault of women themselves choosing to "opt out" (to use a now passé turn of phrase) or is the problem more structural? By structural, we mean that the employer expectations and rules, in conjunction with government policies in employment, child care, and education, result in a workplace which is inherently inaccessible to women with children. To get a feel for this question, think about Rapunzel up in the tower. Is the problem that she is just afraid to jump or that she knows full well that jumping is suicidal? After all, if the tower builders wanted Rapunzel to be able to descend, wouldn't they have built a staircase?

Anne-Marie Slaughter's cover story in *The Atlantic Monthly* in the summer of 2012, "Why Women Still Can't Have It All," presents, in some ways, the opposing side of Sandberg's argument. After years and years of playing the game, Slaughter concludes that the tower is just too tall, no matter whether there are stairs or not. Slaughter, a full professor at Princeton, appears to us, as she must to many of you readers, as a woman who does "have it all," if having it all is husband, kids, and a tenured position at a Research I university. But Slaughter argues that she didn't realize how important the flexibility of time and place of her academic job were to her success until she took the job in Washington with the State Department. In a response piece ten days after her original article was published, Slaughter attributed her success to the fact that she was an academic and had the ability to manage her own schedule. She writes, "That made it possible for me to juggle work and family all the way up through a deanship and again today." In addition to a call for more flexibility in the workplace, Slaughter wants to challenge the expectations of employers who demand unreasonably long hours from salaried employees. She advocates for a reduction in the length of the workday so that both men and women can better balance work and family responsibilities. In other words, Slaughter argues that we should all be spending less time climbing up ladders (or down those towers without stairs).

Slaughter's article fanned the flames of the debate Sandberg's advice had sparked. Can women have it all, and if they don't have it all, is it somehow their own fault? Many people have weighed in on what has become a new cultural touchstone. Fathers pointed out that they couldn't "have it all" either. Many women criticized both Sandberg and Slaughter for focusing only on women at the top. What about the other 99%?, asks Laura McKenna in a blog response at *The Atlantic* website. Others have accused Sandberg of being a lackey of corporate capitalism. In a 2013 piece in *The Baffler* magazine, Susan Faludi points out that Sandberg's admonition for women to "lean in" is really just telling already overworked women to work harder, a message that benefits employers far more than it benefits women. Still others have written about accepting that life has tradeoffs, and questioned the value of "having it all" in the first place. Some choose to scale it down on the work front, while others say they are happy with their frantic juggling lifestyle. In both cases, it is important to accept one's choices, even when those choices are limited by institutional or structural constraints. So how does *Professor Mommy* fit into this larger media debate about work/family balance?

We wrote *Professor Mommy* just before Sandberg gave her TED talk and well before Slaughter's piece in *The Atlantic Monthly*, but we clearly were grappling with the same set of issues. There are things we can do individually to increase our chances of success in the institutional landscape of the academic labor market. This is the parallel to Sandberg's argument. And at the same time, the realities of the academic labor market place higher stumbling blocks in front of women than men, because of the coincidence of tenure clocks and biological clocks. This parallels Slaughter's argument.

Let's consider both perspectives in the context of finding work/family balance in academia, starting with Slaughter. We agree with Slaughter that the flexibility of time and place help academic mothers successfully juggle work and family. This is what we argued when we suggested that women considering an academic job should compare it to the time commitments of alternative career paths. If your alternative career is to become a lawyer, for example, it is unlikely that your work as an attorney will be as flexible in time of day and place as that of an academic. But we also urged our readers to steer clear of the flexibility trap. Just because you have a flexible schedule does not mean that you should always be the one to taxi the kids around or to stay home when they are sick. No one else does your work for you when you are attending to the children. Slaughter is also correct that time expectations for many careers (and we would include academics in this group, though it's not clear whether she would) are very high, and that fact alone makes it very difficult to juggle "full-time" (read "full-time" as lots of overtime) employment with the time demands of very young children. University demands on faculty time are ever increasing; we all need to collectively stand up against the American culture of overwork.

But, before you despair and throw this book back on the shelf, remember the wise words of Rachel's mother, "It gets easier." Some recent academic research of Rachel's with coauthor Jean Kimmel is relevant here. They find that mothers and fathers with preschoolers were happier in their everyday activities if the mother was not employed compared to mothers and fathers with preschool-age children where the mother was employed full time. However, the happiness differential between working moms and stay at home moms disappears when the sample was limited to those mothers and fathers whose youngest child was school aged. In other words, it is the early years that are the hardest ones, but it gets easier.

The most important way in which we agree with Slaughter is that institutions *need to be* part of the solution. In chapter 10, we wrote briefly about the important role that tenured women faculty (who are also mothers) can play in improving the chances for the next generation of professor mommies. We wrote, "Once your kids are older, it is time to give back and make the academy a better place for work-family balance. After you have achieved tenure, lobby for changes at your institution. Institutional changes are essential, but they take time and sustained effort." Slaughter's *Atlantic* piece, in conjunction with conversations we have had with a number of our readers since writing *Professor Mommy*, have convinced us that we should offer some more specific advice on how to achieve institutional change, just as we offered very specific self-help advice. In this updated version of *Professor Mommy*, we have added a new afterword, which focuses on the role that tenured faculty members can play in pushing our institutions toward much needed structural change.

But let's come back to Sandberg; we should not entirely give up on the insights gained from her experiences in both government and the corporate world. One interpretation of what Sandberg is saying is that we can't wait for institutions to change even though we, as women, need to work to make it happen. Instead, says Sandberg, there are three things an individual woman can do for herself that will help her play in the "big leagues." Most of the advice in *Professor Mommy* can be characterized in a similar way. Yes, institutions need to be changed, but in the meantime, there are things that you can do on your own to increase your chances of success. "Know what you want." "Be prepared to make trade-offs." "Use your time wisely, both at work and at home." "Let some of the housework go undone." "Let some the 'extra-curricular' committee work go undone." (We are even so blasphemous as to say, "Let some of the child care go undone." You don't have to attend every soccer practice. You don't have to attend every high school debate. You might even let your child [gasp!] turn in his assignment without checking it first.)

Sandberg's three self-help suggestions do ring true in the employment world we know best, the world of the academy. "Sitting at the table" translates into making sure that you publish and then that you let others know what you have published by presenting papers at conferences and by participating in panels. We discuss "making your partner a real partner" in chapter 3 when we urge you to think about the nature of an academic career and how that will interface with your partner's plans. Having a partner who is doing his or her share of the child care and housework is certainly a wonderful thing (something on which Sandberg and Slaughter agree and with which we are also currently blessed, thanks to our own equal partners), but in chapter 4 we also argue that even the lack of a partner can be worked around. We have talked to enough single professor mommies out there to be able to say with 100% certainty that this too can be done. It requires a willingness to outsource, to compromise, and to prioritize children and work over everything else. We do not mean to minimize the difficulty, but we refuse to shut down the possibility. Our advice is to be creative in finding solutions to your own specific challenges. To abuse the Rapunzel metaphor for a bit longer, why not just grow your hair really long and use it as a rope to get down from that tower?

This brings us back to Sandberg's third piece of advice, to "lean in." Ultimately, *Professor Mommy* is a book for those who want to consider "leaning in" to the world of employment in the academy, even as we recognize that there are growing challenges. We offer many very specific suggestions (not just three general ones) which we hope will help you to be successful at what you do. The suggestions are arranged in chronological order of graduate school, pre-tenure, early post-tenure, and later post-tenure. In each time period, we consider 1) research, 2) teaching, 3) service to your department, the college or university, and your professional organizations, and 4) family issues. Of course, people have children at different times along the academic ladder, so you might want to look ahead or back when you get to the family sections. Our advice about children is much less specific than the advice about maneuvering through hiring, tenure, and promotion since there are many more books out there on child-raising. Where we do make a contribution is in how to combine family life and academic life (such as taking your children along on research trips or to academic conferences), and in how to make good use of the resources of the university for child enrichment. We think our children would agree that a college campus is a very fun place to grow up.

There are great rewards to be had from combining an academic job with parenting. In the jargon of economists, both endeavors offer strong positive long-term gains, but require substantial early investments. Our goal in writing *Professor Mommy* was to help ease some of those early investments so that you can focus on both the finish line and the beautiful scenery along the route. With this new edition and the added afterword, we hope you will share our advice and make the path smoother for the professor parents who will follow in your footsteps.

Rachel and Kristen
Brunswick, Maine

Acknowledgments

Rachel would like to thank her Bowdoin colleagues for making her job the best gig around, and her wonderful cohort of women economists who have been fellow travelers on this experimental journey. We thought we could do it, and we did. Thanks to Michael for totally believing that we could do this and being Da to our children. Finally, thanks to my mother for jumping in on so many occasions. I had the best role model one could want for the Mommy side of my life.

Kristen would like to thank all of her mentors, but especially Pedro Noguera, Irene Tinker, Caren Kaplan, Joan Scott, and Jennifer Scanlon for their support and guidance over the years. She would also like to thank her friends, family members, and wonderful colleagues at Bowdoin for providing backup when it was needed, and especially Scott for being such a supportive partner (and willing editor) and Rachel for her encouragement and advice. Finally, she would like to thank her daughter for her endless patience and understanding when Mommy is working.

Kristen and Rachel would like to thank Martin Connelly, Scott Sehon, Michael Connelly, and Emily Connelly, who read and commented on early drafts of the manuscript and gave us invaluable feedback. Special appreciation goes out to our editor Sarah Stanton at Rowman and Littlefield for encouraging us to write this book and giving us her thoughts and guidance along the way. Most importantly, we would like to thank all the professor/mothers who took time out of their busy days and responded to our surveys, sharing their personal experiences and strategies for success. Although we have changed their names, they know who they are, and we owe them a great debt of gratitude.

Rachel and Kristen
March 2011

Introduction

Why We Decided to Write This Book and Who We Are Anyway

It was in the meeting with the dean and associate dean of academic affairs that Kristen started leaking. She sat mortified, listening to them explain the possible benefits package that she would get if she were lucky enough to be offered the tenure-track job. As the deans spoke about health and dental benefits and how much the college would contribute to her retirement account, she was silently becoming hysterical as the cotton pads in her bra quickly became saturated with milk. Kristen was just finishing up her PhD at Berkeley, and this was her first on-campus interview. She had delivered her baby by caesarean section less than a month earlier, and had been contacted for a telephone interview within a week of leaving the hospital.

Her mind clouded by lack of sleep and a necessary regimen of prescription painkillers, she asked the department to call her cell phone, and she answered their questions from her car because she was terrified that they would hear the cries of a newborn baby in the background. This was 2001, but Kristen had been warned that certain departments would look unfavorably on her status as a new mother, fearing that her family obligations would compromise her ability to publish high-quality scholarship and thereby weaken her chances of getting tenure. It was a logistical feat of Himalayan proportions to leave her little daughter and fly from California to Maine for a two-day interview, all the while pretending that she was just another childless graduate student.

The interviews started at 8:30 a.m. and followed one after another until 3:00 p.m. Lunch was shared with another group of faculty, and even when she found a moment to use the restroom there was never enough time to pump. Some faculty member was always waiting outside to take her to the next interview. Kristen had put the cotton bra pads in as a precaution, but she had never been away from her baby long enough for them to be necessary. And she had pumped for thirty minutes in the morning. She thought that would be sufficient.

Instead, the cotton pads soaked through within moments, and Kristen felt the milk stain spreading out under the sleeve of her brand-new interview suit. She pulled her arms in close to her body, hoping they would not see the ever-widening wet splotch. If they did notice, she hoped they might think it was perspiration and that she was merely nervous and sweating. When they asked her if she had any questions for them, she cheerfully smiled and said, "Not at the moment, but I am sure I might have some later after I read through all of these materials." She grabbed the thick folder that they had prepared and abruptly stood up, extending her hand just enough to shake their hands before mumbling something about wanting to have some time to get ready for her job talk.

According to her preset interview schedule, she was supposed to have half an hour to prepare for her one-hour talk at 4:00. It was 3:36 when she left the deans' office and was finally left alone. Rather than going through her slides or reviewing her main arguments, Kristen spent all twenty-four minutes frantically pumping her milk into a sink while trying to get the wet spot out of her jacket with a wall mounted hand dryer at the same time, praying that no one would walk in. Her little handheld pump needed to be squeezed constantly, and the dryer kept automatically turning off. She caught a glimpse of herself in the mirror, one hand pressed against the large silver button of the dryer, one breast hanging out of her button-down shirt, body oddly contorted to maximize the direct airflow onto the milk stain, the other hand squeezing furiously as thick white streams splashed into the porcelain basin, swearing all sorts of obscenities under her breath and wishing that she had not come.

A wave of doubt overcame her. She felt a hot tear of frustration roll down her cheek. "There is no way I can do this," she thought. "How am I going to start a new job with a new baby? How am I ever going to finish my dissertation? When will I be able to spend time with my daughter? Maybe I should just stay in school for a few more years. Or maybe I should file the dissertation and take a few years off. I'll never get an academic job in California, and I don't know anyone here. It's just too hard."

But Kristen's story worked out in the end. Mammary ducts emptied and suit jacket relatively dry, she gave her job talk and was offered an assistant professorship. Rachel, the chair of the search committee, was outraged when she eventually found out that Kristen had left a twenty-seven-day-old baby at home in California.

"Why didn't you tell us? You could have brought her along."

"I was afraid it would be held against me," Kristen replied. "I wanted to be seen as a young scholar. Not as a new mother."

"But you can be both!"

"It doesn't feel like it," said Kristen. "It really doesn't feel like it."

And it was in that moment, a decade ago, that the initial seed of the idea for this book was planted.

It was our idea to write a book that would refute the false dichotomy set up by those who believe that postponement or opting out are the only choices. These two points of view often dominate the debate, and young women like Kristen feel caught in an impossible dilemma: to have a family or to have an academic career. Yet there are many examples of women in the academy today who have successfully combined the two. The trouble is that their voices are rarely heard. These women are simply too busy to attend meetings on work/family issues or to write about their experiences and offer advice and mentorship to their younger colleagues. Until now. This book is designed as a step-by-step guide to being *both* a parent and a professor, starting from graduate school, through the job search, tenure, and all the way to becoming a full professor. Our goal is not only to explain how it can be done, but how it can be done well, with the minimum amount of guilt and compromise and a maximum amount of sanity and satisfaction.

One look at the growing number of women with new PhDs each year and it is clear that this book is needed now more than ever. Between 1995 and 2005, the percentage of PhDs earned by women grew nearly 20 percent, from 44 percent to 51 percent. Even more striking are the changing demographics of faculties across the United States.[1] In 1995, women made up 35 percent of full-time faculty. Within ten years, that figure had increased to 41 percent. While more women are in the assistant-professor and lecturer/

instructor ranks than in the associate- and full-professor ranks, these latter categories have seen the largest percentage of growth for women. Women in the associate-professor rank have grown from 32 to 39 percent, and women in the full-professor rank have increased from 18 to 25 percent.[2] These results show that many more women are achieving tenure. But can they have tenure and their families too?

While we discuss research that finds that early childbearing is associated with lower rates of tenure attainment and lower publication rates, it is important to note that fully half of women in the sciences and 38 percent of women in the humanities and social sciences do have children in their households when they receive tenure.[3] We know all too well that many young faculty women are nervous and confused about when to start a family and how it will affect their chances of professional success. Many inevitably postpone childbearing until they are of an age when their chances of having children are considerably diminished or to a point at which they are forced to use medical interventions that are physiologically draining as well as costly. Unlike their male peers, women in the academy face what economist Sylvia Ann Hewlett calls "the unforgiving decade": between graduate school, postdoctoral fellowships, and the tenure track, women often lose the thirteen or fourteen years of their life that are most physiologically optimal for childbearing because they are consumed with the demands of research, teaching, and publication.[4] Those who decide not to postpone motherhood face seemingly insurmountable challenges and often outright discrimination in the academy. Finding a non-academic job or opting out of the labor market altogether seems a better path for women who claim to be tired of the "rat race" anyway. But we want to encourage young women not to capitulate to these pressures so easily, no matter how difficult the challenges they face. With a little planning, and a lot of self-knowledge and discipline with your time, it is possible to do both. This book will help you learn how to achieve family and professional success.

CHILDLESSNESS VERSUS OPTING OUT

There is a certain type of woman in the academy who is brilliant, productive, and universally acclaimed for her contributions to the enhancement of collective knowledge of humankind. She has a CV as long as Kant's *Critique of Pure Reason,* and she jets around the world dazzling scholarly audiences with her latest research findings. She sits on the boards of major foundations, and university presses clamor to publish her next tome. She is *Academus superstarus*, the kind of scholar who inhabits the intellectual stratosphere, only rarely descending to cavort with the mere mortals who are her graduate students or less esteemed colleagues. Although she has many things in common with the males of her species, unlike them she is usually childless.

Whether the result of a deliberate choice or the outcome of what Hewlett dubbed the "creeping non-choice" (whereby professional women delay child-bearing to the point of infertility),[5] *Academus superstarus* tends to view her childlessness as an almost necessary precondition for a successful intellectual career. Although women have been making steady advances into the academy over the last three decades, scholarly life in the United States is still a deeply masculinist culture; there is a continued expectation that professors are not the primary caregivers to their children.

This is at least partially the result of yet another creature to be found roaming the halls of the proverbial Ivory Tower—*Spousus supportus*. The unpredictability of the academic job market means that young PhDs have to be ready and willing to move anywhere their careers take them, and their partners have to be ready and willing to follow them. It is not surprising that most of the time the *Spousus supportus* is a woman and that, in addition to supporting her partner's academic career, she throws herself into child rearing once the couple starts a family. These women are often the übermoms who attend all of the PTA meetings, organize the school fundraisers, go to all of the soccer games and band concerts, and then find time to bake cookies using organic wheat grown cooperatively in local community gardens. Although there are more and more men who are involved in parenting these days, there are still a lot of men who have stay-at-home partners, especially at the more elite institutions. *Professorus breadwinnerus* rarely has to worry about being late to pick up the children from day care or about what to do when children are home sick. When a crucial deadline nears, he can toil long into the night and through the weekend, safe in the knowledge that his children are well cared for by their loving, selfless, and dedicated mother.

Then there is this poor creature stuck in the middle—*Professorus momus*. Balancing a career and family, she worries that she will never achieve the academic-superstar status of her childless female colleagues, nor will she ever be as "good" a mother as the stay-at-home partners of her male colleagues. At best, she fears she is destined to be a mediocre scholar and a mediocre mother, never able to fully dedicate herself to either role, constantly trying to find the balance between the two so that one does not overwhelm the other. The number of women in this category is now quite substantial. The frustrations of being a professor and a parent are deeply felt. Many women are starting to speak out about the challenges they face and advocating for changes in the system that would make work-family balance something other than a hopeless fantasy.

A recent book, *Mama, PhD*, and the accompanying blog on the Inside Higher Education website[6] reflect this growing frustration. The editors of *Mama, PhD* have tackled these issues head on, collecting testimonials from a wide array of women in the academy and describing their various experiences on and off the tenure track. The book was an original and much-needed contribution, and we were both delighted to see a collection that specifically addressed the plight of academic mothers. *Mama, PhD* was a necessary first step, but there is something about the tone of the book that deeply disturbs us.

Although the editors tried to represent a wide variety of views from different women, the book seems to focus on the women who decided to opt out of academia and do something else with their degrees so they could spend more time with their children. A large section of the book, called "The Recovering Academic," pathologizes the scholarly life and celebrates the women who were brave enough to abandon the rat race. The early *Mama, PhD* blog also featured proportionally more stories from women who chose to give up the academy for what they perceived as a more fulfilling and family-friendly life. Another recent collection of essays, *Motherhood, the Elephant in the Laboratory: Women Scientists Speak Out*,[7] also contains a plethora of negative messages for young scholars, detailing the near impossibility of having children and being a laboratory research scientist. A faithful reader of these books cannot help but be left with the impression that being a *Professorus momus* is too difficult a task for any normal woman. While the editors of both books probably hoped to be inclusive, to empower and legitimize the choices of different women, the mix of experiences highlighted tends to do the opposite—it may scare many women from their goals before they have even made an attempt to succeed.

We worry particularly about how these messages affect undergraduate students, graduate students, postdocs, and assistant professors. For young women not yet fully participants in the profession, the overall message is that being a mom and a professor is so hard that it might not be worth doing. The testimonials advise young women that there are other uses of their PhDs that will make their lives easier. After all, look at all these smart women who are staying home with their children, free from the awesome pressures and frustrating unpredictability of academic publishing. The academic job market is shrinking, tenure standards are increasing, and the demands made on faculty time are constantly expanding—what person in her right mind would want to become a professor under these circumstances, particularly if it means giving up the opportunity to have a family?

The truth is that many of the women who are successful professors and mothers simply do not have the extra time to write about their experiences, and so their voices are not heard. The women who have opted out of the academy have more free time and the luxury of writing for publication in places other than the peer-reviewed journals that "count" toward tenure and promotion. So it should not be surprising that we will hear more from the point of view of the women who have found alternative uses for their degrees. Although we also struggled to find the time to write a book like this one, we felt it was important to speak out and represent the experience of women who have successfully negotiated this balance.

In addition, we worry that *Mama, PhD* and *Elephant in the Laboratory* implicitly support the myth that outright sex discrimination toward women is largely a thing of the past. This is a dangerous attitude, because sex discrimination is by no means extinct in the academy. Sex discrimination, not parental discrimination, is the reason why women faculty members tend to receive lower student-opinion-form ratings than men.[8] The "old boys' network" continues to operate throughout the academy, through all the old paths and some new ones: Who gets which advisor in graduate school? Who plays basketball with whom at lunchtime? Which job candidate do the senior male faculty members in the department just feel "more comfortable" talking with? We hope this book also helps to persuade women faculty members to be on the lookout for the ugly remnants of sex discrimination as it interacts with discrimination against parents.

Yet another omission of recent books on academic motherhood is the failure to recognize that pursuing an academic career is also difficult for many men with children—although the November 2010 book *Papa, PhD* does begin to address this omission.[9] There is a whole new breed of young male academics who father in ways that also require trade-offs, and who face similar problems with work-family balance (though none of them need to worry about pregnancy or breastfeeding). We do recognize the contribution of fathers and the challenges that men, particularly untenured faculty members, face to be active fathers and scholars, but in this book we will focus on women. We know that there will be plenty of people who will ask why we don't spend an equal amount of time talking about fathers. Without trying to seem biologically deterministic about these things, as we write this book it is still a fact that individuals who bear children—that is, those who get pregnant and gestate fetuses, give birth, and breast-feed—have the reproductive organs associated with the female sex. Perhaps more important, and more specific to academia, is the fact that the timing of the tenure track coincides exactly with the woman's most fertile reproductive years. Given how long it takes most graduate students to earn a PhD, the vast majority of aspiring academics do not begin tenure-track jobs until their early to mid-thirties. Until science can help make it otherwise, women's fertility drastically declines after age thirty-five. This means that the years most women will spend trying to earn tenure will coincide with the last decade of their most fertile years. This is simply not true for men, who can generally still father children well into their fifties. Men cannot get pregnant, and there are no artificial wombs; pregnancy cannot yet be outsourced to machines.[10] Until the current tenure system—which is so heavily modeled on the male biological model that a man can establish himself professionally throughout his thirties and then settle down with a younger partner and have children once he has achieved tenure and scholarly recognition in his field—is completely revamped, we feel that it makes the most sense to focus on women, even if we end up excluding a discussion of the challenges faced by young men on the tenure track.[11]

Our purpose here is simple. Rather than merely celebrating the diversity of choices that PhD students might have, we decided to write a how-to book for those women who want to pursue a position in the professoriate and also have a family. Despite the fact that we will be brutally honest about the challenges that these women will face, our overall message is a positive one. Yes, it can be done. And yes, it is absolutely worth it. No, it will not be painless. But few career paths as prestigious and rewarding as academia are easy. We are not going to pretend that combining academic work and family is simple, but we are convinced that it is not as hard as many young women are led to believe.

And more than just an impassioned celebration of the women who continue to "opt in," we provide a variety of concrete strategies that will help graduate students, junior faculty, and even post-tenured mothers find a better balance between the demands of the academy and the obligations of parenthood.

WHO ARE WE?

We are colleagues at Bowdoin College, two mothers, both internationally recognized scholars with five kids, five books, and more than forty-five journal articles between us. Although we are both tenured professors and mothers, we come from very different backgrounds, are in different fields, and are at different stages in our respective careers. Rachel Connelly is the Bion R. Cram Professor of Economics at Bowdoin College, where she has spent her entire academic career, save for a year in Washington, DC, and several years in Beijing. She received her PhD from the University of Michigan–Ann Arbor in 1985. She was the first woman to receive tenure in the economics department at Bowdoin, the first to be named a full professor, and the first to be named to a chaired professorship. She is also the mother of four children. After tenure, Rachel devoted considerable time and effort to changing the environment for women faculty at Bowdoin. As part of that effort, she served a term as the director of the women's studies program, during which time she participated in the multiyear process that led to Kristen's hiring.

As an economist specializing in the fields of labor and economic demography, Rachel has spent her whole career dedicated to the academic investigation of the intersections between work and family life. Her research into the effect of child care prices on women's labor-market decision making is well known. An active and committed scholar, she has received grants and fellowships from the National Science Foundation, the Russell Sage Foundation, the Rockefeller Foundation, the Ford Foundation, the W. E. Upjohn Institute for Employment Research, the Poverty Institute of the University of Wisconsin, and the American Statistical Association.

Kristen Ghodsee is a relatively junior scholar, earning her PhD from the University of California, Berkeley, in 2002 when her daughter was seven months old. Less than three years later, Kristen became a single parent during the critical middle years of her tenure clock. Far from her family in California and with an ex-husband relocated to Europe, Kristen was incredibly lucky to have mentors like Rachel to turn to for advice when she needed it the most.

After six years, Kristen's daughter started kindergarten, and Kristen was awarded tenure in 2008. She is now the John S. Osterweis Associate Professor of Gender and Women's Studies at Bowdoin College and a dedicated scholar of gender politics and postsocialist transitions in the former Eastern Bloc. Kristen has received multiple honors for her work, including fellowships from Fulbright, the American Council of Learned Societies, the National Science Foundation, the Woodrow Wilson International Center for Scholars, the Institute for Advanced Study in Princeton, New Jersey, and the Radcliffe Institute for Advanced Study at Harvard University.

This book is truly a collaborative effort, not only between Kristen and Rachel, but also between the two of us and some of our colleagues. In 2009 and 2010, we sent out dozens of surveys to a snowball sample of our colleagues and friends who are tenured professors with children. However, of the formal surveys that we sent out, we only received eleven completed responses—from ten women in the humanities and social sciences and one natural scientist, teaching in a variety of institutional settings (although we did not have any survey respondents from a community college). In addition to these surveys, Kristen and Rachel conducted informal interviews in a variety of professional circumstances, including at three national residential fellowship programs. Our intention was never to obtain a representative sample of mothers in academia, but rather to solicit stories and advice from women who have successfully combined these two goals in their lives. We have included relevant quotes from their responses and telling anecdotes from our informal interviews in order to provide a diversity of perspectives beyond our own experiences. Finally, we rely on the published research of our many colleagues who critically examine work-family balance issues in the academy. We have done an extensive literature review of the recent and relevant scholarship in this field, and present the key findings of various studies together with our concrete suggestions and specific advice for how to succeed as a *Professorus momus*.

We've organized the book into nine concise chapters. The next chapter sets the scene with a summary of some of the academic studies of the effect of childbearing on academic success, followed by Rachel's story, told with the clarity of hindsight, to reflect on all that she wished she had known along the way. The second chapter takes on a full complement of myths that need debunking; you may find us unpleasant in our honesty, but it's better to know all of this now. The next two chapters, "Know Thyself, Part I: On Deciding to Become an Academic" and "Know Thyself, Part II: Deciding Whether to Become a Mother, How Many Children to Have, and When to Have Them," are meant for younger scholars who are just starting out in the academy. After these two big-picture chapters, we work our way chronologically through the stages of most academic careers: the last year of graduate school, the early years on the tenure track (perhaps including a few years as a postdoc or an adjunct faculty member), the immediate post-tenure years, and the run-up to full professorship. For all of these stages, we address the different types of challenges academic mothers will face. How we should spend our time differs with the ages of our children and our rank in the university hierarchy. While it is true that having small children before tenure is particularly challenging, Rachel reports that having teenagers brings its own unique set of demands.

The key point that we want to drive home is that women can success-fully combine an academic career with a family if they go into this endeavor with their eyes open and are honest with themselves about what they want. Many young men and women get PhDs without truly understanding the future demands of being a scholar and teacher, and later legitimately change their minds about pursuing an academic career. Surviving in the academy is a tough business, but in our opinion it is one of the most satisfying career options available to educated women today. While we understand that the intense competition and the constant exposure to criticism and rejection are not for everybody, we feel strongly that motherhood should not become the excuse that women who otherwise dislike the scholarly life use to justify their decision to leave a profession that they would have left anyway, even without children. Yes, it is hard to achieve success in the academy, but it is not im-possible. If you really want to be both a mother and a professor, you can be both, and there are thousands of examples of women who have successfully combined tenure and a family on university campuses around the country today. If you would someday like to count yourself among them—read on.

1

A Success Story—Told with the 20/20 Vision of Hindsight

A Hopeful But Cautionary Tale

When we first started talking about writing this book and how we were going to organize it, we had to make a decision about whether we should start with the good news or the bad news. There is already a lot of bad news out there, but there are also many young women who go into the academy not truly realizing what they are up against. So despite the fact that the goal of this book is to encourage some subset of young women to ignore the odds and pursue an academic career despite a battery of obstacles, we decided to start with the bad news: the empirical facts about the relationship between motherhood and academia.

The academic studies of the effect of parenthood in the academy do show a negative correlation between parenthood and tenure for women. According to a study by Joan C. Williams, "The Glass Ceiling and the Maternal Wall in Academia," women who have children soon after earning their doctoral degrees are far less likely to receive tenure than men who have children after finishing the PhD.[1] Williams reviewed more than one hundred different studies in social psychology and tried to provide some answers as to why this finding is persistent across institutions and disciplines. Williams's review is essential reading for anyone entering into academia but particularly for young women, who will face stereotypes and often considerably more hostility than their male colleagues. She identifies two key factors at play in limiting women's possibilities for success in the academy: the "glass ceiling," which applies to all women, and the "maternal wall," which specifically refers to discrimination against mothers. In other words, she finds that it is a combination of sexism and *mommyism* that keeps women from advancement on par with their male colleagues.[2] Williams argues that the glass ceiling and the maternal wall reinforce each other, creating a variety of barriers that women must overcome if they are to achieve tenure.

In a 2004 study, Mary Ann Mason and Marc Goulden examined two large data sets to investigate work-family balance issues in the academy.[3] The study challenged the traditional definition of *gender equity* in higher education, which is often defined as gender parity of graduate students, tenure-track faculty, and ultimately tenured faculty. In other words, when there is a fifty-fifty representation of men and women at all ranks in the academy, there will be gender equity. Mason and Goulden, however, argued that the definition of gender equity should include equity across familial outcomes, such as rates of childbirth, marriage, and divorce. Their study used data from the Survey of Doctorate Recipients as well as data from a 2002–2003 study of work-family issues among the ladder-rank faculty at the nine University of California (UC) campuses. In total, Mason and Goulden examined the career trajectories of more than 30,000 PhDs in all disciplines and surveyed more than 8,500 UC tenured and tenure-track faculty.

Their results were troubling for those of us interested in promoting the idea that it is possible to combine academia with family life for women. The first finding of interest was the effect of children younger than six years old in the household at the time of beginning a tenure-track job (which they defined as up to five years after earning a PhD). Controlling for a variety of factors, the study found that women who had "early" babies were far less likely to achieve tenure than men who had children under the age of six in their households. In the sciences, 77 percent of men with "early babies" earned tenure, compared to only 53 percent of women in the same category. In the humanities and social sciences, 78 percent of men with young children in the household within the first five years after completing the degree earned tenure, compared to 58 percent of women. Most of the women not earning tenure had not been denied tenure. Instead, the authors hypothesized that many women were leaving tenure-track jobs for what they called "second-tier positions"[4] in the academy because of the strains of combining professional work with motherhood and marriage. This was sobering news indeed.

Turning the analysis around, Mason and Goulden also examined the impact that academic careers might have on the family-formation patterns of men and women. Using the Survey of Doctorate Recipients, they examined the family composition of ladder-rank faculty twelve years out from earning their PhDs. Sixty-nine percent of ladder-rank men were married with children, 15 percent were married without children, and 11 percent were single without children. For ladder-rank women, only 41 percent were married with children, while 20 percent were married without children and 28 percent were single without children. Among the population of single parents, 11 percent of ladder-rank women were raising children on their own, compared to only 5 percent of ladder-rank-faculty men. Interestingly, among "second-tier" women, 60 percent were married with children and an additional 20 percent were married without children. Of second-tier women, only 14 percent were single without children, half the percentage points of the ladder-rank-faculty women.

What this all means is that "women who are appointed as ladder rank faculty within three years of receiving their PhDs have a 50 percent lower probability of being married than do men and a 52 percent lower probability of being married than women appointed to second-tier positions."[5] Furthermore, ladder-rank-faculty women had a 144 percent greater probability of being divorced than did ladder-rank men, and a 75 percent greater probability than did second-tier women. Not only did motherhood negatively impact a woman's chances for success in academia (if by *success* we mean achieving tenure in a "first-tier" position), but it seems that academia also negatively impacted a woman's chances for success in her personal life. She was more likely to be single, more likely to be divorced, and more likely to delay child-bearing, potentially until it is too late. Indeed, from their study of UC faculty, Mason and Goulden found that whereas only 20 percent of men claimed that they had fewer children than they wanted, the percentage points were twice as high for women.

As these studies show, women in academia continue to face many inequalities, especially when also trying to be mothers. We do not intend to gloss over the challenges, but we also know many women who have successfully traversed these waters. Finding mentors and learning from the experience of those who have gone before is one of the most important things a young scholar can do to increase her chances for success.[6] So having started this chapter with the bad news, we now present a story that challenges all these studies and statistics. It is Rachel's own story. Rachel is now a full professor and named chair in economics, as well as a mother of four children who has been married for more than thirty years to the same husband. Despite Rachel's nervousness about offering her experience up as a "success story," we include it so that you can get a feel for the types of choices that women in Rachel's generation made when deciding to become professors and moms at the same time. Of course, Rachel's story is just one experience, but important lessons can be drawn by reading about how things were for women in the academy not so long ago and reflecting on how one person made the choices that led to a successful combination of tenure and motherhood. And the really good news is that it is a lot easier these days than it was for Rachel. The number of women in the academy has increased, and the academy as an institution is slowly waking up to the need to make changes to help all parents better balance work and family. But even in places where the old rules are still in effect, it is possible to have your tenure and your family, too.

Planning is something Rachel has always done, but she admits she often makes plans with very little information. That combination doesn't really make sense when she looks back upon it now, but each plan always seemed reasonable at the time. And, so far, most of the plans (as naive as they were) have worked out well. Children were always part of the plan, and she and her husband intended to have four or five of them. They married while still undergraduates, and their plan even at that time was for Rachel to go to graduate school and to get a job as a professor at a small liberal arts college.

When Rachel was a graduate student at the University of Michigan, from 1981 to 1985, there were about fifty faculty members in the economics department. Of these, only three were women, and not one of those women had done what Rachel hoped to do: combine an academic career with having a family. Combining academic work and motherhood wasn't yet a topic of conversation even among the Committee for the Status of Women in the Economics Profession (CSWEP), which was, at that time, just trying to convince "the guys" that women could do math and could compete in the academic game if given half a chance.

Like most starting graduate students, Rachel really didn't understand what the job of an academic entailed. From her vantage point, she had observed her undergraduate professors setting their own hours and coming and going from their offices when they wanted, and she thought that this was a job she could do in conjunction with parenting. Of course, she knows now that she was both right and wrong. One of the myths we would like to dispel in this book is this notion that the academic profession is an *easy* job to combine with parenting. Of course, you can combine academia with parenting as well as any job if you are willing to put the time into it. And being an academic does give you unusual flexibility in terms of where and when you work. Rachel can attend a parent-teacher conference in the middle of the day and her son's soccer game in the late afternoon, but she is careful not to do these things too often. There is no shortcut to sitting still and working. Time away from her desk in the middle of the day means Rachel will need to put in more time later in the evening or on the weekend, when other parents are relaxing with their children at home.

The University of Michigan was a good place to be a woman graduate student in economics in the early 1980s, as the economics department was admitting a sizable number of women graduate students. While it does not bother Rachel to be the only woman in a room, it was nice to have a cohort of other women with whom to study. These women are still among Rachel's closest friends and colleagues. But at the same time, the University of Michigan was not such a good place to be in terms of how the economics faculty treated women. Several professors refused to work with women students, fearing that they would give it all up once they married and/or had children. One faculty member refused to work with Rachel on her dissertation, despite the fact that she was a top student in her class. Her professors were also openly disapproving of her choice to concentrate her job search on small liberal arts schools in Maine. The world they knew and understood was the world of the Research I university; they couldn't fathom why Rachel would not want a job at a Research I. Despite their disapproval, Rachel was very sure of what she wanted. In the end, she convinced them to support her limited job search.

Bowdoin College in the mid-1980s was actively hiring women in order to address an enormous gender imbalance in the faculty, part of the legacy of Bowdoin as a men's college. The tenured faculty in the economics department (all men at the time) were not opposed to the idea of hiring a woman as long as they could be sure that she measured up as an economist. Rachel did not (and still does not) think there was anything wrong with that attitude. She was, however, very isolated in the department when she first arrived. Most of the guys in the department played basketball at lunch and generally worked alone on their research. Weeks would go by with no one in the department talking to her. But slowly, she found her place in the department. It has been a supportive environment to do all that she wanted to do—teach in a place where good teaching is valued, do research in a place where research is supported and success in research is celebrated, and still have time for home, family, and friends.

Rachel had her first child after just one year on the job. There was no maternity leave and no stopping of the tenure clock for childbirth (more on the timing of that decision in chapter 4). The next few years of the tenure track were very difficult. She was struggling to launch a post-dissertation research agenda on very little sleep and even less guidance from her dissertation-committee members and her Bowdoin colleagues. She remembers the middle years of the pre-tenure era as the worst time; after all of the effort she went through to write her new, all-important research paper, it sat on an editor's desk for eighteen months. It seemed like academic success was out of her hands. And so were her fertility desires. Rachel had planned to have children every two or three years (there is that planning thing again), but instead she spent the last three years leading up to tenure trying to get pregnant for a second time, enduring disappointment month after month. Finally, she did get pregnant but had a miscarriage in the middle of a spring semester. Since she hadn't told anyone she was pregnant, she suffered alone, but her student opinion forms that semester sure took a hit.

While it was a very difficult time, not everything was bad. She and her husband had a wonderful little boy and a home full of visitors and friends. Having bought a home big enough for their intended brood, they often had a student or recent graduate staying with them during those years. This provided an extra set of hands and eyes to watch their son and some relief from the other demands of housekeeping. If you are lucky enough to live near family, then be sure to allow other family members to help you during these crunch years. If you don't live near family, create family-like relationships with friends. Find someone who loves your child, and then share your child with him or her. A child's love is not a zero-sum game. If your children also care for a caregiver or an adopted aunt or uncle, there is still plenty of love left for you. Having other people in your children's lives teaches them to enjoy different types of relationships and to celebrate each person's contribution to their lives.

When her son was two, Rachel received a research fellowship to work at the U.S. Census Bureau and enjoyed a year's research leave in Washington, DC. During that year, Rachel really learned the importance of attending professional conferences. Rachel identifies going to conferences as a very important part of her ultimate success in attaining tenure. Conferences provide deadlines and give you the opportunity to meet the other players in the field. Conferences are also important for marking your territory—that is, letting the other players in the field know what you are working on. Always try to go to lunch or coffee with the other panelists in your session. (Visit with friends some other time.) These conversations lead to other invitations to give seminars and to collaborate. While Rachel's earliest collaborators were mostly women she knew from graduate school, her more recent collaborators have been drawn from among the men and women she has met through the years at professional conferences. (Networking will be discussed in greater detail in chapter 6.)

Rachel's infertility saga ended happily with another pregnancy during her sixth year at Bowdoin. Her tenure file was due July 1, and the baby was born July 6. Not necessarily the best time to have a baby, but *there is never really a good time to have a baby*, and once you have suffered through infertility, any time is a welcome time. One positive side effect of the timing was that Rachel didn't have the time or energy to obsess about the tenure process. It was all a sleepless blur, and that is probably just as well. As you already know, Rachel's tenure story ended happily.

One year later, Rachel, her husband, and their two young children left for a year in Beijing. Like many other choices Rachel has made over the years, the decision to go to Beijing was not made to maximize her career trajectory. They went to China so that her husband could improve his Chinese, but it turned out to be a very good decision for Rachel as well. In 1992, there were not many economists studying China, and even fewer were investigating Chinese labor markets. Rachel came home from China with another new baby (there's nothing like tenure to reduce what turned out to be stress-induced infertility) and a new research agenda. Rachel still keeps one foot solidly in research on the U.S. labor market and child care concerns, but now her other foot is firmly planted in the area of human-resource issues in China. This has kept her learning new things and feeling excited about her work. The work of an academic researcher is very self-motivated, and it is much easier to find time for research when you are excited about what you are doing. Sometimes this means expanding or even changing fields.

There is no question that Rachel's research productivity slowed down when her third and fourth children were young, but that period did not last long. She found that having co-authors helped—not because they did more of the work, but because their need to get tenure and be promoted motivated her to do her part of their joint work in a timely manner. Rachel delayed coming up for full professor several years since the demands of work and home did not leave room to add yet another source of work and stress. In addition, the wounds of the tenure process were still with her. But she eventually decided that she needed to just go forth. You can read more about that in chapter 9.

Rachel's years as a full professor have been pleasant ones. Since the waning of that intense period of having three very young children plus one slightly older child, she has had more time and energy to devote to her research and her teaching. The time she spends on both these aspects of her job continues to be enjoyable, and the roller coaster of successes and failures seems more manageable. Articles continue to be produced and published, old projects are finished, and new projects are begun with much less angst. Rachel spends more time thinking about what good teaching is, and that has been rewarding for both her and her students. Even her administrative work, which is often considerable, is sometimes rewarding.

After over a quarter century in the academy, Rachel feels that she has become good at what she does. Of course, it wasn't a cakewalk; she certainly met with her share of frustrations and disappointments along the way. There was the call from the editor of the special issue in which she so desperately wanted to publish that came while she was in the hospital having her second child. There were also all those winter vacation days she spent grading papers while everyone else in the house was out playing in the snow. In addition, she is well aware that her situation was easier than many, since she has a supportive spouse who celebrates what she does and who stays home with the children. Since she had someone else at home, snow days and ear infections were much easier for her to cope with than they were for most of her women colleagues. But she and her husband do a lot of juggling with finances to be able to live on one salary; just the thought of college tuition bills put her into a deep funk for over a year.

In the wonderful clarity of hindsight, there are many things Rachel wishes she had known, and a lot of things that she thought she knew, but that turned out to be wrong. When we started discussing this project, we realized that many myths and expectations about how things would work were still in place when Kristen began her academic career. Somehow Rachel had imagined that these myths would have gone away as more women entered the ranks of the faculty, but they are just as pervasive as ever. In our conversations with colleagues, we found that many women still enter academic life believing these same myths, regardless of discipline and institutional type.

In the next chapter, we have decided to tackle some of these myths head on—not to discourage you, but because you need to arm yourself with knowledge that will help you successfully navigate the challenging seas of academic life. After that, you are asked to think long and hard about the sacrifices and decisions that you will have to make in order to successfully combine motherhood with academic life. It may seem like a lot of bad news all at once, but all the bad stuff is laid out first in order to give you more specific guidance on how to overcome the wide array of difficulties, obstacles, and requirements. As Rachel's story has shown, it can be done. Even with four kids.

The Nefarious Nine, or The Not-So-Pretty Truth about Motherhood and Academia

MYTH 1: AN ACADEMIC JOB WILL ALLOW YOU TO SPEND MORE TIME WITH YOUR KIDS

This is one of the most insidious myths out there, and yet it is easy to see how it is perpetuated. It goes something like this: If you teach at a college or university with a 2-2 load (meaning that you teach two courses each semester, for a total of four courses per academic year), and your total weekly in-class time for each course is three hours, this means that you are actually expected to be in front of a classroom for six hours per week. Out of a forty-hour work week, it could easily seem that you have thirty-four hours of your week that are free for child care and other family-related responsibilities, right? *Wrong.* Your six hours of in-class time does not include the time you need to prepare the classes, to grade the papers, to hold office hours, to meet with students, to attend committee meetings or departmental meetings or faculty meetings or tend to the plethora of other service commitments heaped onto faculty; nor does it include the time required to write letters of recommendation or reply to your emails from students, colleagues, concerned parents, applicants to the college, former students, conference organizers, and administrators. And this is still without factoring in your many scholarly obligations, which are far too numerous to mention here (but which will be discussed in later chapters)— the most important of which is publishing enough work to earn you tenure and promotion. The truth is that even if we only spend six hours a week in front of students, our jobs require us to spend at least fifty hours a week on our other professional responsibilities. Even the idea that we have summers free to be home with our children turns out to be a complete and total illusion. For many of us, it is difficult to do scholarship during the academic year, and we end up with towering backlogs of work to do over the summer, which absorb much of our "free" time.

In their large study of University of California faculty, Mary Ann Mason and Marc Goulden looked at the number of self-reported hours that professors claimed to spend on professional work, housework, or caregiving activities in any given week.[1] Faculty women between the ages of thirty and fifty who had a least one child in the house claimed to spend 101 hours per week on these three activities, reporting that 51 of these hours were spent on professional responsibilities. Men with children reported an average of 80 hours per week engaged in these activities, with 56 hours dedicated to professional responsibilities. Men and women faculty without children claimed an average of 78 hours per week of work, with about 60 of these dedicated to their jobs.[2] These numbers not only show us how much more women faculty are working in the home and for their children, but also that academia is by no means a forty-hour-a-week job for anyone, with or without children.

One of our survey respondents, Elissa, a new mother and newly tenured associate professor of sociology at a large Canadian research university, ruminated:

> I think that the flexibility of academia both works for and against us. On the one hand, I am able to be there for my child, when she needs me, most of the time (e.g., if sick). However, there is also an "elasticity" to academic work that makes it seemingly infinite. In other words, there is always something more to be written, researched, etc. . . . and there are endless emails, letters of recommendation to be written, books to be read. Prior to having a child, I never had a clear sense of how *many* hours I actually spent working. My time was so fluid that work just expanded to fill my life. I now find myself needing to bound it, which is proving a great challenge.

Similarly, Clarice, a full professor of American studies, also recognized that academia can completely take over your entire life.

At least in a research university you can make claims for research, and research gives you more flex time than just teaching. But it also requires you to do a lot of research and publishing and at specific benchmarks, so that's less flexible. I have to work like mad all summer and on "vacations" and during "furloughs" and I am still always behind and feel inadequate to the research requirements and also don't have enough time for family or even for my own health.

Although our time is more flexible than that required in some other jobs, this flexibility should not lull us into thinking that academics is a part-time job. We work just as much, and sometimes much more, than those in many other professions. We just don't always do it between 9:00 a.m. and 7:00 p.m.

How can we fight this myth? Be aware of the trap of flexibility. Don't think that flexibility means fewer hours at your desk. You need to have time to work when you are most productive, and you will have to make up lost time or you will not be able to produce the scholarship required for promotion and tenure.

Arabel, a professor of economics with two children, explained:

One thing I learned along the way was that trying to work at home when my children were little wasn't a great idea. Even though I had the flexibility to work from home, the kids would want my attention and I found myself telling them not to bother me because I was working. One time when my younger daughter was six years old, she came up to me at the computer and started saying something. I turned and looked at her and she immediately said, "I know, don't bother you. You're working." At that point I decided that when I had to work, I would be at work. And when I was home, I was available for them. This meant I spent more time at the office, but I think it was better. When the girls were older, I could work from home more easily because they were more independent. But I still keep in mind that when I'm working from home, I have to be willing to stop sometimes and respond to them without them feeling bad about it.

MYTH 2: BEING SMART AND WORKING HARD IS ENOUGH
Although academia is founded on admirable meritocratic principles, it is not always a meritocracy. Networking and collegiality count for far more

than anyone would like to admit. Take note of what Rachel said in chapter 1 about the importance of attending professional association meetings and marking your territory. You must take the time to give invited talks and to send offprints of your articles to the major players in your field in order to get your name out there. This puts young mothers with primary caregiving responsibilities in a bind because they often do not have the backup that most men have when traveling for professional reasons. Young faculty have to be particularly proactive early in their careers when they are trying to get articles and books published, and for parents of young children this necessitates more time away from the family. You can write a brilliant book, but unless you go out and promote it by giving talks and attending conferences, there is considerable risk that it will be ignored.

Daniel Hamermesh, a well-known economist, writes in "An Old Male Economist's Advice to Young Female Economists":

> Louis XIV remarked that he could not reward someone whom he did not see at court at Versailles. Implicitly the same thing is true in academe. Even with kids it is important for young female professors to attend seminars by internal and external speakers, to interview job candidates at the January meeting, and to talk with them during campus visits. More generally, despite your extra family burdens you must take full part in the professional life of the department and engage in activities that generate the "bonding" that is crucial in any work environment.[3]

Applying for national grants is another way to get your work out there, but many young scholars avoid this endeavor either for fear of rejection or because they have access to ample internal funding. Applying for grants is not always about getting money; it is also about winning prestigious awards and putting your work in the hands of the most senior scholars in your field, who sit on the award committees. In all of these cases, it is very important that people in your field know who you are, and this means doing more than just teaching, research, and service. It means that you have to add networking to the already long list of requirements for a successful academic career. You may not like doing it, but you really, really have to. Being smart is not enough. You have to be visible as well.

MYTH 3: ALL STUDENTS ARE LIKE YOU WERE AS A STUDENT

This may seem self-evident, but many young academics are shocked to find that they have students in their classes who are content with a C when they themselves never earned anything less than an A. Furthermore, there are thousands of young professors out there today who believe that their undergraduate classes should be taught like the graduate seminars they took just before earning their PhDs. We'll deal with this matter in more detail in later chapters, but it is worth mentioning it here because so many aspiring academics make this common mistake and end up creating more work for themselves at the exact moment when they should really be focusing on their research.

The lesson is to think carefully about the students you are teaching. Yes, you want to move them forward, but they cannot and will not be leapfrogged too far from their comfort/ability zone. Take the time to understand the students' expectations. At Bowdoin, for example, it is okay to give frequent problem sets and group projects. Group projects are more difficult at nonresidential schools. But even Bowdoin students balk at two problem sets a week for the same course (including during the week of the midterm exam). One faculty member who did this thought she could convince her students that they could and should do the work. But the students did not agree. Instead, most simply avoided her courses, the others complained vociferously, and she was ejected from the tenure track after her third year.

MYTH 4: THERE IS NO LONGER SEXISM IN THE ACADEMY

There is still plenty of discrimination against women in the academy. It occurs over a full spectrum of forms, ranging from the unbelievably overt to the incredibly subtle. We need to continue to be on guard against differential student evaluations of male and female professors (i.e., he is smart and thought provoking, while she is an opinionated bitch; he is a tough grader, while she is nitpicky).[4] There are also institutional structures that insist that there be a woman on every committee. This is a problem in fields where women are still underrepresented. There are both men and women out there who don't like strong women, but are sure that *they* never discriminate. While it is true that mothers have it particularly bad in the up-or-out system of tenure, women as a whole still suffer in the academy compared to their male peers.[5]

And then there is the troubling reality that the increasing feminization of the academy has coincided with a "silent revolution" in the academy of declining wages, poorer working conditions, and increasing contingency of academic labor. Although no one will like us for saying so, the period of time since women started seeking doctoral degrees has coincided with the period of time during which the ratio of tenure-track jobs to PhDs earned has declined (mainly because PhD programs are churning out lots more PhDs). With the percentage of women pursuing graduate education steadily increasing, there is more competition for academic jobs that were once almost exclusively reserved for men. But we should all understand that correlation does not imply causality. And even if there is some causation here, it is only because women were unjustly shut out of top PhD programs for decades.

In a 2001 article, "Assessing the Silent Revolution: How Changing Demographics Are Reshaping the Academic Profession," Martin J. Finkelstein and Jack H. Schuster point out that the increasing number and diversity of doctoral recipients have coincided with massive structural changes in academic employment. According to the authors, when white, native-born men dominated the ranks of the academy in 1969, non-tenure-track faculty appointments accounted for only 3.3 percent of academic employment. The growth of what they call "non-regular" full-time appointments (i.e., adjunct positions) ballooned in the 1970s and 1980s, and by the mid-1990s, these positions constituted the majority of full-time faculty appointments in the United States. Once a rarity, adjunct positions have slowly become the norm. This trend neatly coincided with the ongoing expansion of women earning PhDs and seeking academic employment. The authors note:

> Consider that white males, especially native-born, historically have comprised the dominant core of the profession. Yet by 1992 they no longer constituted even a majority (43.2 percent) among the new faculty cohort, dropping further to 36.5 percent in 1998. Indeed, to further dramatize the faculty's transformation, if we add a variable to capture the ever-growing tilt toward professional/career fields, we find that by 1992 only one in five (20.5 percent) recently hired full-time faculty was a native-born white male teaching in a liberal arts field, a proportion that shrank further to 18.6 percent by 1998. In other words, it can

be said, with only slight hyperbole, that the prototypical faculty member of a mere few decades ago (the native-born white male based in the liberal arts) may now be approaching endangered status![6]

Most troubling are the insinuations that the willingness of women to accept contingent full-time appointments is somehow responsible for the overall erosion of the tenure system. While Finkelstein and Schuster are careful to state that the increasing presence of women and ethnic minorities in the academy is inherently a good thing, they do point out that women make up the majority of "non-regular" full-time teaching appointments, and present data that show that women "termers" were the most satisfied employees in the academic profession in 2001. They write, "Perhaps the day of the full-service professor—teaching, research, service—is becoming an anachronism. . . . Clearly, for some of these off-track appointees, the more-defined and limited responsibilities associated with term employment may provide for them a better accommodation to life's other demands than does the traditional academic role."[7]

In March 2010, Kristen attended a panel on "Women in Academia" at Indiana University, where five distinguished speakers were discussing various policies that could be put in place to support new mothers and help women find successful work-family balance. At the end of the session, a young man sitting in the front row of the audience made a brave comment. While he was sympathetic to the concerns and challenges of professors having young children in the academy, as a single graduate student about to earn his PhD and hoping to land a position in his discipline he was worried that too many demands for part-time and flexible work at the assistant-professor rank would ultimately undermine his ability to find a solid tenure-track job.

To this young graduate student, demands for different pathways in the academy could too easily be co-opted by corporatizing, market-driven universities trying to cut labor costs and undermine faculty autonomy and academic freedom. He feared that a large population of qualified, hardworking women willing to work for less money and weakened job security in order to have a better work-family balance would destroy the traditional academic career paths and play right into the hands of those hoping to abolish the tenure system once and for all.[8] In other words, parents' demands could become a Trojan horse for a capitalist-driven college and university system.

The implicit message was that while academic mothers may have legitimate concerns, they should keep their collective mouths shut lest they unwittingly destroy the very institution that they are hoping to gain access to, even if that is an institution inherently built around male privilege and male biology. These are subtle and complicated debates, and the philosopher Nancy Fraser has recognized a troubling tendency for liberal feminism to work as a handmaiden of free-market ideologues.[9] We don't purport to know the answers to this dilemma, but we do want to warn young mothers that they may face discrimination from both men and women who fear that greater workplace flexibility will undermine the tenure system.

Thus, arguments against women's increasing presence in the academy can come in two forms. The first form of sexism is the most familiar one: the idea that women are not as good as men in certain disciplines, the hard sciences and math being the best examples. But the second kind of sexism is more subtle: the concept that women may be just as good as men, but once they are "on the inside," the presence of too many women will decrease wages and erode the foundations of the tenure and promotion system. Young women, especially young women with children, can unknowingly be the victims of both forms of critique. Your colleagues may think that you are incompetent or they may think that you are too competent. What can we do about it? Be aware that sexism is still there. Watch for it, and try to figure out who the worst offenders are at your school, or what institutional structures may aggravate the situation. Avoid them pre-tenure, and work to fix things post-tenure (see myths 8 and 9 below). Most of all, work hard and prove them wrong.

MYTH 5: GETTING AND BEING PREGNANT WILL BE EASY
The movement for equal amounts of "parental leave" for both mothers and fathers should be applauded for its underlying egalitarian impulses. This trend, which has taken hold at many universities across the country, unfortunately ignores the realities of biology. Men do not get pregnant. They do not give birth. Their breasts do not produce milk. Their fertility does not decline precipitously after age thirty-five. They are not subject to the same hormonal roller coaster that women must deal with, particularly women who must undergo IVF treatments in order to conceive because they have waited beyond the optimal biological period for becoming pregnant.

When Kristen was at the Institute for Advanced Study in Princeton, she was in the bathroom at the gym when she heard the hiccuping sobs of a colleague in the neighboring stall. The woman was a brilliant historian who was nearing forty and was desperate to have a baby with her husband of seven years. The academic couple had decided to delay childbearing until they were sure that they would both get tenure and achieve career stability. Once they decided to have a child, however, the woman had difficulties conceiving. She began IVF treatments just as she started a one-year fellowship at the Institute. That day in the bathroom, she was hysterical because she felt she simply could not concentrate on her scholarship due to the potency of the hormonal injections she had to take to stimulate ovulation. While her husband plowed away on his newest book project, she could barely get her mind (or body) to cooperate.

While it only takes a few weeks to recover from a normal vaginal delivery, a more complicated delivery, or a caesarean section, can take months out of a woman's precious time on the tenure clock. Fathers, no matter how involved in child care, are rarely forced to write their articles in a standing position because they cannot sit down in front of their computers due to a raging case of labor-induced hemorrhoids. Fathers may have equally disturbed sleep patterns as new mothers, but they are unlikely to suffer from the post-partum depression and fatigue that many women experience. The experiences of pregnancy, labor, and breast-feeding are very intense for most women. They can take a large toll on women's ability to do scholarly work. Unfortunately, many young parents think of their parental leaves as extra time to get more scholarship done; this only works out for the father, who can run off to the office and get away from the baby without having to pump breast milk every two hours or risk a painful case of mastitis.

It is important to go into motherhood knowing what you are getting yourself into.[10] Don't plan to be as productive during your pregnancy or during the six months after the birth of your child as you usually are. There may be things that you can do during that time, but original writing is probably not a reasonable expectation. It might be a good time to be tweaking a final draft of a manuscript, but not a good time to be drafting new sections. It might be a good time to do some statistical work, but not an optimal time to be designing new studies. In the book *Cheaper by the Dozen*, the mother (who was an incredible woman pioneer in the engineering field in the early twentieth century) always proofread her latest book during her "confinement."[11] Make sure that you have some projects that you can work on that will not require your full brain capacity, and don't beat yourself up for not getting as much done as you hoped. Most importantly, get some sleep. Your brain will eventually recover and will thank you for it.

MYTH 6: MOTHERHOOD IS INSTINCTUAL

Babies do not come with instruction manuals. Many intelligent, highly educated women are absolutely flabbergasted when they realize that they have no idea what to do with a baby. Unless you happen to be lucky enough to have your mother nearby or rich enough to afford a nanny, you (and your partner if you have one) will have to figure out all of the mysteries of baby care on your own. (Beware that some of the advice books out there are strongly biased toward the stay-at-home mothering choice.)

At the exact moment when you are trying to impress the academic world with your original contributions to the collected knowledge of the human race, you are standing over a bassinet trying to reinvent the wheel when it comes to effectively dealing with a nasty case of diaper rash. Regardless of what you may think, the motherhood program does not automatically download into your brain after delivery. Accepting this and recognizing that everyone makes mistakes is part of finding your sanity after childbirth, especially when you are also trying to write a book, be a responsible colleague, and teach your college classes.

MYTH 7: CHILD CARE IS ALWAYS LOWER QUALITY
THAN MOTHER CARE

For some strange reasons having to do with residual Cold War politics and the cultural stranglehold of social conservatives on the collective parenting consciousness of the United States, there has been a disinformation campaign against institutional child care in this country for the last sixty years. Many people believe that a mother is always what a child needs, even though many young children thrive in quality child care settings. The key word in that sentence is *quality*. There are plenty of sub-standard child care settings out there, but high-quality child care (this usually means an accredited day care center with educated and/or experienced professionals who have studied child development and infant psychology) is stimulating and healthy for a young child. There is an irony in the rejection of child care since it has been shown that young children in day care develop stronger immune systems than those raised at home. Since strengthening the immune system of babies is one of the main reasons given for extended breast-feeding, it seems peculiar that this same reasoning would be ignored when it comes to the benefits of institutional child care.

Other benefits of child care are that it brings about the earlier socialization of your child to other children, it teaches your child independence, and it allows your child to be surrounded by other caring adults. In addition to giving you the time and space you need to do your own work, good child care can also help make you a better parent. One of our respondents, Helen, a tenured natural scientist at a liberal arts college, explained:

> I think I was very paranoid about daycare early on. I had this idea that children would be deprived if they weren't home full time with a mother or at least one parent. I've come to understand how tremendously positive an excellent day care can be for children. I think it allows them independence when they are ready, but also gives them the love and affection they need. Personally, I learned a ton about being a good parent from the daycare providers I've worked with over the years. I can't quite imagine our lives without having had those experiences or met these wonderful people.

Despite the fact that there are numerous studies showing that young children raised in part by nannies and those attending institutional child care fare no worse than children raised by their biological mothers at home (see textbox 2.1), the truth is that there remains a strong societal view in the United States that mothers should be the primary caregivers of children. Some scholars, such as Susan Douglas and Meredith Michaels,[12] have compellingly argued that the insanely high mothering standards in the United States are a backlash against the gains of feminism and the very real inroads that women have made into corporate America. In *The Mommy Myth*, written by Douglas and Michaels, as well as in Judith Werner's *Perfect Madness*,[13] scholars document how media representations of perfect mothers have risen in tandem with the number of women graduating from universities and entering previously male professions. This myth is a very dangerous one for academic mothers because it inevitably leads to "mother guilt," which we will discuss in subsequent chapters.

TEXTBOX 2.1. THE RESEARCH ON CHILD CARE

A large part of Rachel's academic research has been on the economics of child care. There is now a large body of research on how women's work lives and motherhood choices are affected by the need to care for young children. Women in the United States face large barriers when it comes to child care: we don't trust it, it is expensive, and sometimes it can be hard to find.

Why don't we trust it? It is part of the "traditional family values" strain of American thought, which is correlated with our higher rate of church-going compared to most other developed countries, coupled with our sense of individualism—which means mom care is always the best. So what that most women with young children are, in fact, in the labor market and use some sort of non-parental child care? We still don't trust it, so we seek to minimize its use. We play tag-team parenting; we ask Grandma to take a shift or two; and we muddle along as best we can. (This behavior is also consistent with the next point, that child care is expensive. Tag-team parenting and using relatives are also ways to reduce the cost of child care for the family.)

Why is it expensive? Because child care is highly labor intensive, one teacher oversees a small number of children, and because we as a society do not subsidize it (unlike most European countries). We don't seem to have a problem with subsidizing first grade, or second or third for that matter, but we have a big problem subsidizing the education of three-year-olds. Why? Go back to the first point—because we as a society believe that Mom should be doing it and because it was her choice to have a child in the first place.

Why is it hard to find? Mostly because we don't want to (or can't) pay what it would cost to do it right, and so instead we cut corners here and there. Most families accept mediocre child care. There is no financial aid for child care, the way there is for college; the customers are young families with lots of other demands on their income; and the long-term effects of poor-quality child care are hard to see in your own child. High-quality child care may not even be offered in a given marketplace if there are not enough people who would be willing to pay the price.

Child care serves two roles in our lives: it facilitates our employment, and it provides a structured, caring, and learning-fostering environment for our children. Your job is to find a child care arrangement that does the best job it possibly can do with both of these roles. You may need to accept trade-offs between the two roles: you may need to accept child care that works for you in terms of your job, but is not the highest quality out there. Or you may find yourself making the opposite choice. Either way, understanding child care's dual-personality disorder helps us see the forest through the trees of guilt and financial concerns.

In terms of its role in facilitating employment, you need consistent, dependable child care. You need child care that is available when you need it. The best care imaginable won't do you any good if it is only available from 9:00 to 11:30 a.m. Look for full-time care with an educated provider. We can't guarantee your provider won't quit in the middle of the semester, but the research shows that turnover rates are higher for providers with lower levels of education.[1] Here is a rare situation with no trade-off, since the research also shows that education level of the provider is positively correlated with quality of care.[2]

In terms of providing a structured, caring, and learning-fostering environment for your child, be assured that the child-development research tells us that this matters. Good things come from high-quality care. Bad things come from poor-quality care. There have been hundreds of studies looking for the effects of child care quality on child outcomes, and you may read that the results are mixed, but that is because there was a lot of poor-quality research out there. Two new, large studies with very careful data-collection efforts both show long-term positive effects of high-quality care on child outcomes. These positive effects consider school readiness, math and vocabulary scores, and appropriate social interactions.

The first large data-collection effort was the National Institute of Child Health and Human Development (NICHD) Study of Early Child Care. A large team of researchers collaborated on both the study and

(continued)

the analysis of results. Lots of information about the children, their families, and their child care arrangements was collected during five home visits and four visits to the child care setting, and through measuring child performance on various "tests" spread out from the time the child was one month old until he or she was thirty-six months old. As you can imagine, many studies have been published using these data. A report by Deborah Lowe Vandell and Barbara Wolfe summarizes these many findings. Overall, they found that "the quality of child care during the first three years was related to children's school readiness, expressive language, and receptive language at three years."[3] They found that home environment mattered as well, roughly twice as much as the child care quality scores, but that the child care quality scores "were large enough to be meaningful."

The other important study is the Cost, Quality and Child Outcomes in Child Care Centers Study begun in 1993, which did a very careful job of assessing the quality of child care settings for children in child care centers in four states, and which followed the children into the second grade. This study allows us a longer-term perspective than the NICHD study, which stopped at thirty-six months. The Cost, Quality and Child Outcomes study findings are summarized in the following four statements quoted from the executive summary of their report, "The Children of the Cost, Quality and Outcomes Study Go to School":

- "High quality child care is an important element in achieving the national goal of having all children ready for school."
- "High quality child care continues to positively predict children's performance well into their school careers."
- "Children who have traditionally been at risk of not doing well in school are affected more by the quality of child care experiences than other children."
- "The quality of child care classroom practices was related to children's cognitive development, while the closeness of the child care teacher–child relationship influenced children's social development through the early school years."[4]

They conclude, "It is no surprise that the nature of children's experiences in child care are important, but the results of this study confirm the lasting impact of these early experiences. High quality child care experiences, in terms of both classroom practices and teacher-child relationships, enhance children's abilities to take advantage of the educational opportunities in school."[5]

How can you tell if your provider is providing high-quality care? Some states have instituted rating systems for child care providers. Find out if there is one in your state and, if so, ask whether the provider is participating in the program. If so, what is the provider's score? Ask about the educational credentials of the providers. Ask about the number of children in the group and the number of caregivers. Ask to sit in and observe a class for an hour. You should see teachers talking with and engaging children, not just supervising. You should see warm relationships between caregivers and children. Usually it is considered better pedagogy to give children a choice of activities instead of everyone doing the same activity at the same time. Basic safety measures should also be in place, like fire extinguishers in every room, and lots of hand washing should be going on.

If you don't like what you see, consider a different provider. Ask other parents in the area. Think outside the box. Is there a good preschool program in the area, but of inadequate duration? Might it be possible to combine the preschool program with a home day care arrangement? This can be a good solution if you are not the one doing the transfer. Having to jump up every day at 11:15 a.m. to pick up and move your child to another location is a formula for not getting anything done in the middle of the day.

Don't be tempted to forgo after-school care once your child starts school. A good after-school program can provide physical activity for children who sit too long in school or help them get started on their homework, and in the best of situations it accomplishes both. Get rid of that maternal guilt thing, and celebrate the time your child is happily engaged in activities that don't involve you. There is still plenty of family time left if you make the most of the at-home family time. Wouldn't you rather be playing a board game than hectoring your child to do math homework? Let the after-school program do that prodding.

(continued)

One option a lot of faculty parents use is a nanny or au pair. Au pairs are cheaper, but they are essentially teenagers who live with you. Sometimes that works, and sometimes it doesn't. Also, they can only stay one or two years. It takes time to interview the new ones, orient them to the job, and so on. The advantage is that you get a lot of flexible hours of care and even some light housekeeping tasks (unloading the dishwasher, doing the laundry, making school lunches, etc.). A nanny can do all of these tasks and can stay for longer than a year. A good place to look for a nanny would be the population of recent college graduates with education degrees. In the current labor market you may be able to hire a full-time recent graduate for the same price as an au pair. No, that recent education major is not going to stay forever either. But you don't need a nanny forever. Ask for a one-year commitment, and establish an open, trusting relationship so that your nanny is more likely to tell you when looking for another job.

Another popular option is the university child care center. Make sure you get on the list early. They are usually oversubscribed. One advantage of the university child care center is you will get to know other faculty parents.

No matter what kind of child care you use, banish the guilt and make the most of it. High-quality child care may be the key component in your attempt to successfully combine work with motherhood.

MYTH 8: LIBERAL ACADEMICS WILL LET TENURE STANDARDS SLIDE FOR FAMILY REASONS

Another mistake that young academic parents make is to assume that because some of their colleagues eat organic granola and protested against a war, they are willing to make exceptions for junior faculty who do not get their research done for family-related reasons. It is important to realize that many academics have devoted their entire lives to intellectual pursuits, and many older women academics have chosen the career route over the mothering route (it was much more of an either/or proposition for them). Just because they vote for liberal candidates and progressive legislation and may even be in favor of paid maternity leave doesn't mean that they will grant you tenure if you don't have your research published. They may allow you to extend your clock and may try to lighten your committee assignments, but they will probably stick to their guns when it comes to maintaining what they think of as the appropriate tenure standards.

The solution is to get your research written and published, but also be on your guard. If you are leaving at 3:00 p.m. to pick up the kids, perhaps you don't want to mention that. We are not in favor of completely hiding your kids, but there is nothing wrong with being careful with appearances when you are pre-tenure. Yes, you may see photos of children in the offices of the junior men in your department, but remember that men get extra credit for being involved parents and are less likely to be viewed as slackers when they rush off to tend to a sick kid during a faculty meeting. As a woman, our society grants you no special recognition or heroic honors for being an involved parent. The important thing is to pay careful attention to the institutional culture of your department. If your colleagues don't talk about their children (or they do not have children to talk about), you should exercise some discretion.

MYTH 9: ALL SENIOR WOMEN ON CAMPUS ARE YOUR ALLIES

Perhaps we should list this one as a corollary to the prior one, but it is one of the most dangerous myths, and so we list it separately. There was a time when the feminist movement encouraged us to think of all women as belonging to one big sisterhood. Women thought they could stand together and support each other in a collective fight against patriarchal oppression. The truth is that academia is a competitive business, and the people who have succeeded made lifestyle choices that supported their goals. This is especially true for women of a previous generation who slogged through the ranks without the benefit of tenure-clock-stopping parental leaves and on-site, university-sponsored day care. They were often forced to make a choice between family and career. They paved the way for us, and they paid a high price for their success if they decided not to have children when they really wanted them. Given the sacrifices most of them had to make, they may be even more critical of you than some of your senior male colleagues (who secretly know they had it easier thanks to their stay-at-home spouses). The key thing is to seek out senior female colleagues who will support you and the choices you are making. Tactfully avoid those women most likely to sabotage your efforts to be both a professor and a parent. Senior mentors are essential, but beware of those to whom you might give your confidence if they feel that their own success in academia was predicated on giving up their chances of having a family. Although this is not universally true, senior women with children of their own are probably the ones most sympathetic to your situation. But, of course, they may be too busy with work and family obligations to be active mentors. That is where we come in. The chapters that follow will try to distill the most valuable advice that the senior professor-mothers on your campus may not have time to dispense.

3

Know Thyself, Part I

On Deciding to Become an Academic

I think people did tell me the things I should have been told, but I just didn't understand, internalize, or frankly believe some of them. The fact that it is really tough, that you have to make sacrifices, that your life is sometimes very chaotic. You can hear these things, but you can't experience them in advance or internalize how true they are.

—*Helen, a tenured natural scientist and mother of three*

The challenges of combining work and family in the United States are greater than those in almost any other industrialized country—Americans work longer hours, have higher parenting standards, and inhabit a highly individualistic culture that views child rearing as a purely personal decision and a private responsibility. Unlike countries in Northern Europe, where the state actively supports young families and protects new mothers in the labor market, the United States prizes its "flexible" work force and remains one of only a handful of countries around the world without mandated paid maternity leave. Adding insult to injury are the deep libertarian impulses against publicly sponsored child care and the growing trend of homeschooling. Many Americans simply don't trust public institutions to care for or educate their children, and instead are embracing a type of hands-on motherhood that our own mothers would have balked at. The cultural shift away from the term *housewife* to "stay-at-home mom" indicates an important change in our society. It is no longer acceptable to be a full-time wife—that is just too 1950s, *Leave It to Beaver,* pre–Betty Friedanish. But a full-time mom is another thing; partners should be able to take care of themselves, but our children need us twenty-four hours a day for at least eighteen years. It is a career decision to make a job out of motherhood, a choice that our society accepts for women but rarely for men.

There is a whole school of feminism that enables and encourages us to recognize and respect women's choices, whether the choice is to be a working mother or to stay at home full-time. Indeed, we have decades of the so-called Mommy Wars behind us, with a history of furious skirmishes between the working mothers and the stay-at-homers. And we certainly recognize that there are huge costs, both personal and professional, involved in trying to combine motherhood and a career. We know that successful professional women still tend to be childless at a much higher rate than their male peers. In 2002, Sylvia Ann Hewlett found that 49 percent of what she called "ultra-achieving" career women (those earning $100,000 or more) ages forty-one to fifty-five were childless and 33 percent of "high-achieving women" (those earning $55,000–$66,000) were childless, compared to only 19 percent of ultra-achieving men aged forty-one to fifty-five and 25 percent of high-achieving men.[1] Jane Waldfogel disaggregated the gender wage gap and has shown that while women as a whole only earn seventy cents on a man's dollar, childless women actually earn ninety-five cents, leading to what has been called the "motherhood wage gap."[2] Add to this the high price and limited availability of high-quality child care, the scientific evidence that a newborn's immune system benefits from being breast-fed for at least a year, and the fact that our best physicists have not yet figured out how to put more than twenty-four hours into a day, and you have more than enough factors pushing women out of the work force and back into the home. There are many rational reasons for opting out.

But there are other, less rational reasons why professional women drop out—there is the guilt brought on by the rhetoric that elevates full-time motherhood to the highest pedestal. There are also personal reasons that stem more from having made bad or uninformed decisions. Many young people do not really know what they want out of life before heading down a particular career path. In this case, it is no surprise if some of these young people, both men and women, later find themselves unhappy with their chosen profession. This chapter is dedicated to helping you figure out whether academia is the right place for you before you make the decision to attend graduate school (or to finish graduate school, if you are already there).

It is essential to have this discussion before you decide to get a PhD, and certainly before you go on the job market. While later in the book we give you some tips on how you can make an academic career work for you, we do not see ourselves as being in the business of selling everyone an academic career. In fact, the most important piece of advice in this book is to *know yourself.* You need to determine whether a PhD is worth the investment, given that in many fields teaching at the college level is the most common career linked with the PhD credential. Even if you decide that, yes, this is the path for you, it is useful to distinguish between the women who truly opt out of academia for work-family reasons and the women who use work-family reasons as an excuse to get out of a profession that they don't like anyway. As long as these two categories of women remain lumped together in people's minds, it sends the message that being a professor and a parent is much harder than it really is, and it encourages young scholars to delay childbearing or to give up an academic career before it has even begun.

We warn you: this chapter is not for the faint of heart. One graduate student read an early draft of this chapter and started crying, believing that the whole enterprise was just too hard. But our purpose is not to dissuade you; it is to prepare you for the realities that you may have to face (however unpleasant it may be for you to hear them). If you already have a good handle on the challenges of pursing an academic career, you can skip ahead to the next chapter. Otherwise, brace yourself for some serious but necessary introspection about what kind of person you are and what kind of sacrifices you are really willing to make.

Let's start with the story of a woman we will call Amelia, a hypothetical graduate student in English at a major Research I university. Amelia is a composite of several young women we knew who each made choices that ultimately led them to leave academic careers. Let's say that our Amelia was an English major as an undergraduate because she loved reading novels and poetry and doing comparative critical analysis of contemporary authors. She was an excellent student, eager to please, and a creative thinker. Amelia decided to pursue a graduate degree on the recommendation of both her parents and her professors. Although she wanted ultimately to find a partner and start a family, she was convinced that she was still too young and should further pursue her education. After all, none of her friends were getting married at twenty-two, and certainly no one in her circle was planning to have a baby before the age of thirty.

She was accepted into one of the top English graduate programs in the country, based on strong letters of support and a brilliant writing sample that she had spent the entire final year of college producing as a thesis under the direct supervision of her major adviser. She excelled during the first two years of graduate school, working closely with her classmates and professors on a variety of well-executed critical papers during her coursework. When it came time for her qualifying exams, she began to have trouble. The independent nature of studying for the exams meant that she had to be far more disciplined with herself than she had when she was given specific assignments to complete by specified deadlines. The dissertation proved to be even harder. The long hours spent writing did not appeal to her as much as reading the texts she was analyzing. Amelia needed constant supervision from her dissertation adviser, and found that she repeatedly changed her thesis topic by adding more books to read. However, under the steady guidance of her adviser, she eventually completed the dissertation and earned her PhD.

It is almost automatic at Research I universities, particularly in the humanities and social sciences, that newly minted PhDs are supposed to go on the academic job market. And this is exactly what Amelia did, putting together her dossier and sending out more than fifty applications to colleges and universities across the country. But secretly she was not so sure that the academic life was for her—particularly in a university English department where there would be incredible pressure to publish. The problem was that everyone—her parents, her professors, her colleagues, and her friends—all expected her to get an academic job. After all, why else would one spend six years or more earning a PhD? And her love for literature surely would translate well into the university classroom, where she could teach young college students to savor the joys of close reading and comparative analysis as a vocation.

Her first year on the job market, she had three interviews but no offers. Amelia was stunned. She had always succeeded in everything she had ever tried—up to and including getting into the college and graduate schools of her choice in a subject area that she loved. This was the first real disappointment in her life—although her thesis adviser told her that it was a particularly bad year on the job market, and that she would surely get a job the following year if she could manage to generate a publication or two in the interim. At this stage, Amelia really began to worry that perhaps an academic career was not the right choice for her. But she would not let herself be a quitter, and that is how she would have felt if she'd abandoned the market after that first year. That was certainly the message she got from her advisers, who warned that it could even take a few years before she landed a tenure-track position in an English department. It was, she was told, a very difficult discipline in which to find a job.

"A whole year?" Amelia asked her adviser. "What am I supposed to do for this next year?" A postdoctoral fellowship was arranged so that she could get some teaching experience and spend some time turning her dissertation into a book. She reworked one of the chapters of the thesis into an article and, at the urging of her adviser, sent it out to a top journal. After an excruciatingly long five months under review, the article was rejected. Once again, Amelia was unprepared for the emotional blow she received when she opened the letter. She had never received anything less than an A on any paper she had ever written. The comments from the reviewers were substantive, and she was advised to revise the article immediately and resubmit it elsewhere. In the meantime, Amelia loved teaching her own class, and she found herself putting in a lot more time and preparation than she had planned.

Amelia had also met someone. He was a young lawyer, a friend of a friend. They had been spending a lot of time together. He was thirty-four years old and already well established in a law firm as a junior partner. Amelia was now twenty-eight and beginning to worry that if she waited too long she might not be able to have a baby, something that she knew she wanted. But she managed to carve out some time to make the revisions to the article, and she sent it off to another journal, this one more specific to her field and in the middle range of the journal hierarchy in her discipline.

By the time the job-market cycle came around again, Amelia's article had been accepted and she had taught two classes of her own design. The young lawyer had also asked her to marry him; she had happily accepted. Since he was relatively immobile, she limited her applications to colleges and universities within a five-hundred-mile radius of her future husband, but in truth, she was not really willing to accept a position outside a three-hour drive. Just as her adviser had predicted, she did better on the job market the second year. She was short-listed for five jobs, had four on-campus interviews, and received two offers: one at a nearby Research I, and one at a liberal arts college slightly farther away. All of her advisers and colleagues encouraged her to take the Research I job, and her fiancé also hoped that she would choose the geographically more convenient position. When comparing the offers, however, Amelia realized that she might be happier at the liberal arts college, where the pressure to publish would be much less and where her classes would be smaller and more intimate. In the end, she capitulated to the pressure of wanting what others thought she was supposed to want, and to the desire to be near her future husband. She took the Research I job, starting the following fall.

She was married and already two months pregnant when she began teaching in September. The dissertation had not been revised, and she had yet to send a second article out for review. Her new chair emphasized that a second article publication would be necessary for reappointment, and that he expected her to have a book by tenure-decision time. Amelia hoped that her chair would read drafts of her work and give her helpful feedback, but it soon became clear that the people in her new department were far too occupied with their own scholarship to worry about hers. And between the morning sickness and the fatigue, Amelia could get almost no work done on her scholarship. For the time being, she focused on teaching, hoping that she would be able to return to the book after the baby was born. The demands of her job were many, and her starting salary was abysmally low, not even a third of what her husband earned. More importantly, when she read through the journals to which she hoped to submit, she found herself bored by the scholarship. Amelia was much more interested in novels than the scholarship others produced about them; she found herself questioning the value of her discipline.

Without a thesis adviser to prod her along, Amelia lacked the discipline to pursue the book revision. Slowly, she began to disengage from scholarly commitments. The accepted article had come back with queries from the journal, and Amelia took more than a month to respond to them. She had submitted a proposal to give a paper at the Modern Language Association meetings and it had been accepted, but she pulled out the month before because she did not want to fly at that stage of the pregnancy. Her thesis adviser had recommended that she contribute a chapter to an edited volume. She turned it down by claiming that she needed to focus on peer-reviewed journal articles. After the baby was born, she declined two invitations to give talks, citing child care reasons, but in fact she did not very much like public speaking. When her chair encouraged her to apply for a National Endowment for the Humanities Summer Stipend, she argued that she would be too busy with the baby to make proper use of a grant.

Her university gave her a semester off for maternity leave and offered to extend her tenure clock by a year. But when Amelia prepared to return to campus the following fall, she was shocked to find that her child care costs would absorb more than half of her salary for the year. In addition, a second article that she had sent out at the beginning of the summer had come back as a "revise and resubmit with substantial modifications." Amelia was terribly disheartened, finding herself wounded by yet another rejection. Listening to the publishing woes of her more senior colleagues, she was becoming aware of how difficult it would be to publish a whole book in her discipline, particularly a revised dissertation. As she read through her own dissertation, she became increasingly convinced that she would never get it published and therefore never get tenure. So why should she waste the time trying?

But Amelia pushed on. She managed to stick it out for one more year, putting her son in child care three days a week and working at home with him for the other two. Between breast-feedings and diaper changes, she did a hurried job on the revise and resubmit and eventually got a second-round rejection. When the letter came, she cried for an hour in the bathroom while her baby slept. Her husband came home from work to find her disheveled and almost hysterical with frustration. Her heart nearly burst with joy when he suggested that she "take a few years off" until the baby was a bit older; he could easily support the family on his salary alone. Amelia informed her chair that she was resigning at the end of the spring semester, citing the need to stay home with her son and really "be there" for him. It was just too difficult, she said, to combine motherhood and an academic career.

A story like Amelia's allows us to show how some people might begin academic careers almost by mistake, without ever really knowing what they were getting themselves into and without really knowing what it takes to achieve professional success. No matter where you are in your life, it is very important to examine your motivations. This is especially true if you are still in graduate school. In what follows, we pose some key questions that will help you figure out if an academic career is really what you want, or if it is something you have been led to think that you want by your parents, professors, partners, and friends. Think about your own history and your own goals in life as you read through these next sections.

1. WHY DO YOU WANT TO LIVE THE LIFE OF THE MIND?

It is worth reiterating here that Amelia's choice to opt out of the academy was, of course, influenced by the lack of affordable child care, the legitimate stresses of new motherhood, and the tightness of the academic labor market in her discipline, as well as the murkiness and capriciousness of the publishing process. But if we simply chalked up her leaving to the issues of work-family balance, we would be ignoring the many red flags that should have warned Amelia that she was not really a good fit for the academy, long before she found herself juggling her teaching, research, and motherhood on the tenure track.

In the first place, it seems that Amelia went into graduate school without really understanding what PhDs in English *do* after they finish their degree, or the difference between consuming knowledge and producing it. A PhD is a research degree, and doctors of philosophy are meant to produce original scholarship in their field of expertise. It is not, as many young people believe, a credential that simply allows you to teach a subject at the university level. While there are many institutions that do focus almost exclusively on teaching, these are not the institutions that most successful graduate students aspire to or are taught to aspire to (more on institutional types in chapter 5). Most graduate students on the job market come out of Research I universities, and they are encouraged to seek employment in similar institutions. A position at anything less than a Research I is considered a failure—and graduate students implicitly internalize these expectations, even when they are self-aware enough to know that they might prefer teaching to research. In the overall pecking order of academia, the Research I is always on top; at Research I institutions, independent, original research always takes precedence over teaching. It is clear that Amelia enjoyed the learning and teaching much more than she ever enjoyed the writing, and this should have been a clue that she would be better off seeking a job at a school that valued teaching more than original research, or choosing a career completely outside the academy. (More on this is chapter 5.)

It is also clear that Amelia disliked independent work and thrived in situations where a mentor directly supervised her. Furthermore, Amelia was particularly thin-skinned when it came to rejection, and rejection is an ever-present part of the academic life. Of course, no one likes rejection, but the most successful scholars are those who learn not to take it personally and to accept it as part of the intellectual growth process. A disinclination to independent work, a lack of interest in writing, and a deep aversion to rejection would doom the academic career of even the most brilliant young mind, whether distracted by a baby or not.

Thus, the first set of questions you should ask yourself include the following: Why do I want to live the life of the mind? Do the scholarly debates in my field fascinate and inspire me? Am I willing to toil away independently and often in obscurity, in order to advance the collective knowledge in my field or subfield? Can I handle the professional rejection that will accompany the career of any prolific scholar? Am I willing to make personal and material sacrifices so that I can live in the realm of ideas, surrounded by people who value scholarly abstraction as much as they value a good cup of espresso?

If you are having a difficult time writing your dissertation and you are bored by long hours spent doing research, chances are that an academic job with high research expectations is not for you. If, on the other hand, you wake up every morning thrilled to be diving back into the colossal intellectual endeavor that is an original thesis, or you love every minute that you spend in the archives, in the field, or in the lab, and even the time you spend writing, then you probably have what it takes to be a successful academic. If you meet your adviser only once every two months, and then only at his or her instigation, you are naturally suited for the independent work required for a career at a research university or top liberal arts college. On the other hand, if you feel that you need a steady stream of advice, attention, and input from your thesis adviser in order to finish each individual chapter, then it might be worth passing on the research end of the academic job market. If writing is a tortured and frustrating process, and you fear nothing greater than the next rejection letter telling you that your ideas are hackneyed and your prose is dull, then be honest with yourself now.

One of our respondents, Diana, is a professor in a public-policy school at a large research university and a mother of one. She had this advice for young women entering academia: "Decide from the start that tenure at your school is not the only possible path for your career. Life is not over if you don't get tenure. Many excellent scholars did not get tenure somewhere." Like Diana, we believe that there is absolutely no shame in deciding that your personal priorities do not include becoming a tenured professor at a research university. The important thing is to be honest with yourself about what you want and then do your best to achieve your goals. Getting tenure is hard, and you need to understand that no matter how hard you try, you might just not make it, even if you don't have kids. Realize that if you don't make it, it is not the end of the world, but at least go into it willing to give it your best shot.

Perhaps because of the abundance of American television shows about hospitals, courtrooms, and law firms, young people have a somewhat realistic expectation of how difficult it is to become a doctor or a lawyer. We all know how brutal medical residencies can be, thanks to shows like *ER* and *Grey's Anatomy*, and no one thinks that it is easy to make partner in a law firm. But unfortunately (or fortunately), there are no TV shows about academia that dramatize the trials and tribulations of young (good-looking) academics as they struggle to establish themselves in their profession—probably because watching someone sit and grade papers for fifty-three minutes is not very exciting. But the sacrifices and commitment required are similar, and you should be prepared to work hard.

2. WHAT ARE YOUR PERSONAL GOALS IN LIFE IN TERMS OF FAMILY?

Another key part of Amelia's story is that she ended up in graduate school almost by mistake, propelled by the expectations of parents and mentors and not wanting to start a family too soon. In fact, there are probably many bright and talented women who feel compelled to warehouse themselves in graduate school until they are of the socially acceptable age to get married and have children. The average age of first marriage has steadily increased in the United States over the past four decades, as has the age of first childbirth, particularly for college-educated women. Many of these women will work into their early thirties before settling down with a partner and opting out, a situation that provides them the moral high ground of having sacrificed a potentially successful independent career for the sake of their children. It is really important to know what you want out of life and whether graduate school is (or was) just a holding tank until you felt that you were the "appropriate" age to start your family.

Furthermore, if you entered graduate school because you believed that you would make a good scholar and professor, and then you find yourself changing your mind because it is not quite what you thought it would be, or because you have fallen madly in love with someone and want to put your relationship and family above all other pursuits, don't be afraid to cut your losses early and pursue an alternative career path. No one ever forces anyone to go into the academic job market (although, admittedly, it does feel that way sometimes). If you do decide to seek a job in the academic labor market, think hard about who you are, what you want, and which type of institution is most suited to your personality. Despite the strong pressure to pursue a career at a Research I, explore the other options and be realistic about what the different requirements for tenure look like at different institutions. Even if you land a tenure-track job, you may have a child and find that being a mother really is the more satisfying part of your life, and that scholarship loses its importance. Again, there is no shame in leaving the tenure track early if you are certain of your priorities.

Finally, there are those women who truly want to be both mothers and scholars. If you fall into this camp, then we have good news for you. *It can be done.* Not only can it be done, it has been done by thousands of women at universities around the world. If you head down this path, it is important to be clear about what your expectations about being a mother and a scholar are, and to have a plan for how you are going to meet them. Start by being realistic about the challenges and expectations of others.

3. DO YOU HAVE A CLEAR SENSE OF THE PERSONAL CHALLENGES THAT YOU WILL FACE?

As you consider becoming a successful academic, you will need to think about the labor market, your own work style, your desire for a partner, and possibly a partner's expectations about your relationship. If you do not have a partner yet, you will have to think about where you are going to be located and the likelihood of meeting someone there. If you don't want a partner, think about the availability of support networks to help you raise a child on your own. We have already talked about working independently and the importance of being self-sufficient and self-disciplined in your work, but it is important to recognize that different academic jobs will have varying expectations about teaching, service, and scholarship. Scholarship is often a relatively solitary endeavor compared to teaching and service, so if you have a gregarious personality and prefer to work in teams, choose your future institution accordingly.

Figuring all of this out will take some serious introspection, but the better you understand your own needs and priorities, the better the chance you have of making a successful academic career at an institution suited to what you actually want (and not to what you think you *should* want).

After you do this for yourself, you also need to think long and hard about your partner. Like becoming a doctor or a lawyer or any other professional, academia requires considerable time and effort, and the work and the time it takes will affect any relationship that you have or will have. If you do not already have a partner, how important is it for you to find one? If finding a partner is high on the list of priorities, think before taking a job at a school in a rural area where most of your colleagues could well be already married with children. If you want to find a partner, you might do better to take a job in a large metropolitan area where there will be more single people available. This is especially important if you are looking for a same-sex partner or someone of a particular ethnic or religious background. There is no right answer here, but the key is to be honest with yourself about what *you* want and make your choices accordingly.

If you already have a partner, the decision to become an academic has its own challenges. If your partner already has a career, how flexible is he or she in terms of relocating? An academic couple's relationship can be among the hardest to make work because of the paucity of tenure-track jobs and a still nascent system of spousal hiring. How willing is your partner to support your academic career? How much are you going to ask of your partner, and what do you plan to offer in return? Is your partner willing to follow you? Are you willing to follow your partner? These are all important questions to keep in mind when you are thinking about the job market. No one can become a doctor without putting in the long and grueling hours that a residency requires, and few newly minted PhDs can become professors without being ready and able to move where the right (and sometimes the only) job takes them. Those are the realities of the profession, and they apply equally to men and women, regardless of whether they are parents.

4. DO YOU HAVE A CLEAR SENSE OF WHAT THE PROFESSIONAL SACRIFICES WILL BE?

Every profession has its own internal rules and requirements for success, and academia is no exception. For most professions, these expectations are shaped around male biology and the assumption that the professional is not also a primary caregiver to his or her children.[3] There is also implicit and explicit sex discrimination against women because of the still strong "old boys' network" of senior male scholars who occupy the upper ranks of many disciplines. It would be great if all of these factors could be instantly eliminated by some administrative decree of the American Association of University Professors. The only way things are going to change, however, is for women and mothers (and fathers and husbands aware of these issues) to enter the ranks of the professoriate and start to change things from the inside. We both whole-heartedly advocate for institutional changes that will make academia more family friendly, but we also don't think women should wait for institutional change before starting their careers. For the time being, young scholars should try to work around the obstacles and be realistic about the sacrifices required to become successful academics. We discuss eight major sacrifices here—again, not to scare you away, but to prepare you to make a more informed decision about your future career choice. These are things that we both wish we had known in graduate school.

High Mobility

As already discussed, you have to be willing to move where the next post-doctoral fellowship or tenure-track job takes you. This is particularly true in the sciences, where recent PhDs are often required to do a series of postdoctoral fellowships before starting a tenure-track position. The job market is unpredictable, and you can never know far in advance when or where positions in your field will be available, and what the pool of people with whom you are competing will be like in any given year. There are two key rules here: you should plan to be on the market for at least three years before landing a tenure-track job (up to five years in the sciences), and accept the reality that any job is better than no job. This is not to say that some graduate students do not get jobs immediately after filing their PhD thesis, but merely that if you are serious about pursuing an academic career, you have to go into it accepting the possibility that you will have to move one or two or three times before settling into a tenure-track job. If you don't get a job in your first or second year out, you should regard this as normal and not take it too personally. If you do not get a job after your third or fourth year on the market, you can start to worry. All of this means you have to be willing to move. If you have a partner, he or she has to be willing to move with you or to accept a commuter relationship (not an easy choice, but one that many academic couples make).[4]

Living Someplace Undesirable

Related to the first sacrifice is the reality of having to live somewhere undesirable, by whatever your own criteria are. It could be that you are moving to an unaccustomed climate or that you are moving to a rural area from a big city, or the reverse. You may have to move far away from your partner, your friends, and your extended family. You may have to live in a part of the country populated by people with political views very different from your own, or relocate to a state that you consider to be a cultural backwater. All of these are very real considerations to keep in mind as you go out on the job market; however, the more you limit your search, the harder it will be to find job opportunities. It is much easier to find a job when you already have one—so it is best to take what you can get and then, if you find your current situation unbearable, get back on the job market the very next year to see if you can improve things. The truth, however, is that most new faculty are so overwhelmed with research, teaching, and service commitments that they rarely even notice where they are living—so maybe you won't mind the bitter cold or intense heat, the interminable street noise or the deafening rural silence, as much as you thought you would. You might even come to like the place.

Not Having a Life Outside of Work

Depending on the institution, there will be different expectations for receiving tenure and promotion. Some institutions will focus solely on research, while others will require more teaching and university service. In either case, the early years of any academic career will be consumed by the demands of your job, something that is true for many other professions as well. If you are not truly enamored of the work life of those academics around you who gladly spend all of their free time reading journal articles or toiling in their labs, these will be very difficult years indeed. If you already have children, it will be hard to continue with hobbies or non-work-related activities. The good news is that you may not really mind this if you are living somewhere undesirable in the first place. Furthermore, you probably won't earn enough money to go out much anyway. Which brings us to . . .

Accepting a Lower Starting Salary Than You Expected

To add insult to injury, most academic jobs offer relatively small salaries to the newly initiated. If you have student loans to pay back, this means that your first few years on the tenure track could be spent with less disposable income than you had even as a graduate student. By the time you earn your PhD, many of your classmates from undergraduate school who went straight into the work force will be firmly established in their respective careers, buying cars and houses while you are still living in run-down faculty housing and willing your car to make it another year. Salaries do not stay so low as you move up through the ranks, and indeed at some schools there will be substantial raises at the promotion to associate and full professor. But these beginning years can be very financially challenging, especially if they are accompanied by child care expenses.

Delaying or Limiting Fertility

All of the aforementioned sacrifices apply equally to men and women beginning an academic career, but this sacrifice generally applies to women. It is an unfortunate reality that most young academic women will spend their prime child-bearing years earning their PhDs and then trying to earn tenure. Because these early years are especially stressful, many women consider waiting to have a first baby, or postponing the birth of a second child until after tenure. (We will discuss the timing and spacing of children in more detail in the next chapter.) There are certainly some advantages to postponement, but there are also advantages to having your first child late in graduate school or early on the tenure track. Either way, you will be stuck in a professional culture that often assumes that there is a *Spousus supportus* at home.

Working Long Hours When Your Kids Are Young

If you do have a child while in graduate school or during the early years on the tenure track, you will have to come to terms with working long hours when your kids are very young. This means that "Mama" may not be your child's first word, and that you will probably not see your son take his first step or be there when your daughter reads her first word. For many women, this is the hardest sacrifice to make, because they feel that they are missing important milestones. But these are milestones that are externally defined by society, and we have to ask ourselves if being there to see your child's ninth step is really that much less meaningful than seeing the first. Missing the first word or the first step will not make you less of a mother, any more than missing these events makes a man less of a father. Thinking critically about our society's ever-increasing mothering standards is essential if we are to deal with this particularly difficult sacrifice.

Not Being in Control of Your Destiny

This sacrifice is in some ways the most difficult to bear. The good news is that it applies equally to everyone: men and women, parents and nonparents, senior scholars and newly minted PhDs. Academia is far from the meritocracy we are led to believe it is, and there are certain aspects of the job that make it much harder to bear than other equally prestigious professions. Unlike many other jobs where you are evaluated on your performance immediately by your known superiors, in academia you are evaluated secretly by unknown colleagues over months of prolonged silence. With tenure clocks ticking, there is nothing more frustrating than knowing that your paper (the brilliant paper sent to the top journal in your field that will ultimately make or break your academic career and therefore change the course of your entire life) might well be buried under a stack of *New Yorker* magazines on the desk of some senior academic gatekeeper who has spent the summer kayaking with his buddies on the Chattooga River rather than reading your manuscript. Your papers often go out for double-blind review, your book manuscripts go out for single-blind review (i.e., they know who you are, but you do not know who they are), and your tenure case is decided based on letters that you will probably never see from researchers whose names you may or may not know and anonymous student evaluations of your teaching. Fellowship and grant criteria change from year to year, and you never know who is judging the applications. Your book will be sent out to reviewers who know nothing about your personal circumstances. In short, becoming an academic means putting yourself at the mercy of the unknown. It doesn't matter how smart you think you are or how smart other people say you are; you are only as smart as the blind reviewers are willing to admit. And heaven forbid that you forgot to cite them.

Exposure to Lots of Rejection

This final sacrifice is very much related to the last. If you are thinking about becoming an academic, the best thing to do is convene a group of your closest friends and family members and have them sit around for a few hours pointing out, in excruciating detail, all of your faults and shortcomings. If you can emerge from this sort of harsh treatment as a better person willing to work on improving yourself, then academia is the place for you. Similarly, if you are able to listen to their criticism and convince yourself of their inferior intellectual abilities and be confident that you are, after all, one of the most intelligent, hardworking, and compassionate people you know, then you will have a great future in the Ivory Tower. If, instead, you sit there seething at your loved ones, determined never to speak to them again, or, worse, you find yourself contemplating joining a convent or monastery, then the academic life is definitely not for you. Being an academic means being able to handle a sometimes overwhelming amount of rejection. Your grant applications will be rejected. Your articles will be rejected. Your book proposals will be rejected. There will be students who don't like you and make that clear in their student evaluations. But if you want to stay in this business, you will have to develop a pretty thick skin, and learn to take the good with the bad. The flip side of all of this rejection is that when you do get a journal article or book manuscript accepted, the pleasure, satisfaction, and relief are enormous. If you are into instant gratification or have a delicate ego, get out now. You will live a miserable life in the academy if you cannot roll with the punches.

5. HAVE YOU THOUGHT ABOUT ACADEMIA VERSUS OTHER PROFESSIONAL CAREER PATHS?

After that long list of negatives, you must be ready to quit your PhD program and give up on the academy altogether. As reasonable as this impulse may seem, what will you do instead? Will you quit working altogether? Or will you look for employment in another profession? Not working—that is, letting your partner support you—is potentially opening yourself up to some huge costs in the case of death, disability, or divorce. Leslie Bennetts's 2007 book, *The Feminine Mistake*, is a "must-read" for anyone who is convinced that a man is the best plan.[5] Even with alimony and child support, the standard of living of most divorced women plummets after marital dissolution, and it is very difficult to get back into the labor market after one has been out of it for an extended period of time. In academia, an extended period out of your field leaves you out of touch with the literature and the current debates, and this problem is even greater for those working in the natural sciences, where scholarship moves at break-neck speed. Long gaps in a CV make it difficult to find a tenure-track position if you try to return to the academy. It would be wonderful if there were more on and off ramps in academia, so that parents could spend a few key years home with their children and then resume right where they left off, but there are few, and, sadly, that is unlikely to change anytime soon. The excess supply of PhDs in most fields guarantees that there is always someone eager to take your place.

The other alternative is to find a non-academic job, something that is strongly encouraged by some books like *Mama, PhD*. But the key thing is to realize that other jobs have trade-offs as well. For instance, working for a non-profit organization may require just as much time and be as badly paid as an assistant professorship. Our advice is to keep in mind the sacrifices that we have listed above and to make a similar list of sacrifices required for whatever other careers you are considering. It is also worthwhile to keep in mind the rewards of the academic life (yes, we honestly do think there are many, despite the negativity of the discussion above). Some of the advantages of the academic life we count: being paid to read and think; self-directed research on a topic of your choosing; international collaborations with colleagues in your field; creative writing; working with young people; making a difference; flexible scheduling (especially during the summer months); sabbatical years off from teaching that provide long, uninterrupted stretches of time for research; working in a relatively prestigious profession; and being paid a decent salary (eventually). This list can go on and will be different for different people in different disciplines.

Indeed, there are those among us who speak in reverential terms about their jobs and the pleasures they bring. For instance, Susan Athey, the first woman to win the American Economist Association's John Bates Clark Medal in economics for the top American economist under age forty, wrote in an interview in 2001:

> I love being in the middle of the research process, or the beginning. Coming up with a new theory, and developing a model and proving some results, and then changing the model, and getting to the point where you have just the right model and into discovering how it works—just the moment when the model really "sings" to you—is just a "high" that it's [*sic*] hard to match anywhere else. Sometimes I get a hard time from my friends about how hard I work, and sometimes they may be right, but I have to say that that kind of "rush" from

solving models is a lot more interesting than a lot of other things that I could think of doing. The other part [of the job] that I've really loved is working with students; in particular, mentoring students and watching their careers develop. That gives me a lot of meaning—it feels like the impact that I have there will outlast a lot of the other things that I do.[6]

All the academic mothers we interviewed expressed sentiments similar to these, differing only in the specifics of the respondent's academic discipline. Beyond enjoying the primary work of research and teaching, almost every one of our respondents claimed that one of academia's most positive aspects is flexibility. While they all acknowledged that academics must work exceptionally hard and that they put in many hours, the ability to set one's own hours and to be more or less one's own boss appealed greatly to the women we surveyed. Miriam, an associate professor of history at a large Research I university who is the mother of one child, claimed there were important pros to working in academia, particularly

[the] ability to control [my own] schedule and time on campus when necessary; flexibility of work schedule except for teaching and meetings. Research and writing can be organized according to one's own schedule and familial patterns, [and one has the] ability to work, vacation, and travel because of research interests. I chose academia for the above reasons and as a working parent, this is the best situation for professional parents in regard to family and work balance. We might work hard but it is on our terms—especially after tenure.

Belinda, an assistant professor of women's studies at a large comprehensive state university who had a child on her own when she was forty, told us:

I think the academy is a great place to be a parent. Even though I may complain, we have such a huge amount of independence and flexibility in our schedule and that is very helpful with children. Of course, the fact that our job is never really done and we bring it home with us all of the time is a bit of a con and requires that you be very well organized.

The ability to take sabbaticals and to win grants to buy time off from teaching is also quite unique to the academy. At many institutions, faculty are given a full semester of paid leave after twelve semesters of teaching, meaning a professor would have a sabbatical about once every seven years. Some professors are able to get enough money to take the entire year off, and others can sometimes extend their leave to two years if they have the external funding. At top institutions, such as Princeton, Yale, or Harvard, faculty earn a sabbatical semester every three years, and even liberal arts colleges like Bowdoin are trying to reduce the number of years of teaching between sabbaticals from six to five. For many women in the academy with children, sabbatical years are a wonderful fringe benefit of working at a university. Diana, the professor of public policy, explained:

> Sabbaticals are a huge advantage of the academy. . . . Start planning sabbaticals away from your institution several years in advance. Figure out how to go away, and do it as soon as you become eligible. Take the whole year at half pay, even if you have to use up savings. Sabbaticals are a lifesaver. They can be a good time to do a lot of research, or just a breather from the usual nonstop routine—a time when you really can go to the gym three times per week. I have come back refreshed and reinterested in my courses and research.

The advantages of flexibility and time off were repeated over and over again by professor parents, but others talked about the rich personal and political rewards of being an educator and a creator of knowledge. Marissa is full professor of history at a Research I university and has two children. She told us that an academic position offers

> flexibility in the work schedule, a more gender meritocratic system (we complain a lot, but I wouldn't dare imagine what sexism in the workplace looks like in a high-powered corporation), and the ability to control a lot of the content of what I do (meaning teaching what I want), and of at least being able to stand behind my "product" intellectually and ethically, with a sense of making a difference for the greater good. As an educator, I might be frustrated by lazy students, but my expectations are always linked to my own sense of my intellectual and ethical self, and if I am able to communicate my ideas somewhat effectively to at least some of my audiences, I can go home without worries about being an agent of good in the world.

For the women we interviewed, the sacrifices were ultimately worth the rewards. But whether the sacrifices are worth the rewards is up to you to decide. For instance, things that are positive aspects for some (the ability to travel for research) may be negative aspects for others (the necessity of traveling for your research). You should make your own list of pros and cons given some of the sacrifices we have outlined above, and then make the decision that is right for you.

6. ARE YOU WILLING TO ACCEPT THE CONSEQUENCES OF YOUR CHOICES?

Of all the things that we advise you to do in this book, this will be the hardest to follow: accept the consequences of your choices. You cannot be everything to everyone all at the same time—a super-scholar, a super-teacher, and a super-mother. However, you can be a well-respected scholar, a good and conscientious teacher, and a loving and attentive mother. That needs to be good enough. There will always be people who are smarter than you are, more productive than you are, more dedicated than you are, and more successful. It is good to keep in mind that this is also true if you don't have children, but it will be true to a greater degree if you do. Yes, men will have it easier, especially those of your colleagues with partners at home, but it is just not worth worrying about. More importantly, it might be worth remembering that there will be senior women out there who would gladly give up half of the publications on their CVs for a child, and that they could be as envious of your life as you are of theirs. There is some truth in the old adage about the grass always being greener on the other side of the fence. It is natural for us to compare ourselves to others, but we should also be realistic about how much we can actually expect ourselves to do. Helen, the tenured mother of three, explains:

> The "having it all" myth is something I still want to believe in—or at least some sort of internal standard I hold myself up against. For example, when I visit someone else's house and it seems so neat and tidy, it makes me feel like I'm not doing my job as a mom well enough. Or, when I see others excel professionally in ways that I haven't yet, it makes me question my abilities to juggle everything. That idea that I really should be able to do everything very well—because there appears to be evidence that others are doing this all around me—is difficult to let go or shake off.

You must have reasonable expectations of yourself. Yes, you can do it all. But no, you cannot do it all perfectly. If you can accept this, you will already be one step ahead of the game.

Know Thyself, Part II

Deciding Whether to Become a Mother, How Many Children to Have, and When to Have Them

According to a 2006 study, the average age for women to complete the PhD degree is almost thirty-four years, and the average age for achieving tenure for women is thirty-nine years.[1] A study of women graduates from Harvard University by Jane Herr and Catherine Wolfram found that women with PhDs were the least likely to have children, compared with their fellow Harvard graduates who either stopped with the BA or went on to get a JD, an MD, an MA, or an MBA.[2] They also found that Harvard women with PhDs had the lowest rate of marriage (still a fairly high 73.5 percent) and the lowest rate of becoming parents given that they were married. Combining these two statistics, they reported that 53.4 percent of the 219 women PhDs in the sample were married and had at least one child fifteen years after graduation. This can be compared with 69.1 percent of MDs, 63.0 percent of JDs, 65.7 percent of MBAs, 58.2 percent of MAs, and 59.5 percent of those with no advanced degree.[3] The average number of children PhDs had was 1.74, compared to 1.84 for women who had gone on to earn MDs, 1.94 for JDs, 1.88 for MBAs, 1.84 for MAs, and 1.97 for those with no advanced degree. It is possible that women PhDs are simply delaying their childbirth longer than other Harvard grads, but the average age of first birth is amazingly similar across the advanced-degree categories. Instead, it appears that women PhDs are simply more likely to be childless, and those who have children are having slightly fewer children. Although the number of PhD students having children appears to be on the rise,[4] these numbers are still rather low compared to other degree seekers. Other studies have confirmed these findings, and have found that many academic women believe that childlessness is a necessary condition for academic success.[5] In the sciences, the long time spent doing postdocs, the demands of laboratory research, and the more limited choices when it comes to choosing an institution taken together make having children even more difficult to combine with an academic career.[6] Although these figures are disquieting, it does not have to be this way.

When it comes to having children, we believe that there are three kinds of women: those who know with certainty they want to have children no matter what, those who have decided that they don't want children, and those who are open to the idea of having children but are also comfortable with the idea of not having children. We will not venture a guess as to the relative size of the three groups; for our purposes, it does not matter. Of course, we understand that sometimes women change groups, but mostly you know which type you are.

For the woman who knows she wants to have children, the issues are when, how many, and, for some of you, with whom. This chapter focuses on these questions. There are no easy answers, but we will take you through the possibilities. If you are in this first group, then you need to think about having children as a goal, in the same way that you think about finishing that dissertation or landing that tenure-track job as a goal. For you, the next question is whether you are willing to have children without a partner. Many single women in academia adopt children or go the route of the anonymous sperm donor. If single parenthood doesn't seem like the thing for you and you don't yet have a partner, then add "find a partner" to your list of goals as well. One of our colleagues pursued finding a partner and having a child with a similar strategy to that which she used to get tenure. When writing her book, she set goals on how many pages she would get done in a week. When looking for a partner, she set targets for how many dates she would have in a given weekend, giving each man no more than an hour of her time. It may seem cold blooded, but women with PhDs are usually highly motivated and pressed for time. If children are important to you, there is no reason you should be sitting around waiting for Prince or Princess Charming to show up on your doorstep, just as you are not sitting around waiting for your dissertation to write itself.

For those of you in the second group, not having children at all is a perfectly acceptable option, and you will find yourself in good company in academia. Consider the flip side of the Mason and Goulden statistics we quoted earlier in the book: 50 percent of women in the sciences and 62 percent of those in the humanities and social sciences do not have children at tenure time. While some may be using the "tenure first" strategy, many will remain permanently childless. The number of childless women appears to be higher at the highest ranks of academia. While Kristen was at the Institute for Advanced Study in Princeton and the Radcliffe Institute for Advanced Study at Harvard University, roughly two-thirds of the women who were fellows had no children. When Kristen asked a tenured professor at Harvard with no children to provide the names of some colleagues who were mothers, the faculty member scratched her head and replied, "I can't think of any tenured women with children here." But if you are so sure you don't want to have children, then why did you pick up this book? Perhaps you are actually undecided. Or perhaps you have been convinced that it is impossible to do both. Remember: *it is not impossible to do both.*

Which brings us to the third group: you can imagine your life either with children or without. Do you currently have a life partner? Check in with him or her. Are your feelings toward children shared by your partner? If not, take the time to have *that* conversation. It is always better to have that conversation sooner rather than later. After the conversation, some of you will move into the first category, while others will have decided that children are not in your future. Still solidly in the maybe category? Read on, but the timing issue is easier for you. For you, waiting until after tenure might be a good choice, but note that there are substantial psychological, as well as monetary, costs of infertility.

IF YOU KNOW YOU WANT CHILDREN

For those in the first category, those of you who are sure you want to have children, our main message is don't wait too long. It is, after all, one of your life goals. You should not be embarrassed that "having children" is on your list of things to do. It does not make you less committed to your scholarship or less committed to your university. It is true you may not want to share your goal with the hiring committee, or with your graduate advisor, but that doesn't mean you shouldn't acknowledge it to yourself. Being self-aware is a critical part of being able to get what you want.

What do we mean by "don't wait too long"? Essentially, it means you should not feel like you have to wait until after tenure. If you are a woman in the sciences, you cannot really wait until tenure, and we don't think you have to wait until you have a tenure-track job. You might decide to wait, if you have made your way quickly through graduate school and the number of children you want is small (one or two). But most women should not wait until post-tenure. The physiology of fecundity just does not support that. Fecundity declines for even well-nourished, healthy women by age thirty and takes a very steep change in the rate of decline at age thirty-five. Yes, it is true, some women are able to have children during their early forties, some requiring medical intervention, but you would rather not do it that way. It is expensive, many insurance plans won't pay for it, and the hormone injections can really mess with your mind. Of course, there are some lucky women who will be able to naturally conceive in their late thirties or early forties, but the chances are substantially lower, and you won't know whether you will be one of the lucky ones until you start trying. It comes back to the question, how important is it to you to have children? For women who don't like to fail, failing to conceive can have devastating emotional ramifications.

Waiting until it is a "good time" is one criterion that does not ever work as a decision-making rule about the timing of children. There is never a "good time" to have children, in the sense that children, especially very young children, take up a lot of time, and none of us are ever idle. There is always a set of papers to read, a deadline to meet, and an article that needs revising. So don't wait for a good time to have children, because there is no such thing. Instead make the time you choose be a good time. Whenever they come, children are fun to have around and psychologically rewarding. That's why you are in the first category in the first place or maybe exploring your status in the third category.

Sonia, an associate professor of history, concurs with our advice. When we asked her when she thought a good time to have children was, she replied:

> There is *no* good time to have kids, but if you can, try and get your dissertation or book well under way (ideally done) first. Make sure you have a supportive partner, and use your time well. In fact, many of the academic mothers I know are more productive than our childless counterparts because we feel compelled to use our time well.

In fact, Sonia might be on to something. One study found that the number of young children in the household was *positively* related to increased scholarly productivity.[7] Controlling for a variety of factors, Steven Stack found that PhDs with children under the age of eleven were actually substantially more productive than their colleagues with no children. Stack argues that it may be that young children motivate faculty scientists to work harder because they want to provide a stable life for their children, and he found that this result held even when controlling for career stage—meaning that even if you have your children after tenure, you are more likely to be productive than your childless colleagues. Stack also found that there was no significant difference between research productivity of men and women with young children in the fields of sociology and criminal justice, two disciplines with relatively higher proportions of female faculty. Although Stack argues that there are measurable productivity gains for all faculty with children, when it came to the group of professors with children under five years old, men had noticeably higher productivity than women. Although there still remains a gendered differential, this is encouraging news for mothers and lends some credence to Sonia's hunch that mothers are more productive than nonmothers.

So what does this all mean? Should you have your first child while you are in graduate school or as an assistant professor? A lot more women these days are having babies in graduate school than when Rachel was in graduate school,[8] but this is still the exception rather than the rule. A 2004 study of Canadian women faculty found that most women on the tenure track believed that having children too early in their careers would be damaging to their prospects for success. In the article "May Babies and Posttenure Babies," Carmen Armenti finds that many Canadian faculty women intentionally try to plan their pregnancies so that they can give birth in May or delay childbearing until after they have achieved tenure.[9] Obviously, women are not always able to get pregnant when they want to, and so Armenti was surprised to find the discussion of having May babies so pervasive among her interviewees. The Canadian faculty she interviewed feared more than anything else having a delivery date in the middle of the semester. Armenti also found that many women gleefully threw away their birth control as soon as they got the much-awaited call from the dean telling them that they had achieved tenure. When they did get pregnant (either before or after tenure), the women she interviewed did everything to hide their pregnancies, for fear that they would be thought less productive workers once they became mothers. Lisa Wolf-Wendel and Kelly Ward report similar feelings of fear from U.S. academics: "We were struck and troubled by the extent to which the entire work process for new parents was imbued with fear. Faculty talked about fear of using [parental leave] policies, as well as fear about not getting tenure. Faculty also expressed fear that having a baby would be viewed as a sign of not being serious and fear that colleagues would be harsh critics about the choice to have a baby."[10]

The worries of these women are not unfounded. It was not without reason that Kristen hid her status as a new mother from the hiring committee at Bowdoin. In another study, Mary Ann Mason and Marc Goulden found that the timing of babies was very important for the achieving of tenure.[11] Across the disciplines and across different types of institutions, women who have early babies are far less likely than men who have early babies to achieve tenure. What is interesting, however, is that women who have late babies (defined as children who join the household six or more years after the mother has earned her PhD) achieve tenure at about the same rate as women with no children. Presumably, this is because women with late babies have already achieved job security and because women with late babies are more likely to have only one child.

Exactly when to have children really depends on who you are and where you are in your life; at the risk of sounding repetitive, we want to emphasize that there really isn't ever a good time. Rachel waited until she was an assistant professor to have her first child. Kristen had her daughter the year she was finishing up her dissertation and looking for a job. As we talk about these choices there are, as with any decision, trade-offs. For Rachel, her goals were very clear: finish the dissertation, then have a baby. Rachel was afraid of living with the stress of an unfinished dissertation. A bad experience with her undergraduate senior honors thesis had convinced her of that. Also, there was the advantage of having good health insurance provided by the university and a job to return to. What she hadn't planned on was morning sickness. People often talk about how much work it is to raise a child (and it is), but they seldom talk about how much work it is to "make" a child. In retrospect, being pregnant her very first semester of teaching probably wasn't the best idea Rachel ever had, but the morning sickness did, as it usually does, ultimately become more manageable.

Beth Ingram, professor of economics at the University of Iowa, wrote in her article "Combining Childbearing with a Career," "My first pregnancy was a (relative) breeze; with Kathy [her second child] I had morning, noon and night sickness. I couldn't eat most of the time, and my productivity really suffered. I had a normal pregnancy, and still lost a lot of time that I hadn't planned on losing."[12]

Kristen, who suffered from debilitating fatigue when she was pregnant, cannot imagine trying to be pregnant on the tenure track. No one knows what kind of pregnancy she might have (and it may well be different with each child), so it is best to assume that it will involve some degree of disability. Thus, the question of timing is a very delicate and personal issue, but it is a very important one, since we know that having a child disproportionately affects mothers more than it affects fathers. Linda, an associate professor of sociology, had her first child when she was forty, after achieving tenure. When we asked her what her advice would be to young women hoping to be mothers and academics, she offered the following:

> Wait as long as you can (but not *too long*!). Being a parent/mother is terrifically demanding and exhausting (particularly in the early years). Unfortunately, there still aren't enough mechanisms in place to really level the playing field in academia between men and women and the reality is that motherhood ends up penalizing women.

Arabel, an economics professor who had her first child while on the tenure track and her second child after tenure, believed her motherhood timing was "okay." From her perspective, she couldn't even "imagine having kids while still in graduate school." For Kristen, however, the flexibility of her last year of graduate school, with time off from teaching and most of the fieldwork done, seemed like a good time to have a baby. Indeed, Kristen had a caring dissertation adviser, who wanted to see his graduate students succeed in all aspects of their lives. Since Kristen was already married, he suggested that the final year of graduate school was an ideal time to have a baby. She had just come back from fourteen months in Bulgaria and would spend an entire year (or possibly two) writing. The university had great health insurance and maternity benefits. So when Kristen found out she was pregnant and was told that the child would be due around November 14, she set that date as the deadline for finishing her dissertation. Despite the fatigue and a painful case of pregnancy-related sciatica, she wrote the last sentence of her dissertation's conclusion on November 10, three days before her daughter was born.

Helen also had her first child while she was in graduate school, and found that the model worked well for her:

I ended up with an unusual timing pattern for a science grad student—a baby during grad school. Supposedly I was the first student in the sciences at [University X] to have had a baby during grad school, which is surprising, and may not be true. So, there was no policy in place for leave—something I had not anticipated when deciding to start my family. Luckily, my boss was great and told everyone else that I would have three months off, and it was taken care of. I do think that early on in graduate school I decided I wasn't going to wait until I had tenure somewhere before having kids. I had seen too many women suffer the consequences of that decision—meaning that they didn't get tenure anyway, and didn't have a family either, or once they finally achieved tenure, they had trouble getting pregnant (I saw quite a few cases of that in successful women in my field, and I decided I didn't want to be in that boat). . . . I'm glad I timed things the way I did—one child in grad school, one in my post-doc year, which is admittedly crazy, and one child here at [College Y]. I think it worked out quite well for me and can't really imagine a much better scenario.

Juliet, an associate professor of history at a highly ranked liberal arts college, had two children while in graduate school and two more children while on the tenure track, but not without great personal costs. Unlike Helen, who was more conscious of trying to control when she was going to get pregnant, Juliet had less luck in timing her pregnancies.

I have four children, but I've gone through five pregnancies since I began grad school. With my first pregnancy, I did not have a chance to think strategically, as I discovered that I was pregnant just as I was about to leave the country on a year-long grant to do my dissertation research abroad. Since the conditions in my country of study were too unhealthy and uncertain to give birth there, and there were no provisions for deferring the grant for parental reasons, I lost the funding altogether. [Then, tragically, she lost the baby at birth.] Pregnancy #2 was planned, after I returned from my dissertation research trip. Baby #2 (third pregnancy) arrived two months after I turned in my dissertation (and before I had a job). Pregnancy #4 took me a bit by surprise (I found out midway through my first year of teaching, and the baby was born in the middle of the fall semester, so I had to take a leave for the entire semester). By my final pregnancy, I had it all figured out—the baby arrived conveniently in June, and I didn't miss any teaching (although my research suffered).

When we asked Juliet about the consequences of her fertility choices, she admitted that it had not been easy for her:

It has definitely been extremely difficult at times, in no small part because I am married to an academic whose work-related needs are often similar to mine. I was sleep-deprived for about ten years (no exaggeration), and this had a major impact on my ability to perform both at work and at home. I always feel stretched. More than this, when it came time to go through the tenure process, I really don't think I was ready—nor do I think that my lack of readiness had anything to do with my capabilities or my work ethic. It was simply a matter of timing. I asked my dean if I could have another year before going through the process (since I had recently had another baby, but no additional time off), but my request was denied. Since there was no structural way to account for the fact that I had taken time to raise four (as opposed to one or two) children, my choice to have those children proved to be directly at odds with what was expected of me at tenure. At tenure, and at other times, I have felt that my identity as a mother of four has been taken as a sign that I am not really dedicated to the profession. I prefer to look at it the other way around—that in spite of my choice to have a large family, I remain an enthusiastic teacher and an active scholar because I am completely dedicated to it. In any case, when I look back on my years as a junior scholar, I realize how desperately I needed someone to mentor me about work-family issues—now that I'm the one with the experience, I try my best to offer support to my younger colleagues.

Juliet is certainly an exceptional case, as there are very few women who could have four children and still get tenure. But her example should be a comfort to those who are only hoping to have one or two children. Despite success stories like Rachel's and Juliet's, however, many women are still too scared to have babies before tenure. Indeed, most of the mothers we interviewed at research universities were those who had waited until after forty to have their first child. Belinda, an assistant professor of women's studies at a large state university in California who went the single parent route, explained:

I have one son and he is five months old. I waited (I was forty when he was born) to have him for two main reasons. First, I am single and I knew I wanted to have a child and it was time so I went ahead on my own. Second, I waited until after I had fulfilled all of the tenure requirements at my institution. This was especially important because I am a single mom and I knew it would be difficult to get a lot done once the baby was here and I was right!

Linda, the sociology professor in Canada, waited until she was tenured to have her first child.

I have one child. I got pregnant, at the age of forty, several months after the submission of my tenure dossier and gave birth to her four months after being awarded tenure, at the age of forty-one. As far as the decision regarding the timing of her "arrival," it was a combination of factors. There was little uncertainty in my mind that I wanted to have a child at some point; however, I spent a considerable portion of my twenties and thirties in graduate school and abroad (e.g., learning the language I would need for my doctoral research, doing field-work). In my mid-thirties, I moved out of the U.S. and took up a tenure-track job at a top Canadian university (another major life change). In hindsight, I think I had many goals and challenges (most very rewarding) with respect to my academic career that consumed a terrific amount of my energy and atten-tion. And, I think I struggled a fair amount with balancing the demands of academia with my personal life. I also think that being a high-achieving/driven woman shaped my choices and options. While I dated a fair bit, it took me a long time to meet someone I could actually imagine spending my life with and/ or having a child [with]. I really wanted someone who would be a partner and would be supportive of my ambitions. This proved tough to find. In my mid-thirties, I began toying with the idea of artificial insemination; however, I didn't really want to raise a child alone and really pushed my biological clock until the eleventh hour. At the age of thirty-nine, I met a sweet man with whom I could imagine having a child. In all honesty, I'm not sure that either of us was 100 percent convinced that we would spend the rest of our lives together but we knew we loved each other and that we would have a very loved child. Today, we are together and have a beautiful, very loved little girl.

Diana, the economics professor, also waited until she was tenured to have children, but this was partially because she was in a commuter relationship with her partner for a long time, a situation common among dual academic couples.

It would have been easier, physically, to chase after a toddler when I was thirty instead of forty. I wish I had started earlier. We might also have thought about having more than one child, if we had started earlier. But my partner and I commuted for many years, so we had many challenges to overcome on the way to parenthood.

Clarice, a full professor of American studies at a major research university on the West Coast, blamed her decision to wait until after forty to adopt her daughter on the lack of senior mentors:

> I wish I had been encouraged. I was discouraged. I had almost no viable role models (the female academics I knew had all put their careers on hold in some way or seemed permanently furious at their spouses). I became uninterested in being a parent because I couldn't see how I could possibly do it and also have the kind of career I wanted. I try to encourage my grad students to go ahead if they want to and assure them I'll help them as much as I can, and I try to talk honestly about pros and cons. None of my professors ever said a word about it, and if I had asked them they would have been embarrassed and uninformative. They were mostly men or women without children, the ones I worked closest with.

Similarly, Miriam, who also waited until she was past forty and tenured to adopt a child, felt that the lack of mentors was crucial to her decision to delay becoming a parent:

> [When to have children was] never really discussed in graduate school but it would have been nice to hear that it is possible to start a family before being tenured. However, this means having a supportive institution and department but it also means learning how to juggle these two obligations (which many American families already do).

Although there is no good time to have a baby, some times are generally agreed to be worse than others. When Mary Ann Mason was the dean of graduate studies at the University of California, Berkeley, she started an online discussion about parenting in academia on the website of the Berkeley Parents Network,[13] and those giving advice about when to have a baby generally agreed that the years of the tenure track were the worst time. One parent wrote in:

> The two best times, in my experience/observation, to have a baby as a female academic are early or late, that is as a graduate student or as a tenured faculty member. If one does so as a graduate student in the humanities, one needs to be able to focus to finish a dissertation, but the extra year or two will not cost you much professionally. What will cost you enormously is, prejudice against women and against mothers in particular aside, the flexibility to apply for jobs around the country, unless you have an unusually accommodating spouse, and to move up the ladder to a second university quickly once you have relocated from the institution where you attended graduate school. If you wait until after tenure, it may well be too late, but by this point you have a pretty big buffer. Your career will probably go on autopilot for several years, and if you teach at Berkeley you can still expect all kinds of extra trouble in moving up the ladder, but you are in a far, far stronger position. Of the mothers (out of twice that number of women) in my department, all fit one of these two models.

So given all of these diverse experiences, when should you have your first child if you want to be a successful academic and get tenure? Whenever. You can make any timing work as long as you remember to plan for the time that the pregnancy and first few months of motherhood do take. Being overly optimistic about a seamless pregnancy or expecting to be able to return to full productivity in short order seems to us a recipe for disappointment. So who can you get to help you? Could your partner take a leave? Would your parents or siblings have time to help out? Can you afford a full-time caregiver for those early months? Don't be afraid to ask for help. If no one is going to be able to help, then you need to plan for some nonproductive time (nonproductive in terms of your career; you are being very productive in terms of your other life goals). The period after your prelims (qualifying exams) and before work on the dissertation begins in earnest might work for some. Taking two years to finish the dissertation instead of one might work for others (as long as you don't just teach more to make up the lost income). If you are an assistant professor and your college or university offers you a paid leave, take it. Don't worry about what your colleagues are going to think. They are going to think whatever they would think about your commitment or lack of commitment to your profession based on the "crime" of having a child, so it won't be any worse if you take the leave. We all need to use those leaves, so that they become as ordinary as a paid vacation week for an administrator or a sick leave for someone who has recently been diagnosed with a severe illness. Using them will help remove any stigma that currently accompanies them.

Should you try to have a child over summer "break"? No. Rachel made this mistake with her first child. He was very carefully planned so that he would be born at the beginning of summer break. First, it is foolhardy to think that you can plan so precisely. Talk about adding stress to one's life. But even more importantly, the beginning of summer break turns out to be the best time for the university, but the worst time for you. Why? Do you really take a break during "break"? No, that is when you get your research done. That is when you do a substantial amount of writing or put in the long hours at the lab, in the field, or in the archives. If our job is both teaching and research, why should only research time be interrupted by childbirth? Mostly, you should give up the idea that you can plan a birth down to the month, but if your body chooses to cooperate, aim for right smack in the middle of teaching term. If you're lucky, you will get a few weeks of teaching off before the baby comes to make up for your lost research time once the baby does arrive.

If the baby comes in the summer, you may still be eligible for a leave in the fall. If you are, take it. As we have argued, you must expect some reduction in your productivity after the baby is born. The leave from teaching will allow you to spend more time on both the baby and your research. Would a reduced teaching load for two terms work better for you than a term with no teaching? If so, ask for it. If not, relish your term off. If this is your second baby, continue to use the same day care situation you were using before the second baby arrived. The stability will help your first child, you will have more energy for positive interaction with your firstborn after day care, and you might get a little writing done during the baby's nap. Or even better, you might be able to have a nap yourself.

What about the timing of the second baby relative to the first? Our vote is to spread them out as much as you can, given again your age and the number of children you want. Why? Mostly, because having kids is not something to get out of the way. It is something to enjoy, and you will be able to enjoy the new baby and the older sibling more if you are not constantly in the throes of a desperate time-crunch crisis. Second, because you want to stay in the game.

If you want to withdraw from the academic game, then the timing of the second child relative to the first matters less. But if you do withdraw, do it with full knowledge that it is very difficult, sometimes impossible, to return, at least at the same level. Karen Conway, professor of economics at the University of New Hampshire, wrote, "Work interruptions to raise children are more punitive [than they used to be before the research bar was raised]. It is not that difficult to teach a course after five years off; it is very difficult to convince people that you can and will do research after five years off."[14] Not returning at the same level may be acceptable to you, but it doesn't have to be that way. If you have one baby at a time, use plenty of help (paid, unpaid, relative's, partner's), and take the leaves you are entitled to, you can keep all the balls in the air. Another reason for spreading out the time between children is that you may be able to wait until after tenure for the second baby. Again, you need to be very clear with yourself about how important that second child is. For both Kristen and Rachel, it was really important to have one. The second one was much more optional. Our sense is that many of you also feel that way.

HOW MANY CHILDREN DO YOU WANT?

So how many should you have? Kristen has one, Rachel has four. Given that, you may not be surprised that we think the answer is somewhere between one and four. One is great. Forget all that stuff about the lonely or spoiled only child. An only child gets lots of attention, and attention is good. You get to fully enjoy every age without having to juggle the needs of another child. You have enough other things to juggle: your partner's needs, your workload, your own needs, and so on. The only child is very much a child who enjoys spending time with adults, so you will spend more time together overall. Plus, if the child is in day care, most of the time there is spent constantly surrounded by other children anyway.

Two? Well, you enjoyed one toddler learning to walk, and one preschooler learning to count, so why wouldn't you want to do it again? Two lets you do that, plus they have each other. Sometimes that is not a plus, but other times having a sibling can be nice—someone to toss the ball with before dinner. Also, sometimes the fact that your child has a sibling is useful to you, like when Rachel's younger son was having teenage relationship problems, and she asked her older son to talk with the younger one. (He certainly wasn't going to talk to his mother or father about it.)

Three? Moving to three can be a bit scary, as you can't use the "divide and conquer" strategy of parenting. (Those of you who are single parents lost that option with the birth of the second child.) You and your partner will be outnumbered. But having three children leads to a lively, childcentric home. Some of us enjoy that; others are definitely not going there.

Four? "Don't you know how to stop this from happening?" That is what a colleague's wife said to Rachel when it became obvious that she was pregnant with the fourth child. Four had, in fact, always been Rachel's goal, but it was clear from people's reaction that Rachel was pushing the limits of their tolerance. Robin Wilson recently published an article in the *Chronicle of Higher Education* titled "Is Having More Than Two Children an Unspoken Taboo?,"[15] in which she discusses why it may be that two is the unwritten limit. There is a sense that more than two is somehow greedy, or that you are not serious enough about your job. This is certainly the impression that Juliet, the history professor, got as well—four just isn't serious. Andrea O'Reilly, based on her study of sixty academic women with children, explains, "You're supposed to be this go-getter, and your work is your life. You're not supposed to be encumbered."[16] Yes, there will be some raised eyebrows if you have three or four children, but don't forget that there were raised eyebrows about having one child as well. You need to decide how much you can push the envelope, but more importantly how many is right for you and your partner and for your other kids. Those college tuition bills come all too soon, and the orthodontist bills come even sooner!

What if you are sure you want to have children, and you know how many you want, but you don't yet have a partner? You need to figure out if you are willing to have a child without a partner. Like all the other questions in this chapter, it is a very difficult consideration, one that some will answer one way and others differently. If you are still holding out for a partner, make that a priority. You need to invest some time in the partner-locating endeavor, just like any of your other goals. You should think about it especially during your job search, as there will be fewer eligible partners in some places than others. If you are willing to go it alone, seek out other women who have made this choice (a great place to start is the website www.searchmothers.com). You are not the only woman academic to have made this choice. In fact, there are so many academic women who adopt children that there are an ever-growing number of monographs and edited volumes about experiences with the domestic or the international adoption system. Many professors in the social sciences who do research abroad will adopt babies from the countries they work in. Others go through the foster-care system. One of Kristen's colleagues went through a special adoption agency that works specifically with single professional women, and she now has a beautiful daughter from Guatemala. In addition to the adoption option there is also the artificial insemination route to childbearing.

Are you a lesbian couple thinking about having children? The same handicaps apply to you if you decide to be the birth mother, so you should understand that your partner will have it easier. The physical acts of gestation and then birth and subsequent breast-feeding are hard on your body. Many universities now extend health-insurance benefits to same-sex domestic partners. You may be entitled to a parental leave based on the birth of your partner's child, or based on the adoption of a young child. To echo one of the themes of this chapter, if you are entitled to benefits, take them.

Are you on the job market? Ask for a copy of the faculty handbook before you accept a job. If you have a choice, think about the differences in the "family friendliness" of the benefits packages. Once you are at the university, see who is on the benefits committee and quietly lobby the members of that committee to push for tenure-clock-stopping leaves and paid parental leaves. Enough schools are providing them now that your school may be willing to consider them, not because they care, but because they are worried about the competitiveness of their offers. Several of the women we surveyed complained about not having these options available. Sonia, an associate professor of history at a public university in the South, explained:

> There was no maternity leave (only unpaid leave) until *after* (the year after) I had my twins. So I got *no* paid leave whatsoever and there was no effort to make amends for all the unpaid time I had to take. Also, I was told point blank that people thought I was being a "slacker" for taking unpaid leave—a year for each child—*and* I was expected to produce scholarship during those unpaid years. I had *higher* expectations at tenure time because of my leave (frankly even higher than many childless colleagues with the same number of clock stops).

TEXTBOX 4.1.   FAMILY-FRIENDLY
POLICIES

Support for combining motherhood and academia is still a relatively new phenomenon. After years of academic mothers struggling against unmoving institutions with rigid tenure timetables and a sense that any time off should happen during teaching breaks, things are beginning to change. The Family and Medical Leave Act (FMLA) passed in 1993 says that any U.S. employee who has been on the job for more than one year (not necessarily consecutive), who has worked more than 1,250 hours in the last twelve months, and who works for a company that has more than fifty employees (or is a public employee) is eligible for job-holding unpaid leave of up to twelve weeks for the birth or adoption of a child, or to care for serious health issues involving him- or herself, a spouse, children, or parents. This is the right of *every* worker in the United States. It is not a special privilege to be grudgingly handed out to you by your dean.

In addition to FMLA, 40 percent of colleges and universities provide leaves longer than the twelve-week minimum, and about half have on-site child care. Other policies more recently adopted by a growing number of institutions (but still a minority) include tenure-clock-stopping leaves, flexible scheduling to meet family needs, subsidized child care, paid parental leaves, and help with spousal employment. Hollenshead, Sullivan, and Smith from the Center for the Education of Women at the University of Michigan surveyed 255 colleges and universities in 2000, asking about a large set of potential family-friendly policies.[1] In total, 43 percent of the institutions reported having tenure-clock-stopping leave, but the leave details varied greatly by type. Research universities are the most likely to offer tenure-clock-stopping leaves—86 percent, compared to only 23 percent of colleges. This difference in opportunities across institutions leads Saranna Thornton, a strong advocate for strengthening institutional support for faculty families, to advise that you consider *where* to have your baby instead of *when* to have your baby.[2]

(continued)

Universities and colleges have been less quick to adopt policies that cost money. Only 22 percent of research universities in the study offered paid leave for dependent care; 32 percent offered course-release policies; 29 percent offered reduced appointments; and 22 percent allowed tenure-track faculty to have part-time appointments or to job share. Certainly you should consider the availability of these policies as one of the criteria you use should you be lucky enough to be choosing among job offers. Most universities now post their faculty handbooks online, making it easy to find out what the parental leave policy is without "outing" yourself to the dean.

If you already have tenure, push your university to adopt as many family-friendly policies as you can. We hope you will never have to benefit from a policy that provides paid leave if you are unable to teach because of a serious illness of your child or spouse, but you never know. It is important to remind administrators that they have the option of taking paid vacation days to cope with the illness of a family member, while faculty do not accrue vacation days. One could imagine a policy where faculty members accrued "emergency leave" days in the same way that administrators accrue vacation days.

Having formal policies on the books is not enough. Whether you are looking for a family-friendly institution or trying to create one, you need to think about whether faculty members feel free to use the policies. There have been a number of studies that show that family-friendly policies tend to be underused by faculty. When asked why, faculty indicate that they are afraid to use them because they do not want to signal that they are not serious about their jobs. Kelly Ward and Lisa Wolf-Wendel, who have done considerable research on the academy and motherhood, call this the "fear factor."[3] Faculty members are afraid to use these policies (many of which are very clunky), and administrators are afraid to make better policies for fear of being seen as "giving away the store" or favoring one group over another. Institutions need to go beyond policies to truly create a family-friendly climate. Department heads need to make it clear to both junior and senior colleagues that having a family does not disqualify one as a scholar. Once you have tenure, talk about your own children, invite children to department get-togethers, and don't hold faculty meetings at 4:30 in the afternoon. Mary Ann Mason and her colleagues at the University of California, Berkeley, make a strong case for changing conditions in the academy to make things more baby neutral. They argue that the best and the brightest PhDs are turning away from the academy because it is perceived as not allowing a satisfying work/life balance.[4] This can and must be changed.

Marissa, a full professor of history at a large public university in the Midwest, had a similar experience:

I work at a state university with a Research I profile and a really crappy parental leave policy (less so now than when I had kids, I worked to change it to twelve weeks from six). If you want to have a kid the old-fashioned way (and even with adoption, there are terrible costs to one's relationship to the child, in many environments with little/no parental leave), at most universities in the U.S. you are dealing with the FMLA leave as the policy of record, so you have six weeks to get your infant and yourself in a place where you can be mutually autonomous for five to seven hours a day. Good luck to all with that. I remember nothing from my two semesters when I had tiny babies, was nursing, and had to teach after the magnanimous six-week leave. I am the primary breadwinner in my family and couldn't afford to take a leave without pay. I tried to work around many limitations and was very lucky to have a partner who is flexible, in love with the kids, and ready to take over when need be. But nursing is nursing, and that he couldn't do. In addition, hormonally I was in a crazy place that put me in the position of teaching via automatic pilot. That was the hardest period.

Finally, as we make it to the senior ranks, it is our job to talk with junior colleagues about their options and to really push our colleagues to accept that a parental leave is not a research leave in disguise. Be careful that your tenure committee or your external reviewers do not expect more scholarship from you, given all of the "time off" that you have had. This problem is especially acute in the disciplines where peer-reviewed articles are more important than books. Because your work was out there in the pipeline for a longer period of time, some may expect that your tenure dossier should contain more published work.

The important thing is to know the institutional culture of the place where you are hoping to land a job, and to have a clear sense of what you need to accomplish in order to achieve tenure there. It is to these questions that we now turn.

5

The Last Year of Graduate School

Heading for the Job Market and Choosing the Right Institution

The juggling act that is the life of an academic begins sometime during your years of graduate study. After your course work is done, you will often have classes to teach, papers to grade, office hours to hold, and, of course, a dissertation to write. You also need to be out there finding a partner if you want one, or else devoting at least a little time to the partner you already have, and maybe you already have children to add to the mix. It is important to realize that your life as a professor is pretty much the same as the life you experience as a graduate student. If you hate this mix and think life will be easier as soon as you have the title "Doctor" in front of your name, you need to think again about a job in the academy. The time allocation across the various parts of your job may change somewhat over time, but all the basic tasks are already in place.

Of course, the most important thing for you to do while in graduate school is finish your dissertation. Make that your priority, just as we later suggest you make research your priority during your years pre-tenure. All the advice in chapter 6 and chapter 7 about time use in the early years of the tenure track applies to you here as well. Your dissertation does not have to be perfect. What it needs to be is good enough for your committee and good enough to be a strong foundation for some publications soon after you finish the dissertation. The best dissertation is a completed dissertation.

Be sure to listen carefully to each of your dissertation advisers. They are giving you clues about what they need you to do in order for them to sign off on your thesis, and they will have advice on what changes will need to be made for publication. Check in with your advisers regularly. Use these meetings or even email exchanges to update them on your progress and to commit to interim deadlines, such as "I plan to have the third chapter done by this date, and I will submit an abstract for a paper that will turn into the fourth chapter by that date."

Your fellow graduate students are your future colleagues and collaborators. In some disciplines co-authored articles are beginning to be accepted for dissertation chapters. At the present time, however, we would recommend against doing this, as most departments still wonder about who did what on co-authored projects. Instead, this is the time to map out a collaborative project with a graduate-school colleague that you two can start when you near the end of the dissertation process. Writing a joint grant proposal for a multi-year project is the perfect way to create a concrete research agenda that you can complete in the future. If you are in the sciences, foster good relationships with your lab partners and think about joint projects for the future. If you are in the humanities you will probably be doing solo work for a while, but it is still a good idea to develop close relationships with graduate students in your cohort, some of whom may go on to be book or journal editors, conference organizers, and manuscript and grant reviewers in your field. In all disciplines, you and your graduate-student colleagues can organize panels for national conventions and colloquia at your institutions, where you can give papers and develop your ideas.

If teaching is a component of your graduate-school experience, you need to begin the practice of devoting enough time, but not too much time, to your teaching. We know that is easier said than done, so you need to be very conscious of how you are spending your precious hours each day. Find out as much as you can about student expectations. If everyone else is assigning four problem sets, don't assign eight. If everyone else gives two midterms and a final, you probably don't want to just give a final. A well-constructed exam or writing assignment is easier to grade than a poorly constructed one. Don't be in a rush when writing exams or assignments. Write them in enough time to let them sit overnight. The next day, revisit the exam, thinking about the amount of time that will be needed for grading it. Often one question can be deleted at this point. You will be happy you deleted the question (even if it is a great question), and the answers to the other questions will be better since the students will have more time to answer them carefully. This same principle applies to the readings you assign for each class. Often two articles will do as well as three, or taking two days to cover the monograph instead of one results in a better understanding of the key points with less overall reading for you. Potential employers will look at your student-opinion forms from your graduate-school years, but they also understand that teaching is something we get better at over time.

If you have children during the time that you are writing your dissertation, all the advice in chapter 7 holds for you now as well. Writing your dissertation is a job, a job that you need to have the time to do well. Make sure you have time on your own at least five days a week that is solely dedicated to working on the dissertation. As little as three solid hours a day is reasonable (although more time is always better), as long as you *only* work on your thesis during that time (no web surfing or checking email). Money is, of course, an issue while in graduate school, but good child care is a sound investment. The sooner you get your dissertation finished, the sooner you can go on the job market and the sooner your salary will increase to help pay for that expensive child care.

One last thing to consider is when to go on the job market relative to when you finish your PhD. Since most programs do not have an upper limit on how long it should take before you file your dissertation, it's not a bad idea to go out on the job market before you file your dissertation. The key is to be almost done, so that your letter writers can confidently explain that you will have your doctoral degree before you start any job. If you do not get a job, you can delay the filing of your dissertation until the following year and use the extra time as a graduate student to start turning your dissertation into a book or a series of journal articles. Kristen's daughter was due on November 14, and Kristen finished writing her dissertation a few days before that. She had given an almost-complete draft to her dissertation committee members, who had all given her feedback and comments. They were generally confident that they would sign off on it once the revisions were made. Kristen went on the job market while she was pregnant, but she had decided not to file the final dissertation until she had a job, even if that meant she would be supposedly revising for another three semesters. Berkeley had very good health insurance, and Kristen had a research fellowship and was also teaching. She could afford to delay if necessary. As it happened, Bowdoin was her first campus visit and her first job offer, which she accepted well before any of the other schools to which she had applied made their short lists. She happily accepted the offer, and only filed her dissertation once she had returned the signed employment contract to Bowdoin and actually moved to Maine.

Although every discipline is different, thinking strategically about when to go on the job market and what kinds of institutions you will apply to is one of the most important parts of your graduate-school career. The decisions that you make about when and where to apply will affect your work and family life for many years to come. Although these decisions are never set in stone, they are certainly important enough to invest the time and effort needed to gather as much information as you can about the process. It is to the question of choosing an institution that we now turn.

THE JOB MARKET

It is important to understand that academia is like a pyramid; a lot of people enter into the profession by pursuing graduate degrees, but the number of people who can move up in the profession dwindles at each stage. The pyramid of academia becomes sharply narrower exactly at the point where you finish your PhD and head out onto the job market. According to a 2003 report from the American Association of University Professors, three out of four hires in the 1990s were appointed to non-tenure-track jobs. A more recent report from the same organization in 2006 found that although in 1975, 56.8 percent of faculty positions were tenured or on the tenure track, by 2003 this percentage had dropped to 35.1 percent.[1] In 2004, the American Historical Association reported that only 32 percent of those who had received their PhDs in history between 1990 and 2004 had obtained and currently held a position in a college or university history department.[2] In sociology, longitudinal research on the 1996–1997 PhD sociology cohort counted doctoral students who were in a tenure-track position by the year 2001. The study found that 36 percent of men with no children who received a PhD in sociology in 1996–1997 had secured a tenure-track position, as did 33 percent of women with doctorates in sociology without children. As for those sociology PhDs who had children in graduate school, 25 percent of the men with children had a tenure-track job by 2001, and 24 percent of the women with sociology PhDs and children had tenure-track positions.[3] This means that even for those men with no children, two-thirds of sociology PhD holders had not landed a tenure-track job (or perhaps did not want to land a tenure-track job) by 2001. These figures clearly indicate that there are many more PhDs granted than there are jobs in the academy, and that competition for these jobs is fierce.

So even if you do not have children, in many fields the chances are not in favor of your landing a tenure-track job, and you may be forced into accepting an adjunct position for several years. (See our advice on being an adjunct in the chapter 6 textbox.) For many graduate students, the academic job market is their first real ego-bashing. It can be incredibly disheartening to send out more than sixty applications and garner not a single campus interview. Yet this is a common occurrence for those on the job market. It takes a particular type of thick-skinned individual to gather up her courage and go out onto the market year after year. But this is the only way to land a tenure-track position for most newly minted PhDs.

If you have read this far in the book, then we assume you are really committed to this career path, and so you need to be thinking about what kind of institution will be the best suited for your particular personal and professional goals. Of course, we understand that most graduate students don't have much choice in the matter, that the academic job market is very fickle, and that most graduate students aren't in a position to be choosy about where they take their first job. But you might have some choice this year, or you may need to decide whether to go back on the market next year to change institutions if your first job is not at the type of institution that best suits your goals and skill set. The vast majority of PhD students come from research universities where their mentors and role models are professors who have chosen to teach at a research university. This often means that graduate students are encouraged, either explicitly or implicitly, to seek employment in similar types of institutions. But there is an enormous variety of academic institutions in the United States for which you will see jobs advertised.

There are many stereotypes about the working conditions and tenure expectations at different institutions. For the purposes of this chapter we use the classification system of the Carnegie Foundation for the Advancement of Teaching, which was updated in 2010. We focus on four general types of institutions: the Research I universities (the top tier of the doctoral-granting universities), the comprehensive university (formerly the Research II and Research III universities), the liberal arts college, and the associate's college. When faced with job ads from this wide range of institutions, graduate students often get little or no

guidance about the working conditions outside of the research-university setting and so have little to go on when deciding how well a particular institution
will fit with their own ideas of work/family balance. Our goal in this section of
the chapter is to inform you about what you're up against when starting out on
the tenure track in different places, and to address the accuracy of stereotypes
about these places based on empirical research that has been done on mothers
working their way up the ranks in different types of institutions.

For instance, one stereotype is that research universities are incredibly
unfriendly to anyone with small children, or indeed to anyone with personal
obligations that take them away from their research and monklike devotion to
scholarly inquiry. And this is true to a certain extent, because of the quantity
of research required of professors on the tenure track at research institutions.
But the "publish or perish" mentality at research universities is clearly spelled
out for young professors, and junior faculty know that research is the number one goal they must meet in order to get tenure. Teaching and service are
much less important, and junior faculty can focus their best efforts on their
research. At other types of institutions, where teaching is more important,
service burdens are much higher, and where professors are expected to cater
to undergraduate students, productivity requirements can seem overwhelming. Tenure expectations here will include both high-quality research and
good teaching as well as time devoted to service obligations. A study by Lisa
Wolf-Wendel and Kelly Ward found that women who had small children at
research universities believed that it would be easier for them to achieve tenure than women with small children at liberal arts colleges.[4] Indeed, this same
study found that women with young children employed at liberal arts colleges
were far more nervous about their chances of achieving tenure because they
felt the standards were so subjective. And this is without taking into account
that, in recent years, many large research universities have put in place much
more progressive parental-leave policies.[5]

The irony, of course, is that many women will accept a position at a liberal-
arts college over a research university because they believe the liberal arts
college to be more family friendly. A study by Carol S. Hollenshead, Beth Sullivan, and Gilia Smith does show that private universities are more likely than
public universities to have paid parental leave, which may be the source of the
sense that liberal arts colleges are more family friendly.[6] The main thing you
need to do is check the faculty handbook at the school you are considering,

and watch for clues when you are on campus for an interview. A given top research university may be more family friendly in terms of parental leaves and extensions of the tenure clock than a regional comprehensive university that will grant tenure for less research. Admittedly, sometimes institutions are simply apples and oranges, and geographic factors as well as family commitments will weigh heavily on where graduate students choose to go. But it is important to think about institutional types, and to recognize that there is considerable variation among institutions within the same category. In our experience, graduate students are woefully uninformed about the differences among institutions.

RESEARCH UNIVERSITIES

Research universities are institutions that award twenty or more doctoral degrees (not including professional degrees such as law, medicine, etc.). The top tier of the research universities in North America are the sixty-one American and two Canadian universities affiliated with the Association of American Universities, an organization that caters to the "research intensive" university. (See appendix 1 for a full list of AAU affiliates.) These are sometimes referred to as Research I universities, and this distinction is earned by having, among other factors, a certain number of doctoral programs, a certain total amount of research funding, and a certain level of faculty research productivity. A subset of these institutions constitutes the Ivy League: Brown, Columbia, Cornell, Dartmouth, Harvard, Penn, Princeton, and Yale. Together with other institutions, which include MIT, Stanford, Berkeley, Duke, UCLA, Michigan, NYU, and the University of Chicago, these institutions comprise the top stratum of the research-university heap. (This, of course, does not include the top universities abroad, of which there are many, but they are beyond the scope of this book.)

Research universities are the places where research is prioritized well above teaching and service and the publication expectations are the highest. Teaching loads are low, usually only two courses per semester and in some cases only one course per semester, depending on your discipline. This is the true "publish or perish" atmosphere and the atmosphere with which you are probably most familiar, since chances are you attended one of the universities in this category as a graduate student. Service expectations are also limited, although you must take into account committee meetings in your department as well as graduate-student admissions and graduate-student advising, which can take up a considerable amount of your time. In general, one can assume that undergraduate teaching is not a high priority, and you will not be expected to put as much effort into teaching your undergraduate classes as you would at another type of institution. Universities such as these often rely on graduate-student teaching assistants to lead discussion sections of your classes and to do some if not all of your grading. When Kristen worked as an adjunct professor at Berkeley in 2000, she was surprised to find that paid graduate-student assistants did all of the grading for the seventy students in the lecture class. Her primary responsibilities consisted of designing the syllabus, delivering the lectures, and holding office hours. In contrast, even as a tenured associate professor at Bowdoin, she often finds herself grading seventy undergraduate papers or exams by herself.

But where service and teaching commitments are light, research commitments are high. These research commitments take up an incredible amount of time and often depend on circumstances beyond your control. Recall Rachel's story in chapter 1, when her key article sat on the editor's desk for eighteen months and then came back "revise and resubmit." Since most journals won't allow you to simultaneously submit articles to other journals, your research can be held in limbo for years before being published. Not only does this increase the chances of your results or ideas being scooped by another scholar, but you also run the risk of having your research overtaken by events in certain fields, particularly in the social sciences. (You can overcome some of these problems by making your papers available in a working-paper series, or even just on your website.) This may lead young scholars to submit to journals that have a less rigorous peer-review process, but this strategy is not a good one at a research university. Your external reviewers will look at the ranking of the journals in your particular field when you are being judged for tenure. This is an extremely frustrating double bind for junior faculty who have only a certain number of years to publish in the top journals in their field before they come up for promotion.

Another common requirement at research universities (depending on the discipline) is the ability to bring in large external grants or to win prestigious fellowships. Writing grant and fellowship applications can take an enormous amount of time and energy, but in certain fields, successful grant writing is also a requirement of tenure. You should not necessarily think of it as time away from scholarship, since the research you do in writing the grant will be useful to you in doing the project. In the sciences, at large research institutions, grant writing is a necessity, and many universities expect that junior faculty will bring in funds to support their lab.

Attending conferences and seminars and giving talks at other major research universities is also taken as evidence of your research prowess, either directly or because these activities lead to additional citations, which matter for some tenure-decision-making processes. All of these things take time, and many people avoid the research-university setting because they believe they will be unable to have a family and publish the required amount needed to achieve tenure in their field. Tenure denials at research universities are inevitably for lack of research productivity.

Another reality that young, newly minted PhDs should be aware of is that many of the top institutions have a so-called revolving door policy when it comes to tenure. At places like Harvard, Yale, Princeton, Columbia, and others, it is nearly impossible for a young faculty member to achieve tenure. This means that assistant professorships at these types of institutions should be looked upon as extended postdocs. The good news is that even if you are denied tenure at a top research university, you can usually get a tenured position at a lower-ranked research university. Of course, this means uprooting your life and having to deal with the rejection of your colleagues, never an easy task. It means that most young assistant professors at these institutions are constantly on the job market before they come up for tenure, hoping to be poached away by another university of similar caliber. These are the realities of working in the Research I setting. You should accept one of these jobs clearly understanding the challenges in front of you.

Despite the high tenure standards for research, however, there are many advantages of working at a doctoral-granting institution. First of all, these are the institutions that are the highest on the totem pole of academic status and confer the most prestige upon individual scholars. If that kind of thing is important to you, then you should be honest with yourself. If you want to be at an institution like Yale, settling for anything else is a true pathway to misery because you will always be comparing your home institution with the fantasy of some Ivy League school. Another advantage of a position at a research university is that the opportunity to work with really good graduate students and excellent colleagues can be invigorating and can push your research in new and exciting directions. You will also be immersed in an active intellectual community where guest lecturers, seminars, and conferences are constantly available to you. You will be on the cutting edge of knowledge production in your field. Indeed, for many scientists who work in laboratory settings, the large research university may be your only option, particularly if you need graduate students to help with your experiments. Many of these institutions also have generous internal funds earmarked to help support the start-up of junior-faculty research. Finally, these institutions have excellent library re-sources, and, if you are in the sciences, they are the ones that can provide you with the most elaborate and best-equipped laboratories.

Because these universities are usually quite large, they also tend to have a lot more support for faculty and graduate students with young children. Many research universities have on-campus day care centers and may even have lab schools attached to them. Because research universities have come under fire in recent years for disproportionately denying tenure to women with small children, or for just being family unfriendly in general, the better-endowed research universities have recently made big steps in trying to equalize the playing field between professors with young children and those without. For instance, both Harvard and the University of Chicago now give new faculty moms and dads one full year on the tenure clock for each child born. Harvard also has an emergency child care fund and provides special support to junior faculty so that they can arrange child care in order to attend professional con-ventions.[7] Even with these new policies in place, however, the extra time and funding is not always enough to meet the publication expectations of junior faculty at these institutions.

Despite this, in their study of job satisfaction and work-family balance by various institutional types, Wolf-Wendel and Ward found that the women with children they interviewed at research universities were relatively satisfied with their jobs.[8] The researchers found that these new mothers believed that it would take particular dedication to get tenure and that it would require all of their personal resources, but they still thought they had a chance and were generally happy with their institutions. Wolf-Wendel and Ward argue that this was because the tenure expectations at Research I universities were per-ceived as being more clearly defined.[9] Junior faculty members knew, without any doubt, that the most important thing was research. Publications were the coin of the realm, and maintaining a steady pace of research and writing were the keys to academic success. As we will see below, women at lower-ranked institutions, who we might have thought would have more flexibility and certainly have less pressure to publish, often feel greater insecurity about their chances for tenure because the tenure standards at their institutions are more opaque or constantly changing.

Mary Ann Mason found that graduate students with children were more likely than others to shy away from research universities, citing a desire for work-family balance as the reason for their decision to apply to other types of academic institutions.[10] While it is true that the research-university atmosphere is not for everyone, and that you may be able to move to a research university at a later point in your career (as long as you keep on publishing, and stay current in your field by attending professional-association meetings and giving invited lectures and talks to colleagues in other departments around the country), the message here is not to automatically assume that research universities are less family friendly than other types of institutions. The research standards there are definitely high, but there is a reduction of other pressures. Wolf-Wendel and Ward claim that, in general, "tenure track mothers at research universities found that they could navigate the challenges of combining motherhood with their academic careers, although the effort required personal commitment and endurance."[11]

COMPREHENSIVE UNIVERSITIES

Comprehensive universities are institutions that award more than fifty master's degrees and fewer than twenty doctoral degrees. These are sometimes referred to as Research II and Research III institutions, although the Carnegie Classification System no longer employs these terms. Wolf-Wendel and Ward divide these universities into two types: *regional comprehensives* and *striving comprehensives*. There are many institutions that fall into this category, so we will be making some broad generalizations here. The best thing to do is research the institutions to which you are applying or from which you have been offered a job and carefully consider the type of institution. Regional comprehensives are universities that try to have comprehensive coverage over a wide variety of disciplines and an undergraduate population that is largely drawn from the surrounding region and which may be less prepared for college than students at the more elite institutions. Teaching loads at these institutions are higher than at Research Is, as high as three or four courses per semester (although professors may be teaching multiple sections of the same course). In California, most of the University of California system universities would be considered Research I tier, whereas the California State University system would be regarded as regional comprehensives.

Striving comprehensives are regional comprehensives that aspire to join the ranks of the Research I universities. Think of them as Research I wannabes. At these institutions, tenure standards can be quite unclear, and the administration may demand that junior faculty distinguish themselves in both teaching and research, as well as taking on a considerable amount of institutional service. Wolf-Wendel and Ward found that women with young children at these universities were the least satisfied because they felt that tenure standards were constantly changing and they did not know what they needed to do in order to ensure their academic and professional success. Furthermore, even though these institutions were now requiring more research and a greater number of publications, they did not have the resources to fund faculty research or faculty conference travel in order to facilitate this increased demand for research productivity. They also put pressure on faculty to bring in grants and win fellowships while at the same time maintaining a high teaching load and considerable service commitments. Wolf-Wendel and Ward found that "this pressure was exacerbated by the absence of a research culture and an institution where senior faculty had limited publication records, and so were not helpful or realistic in terms of setting expectations."[12]

Research expectations are considerably lower at most regional comprehensives than at the Research Is or the striving comprehensives. A colleague of Kristen's who teaches at one of the California State University campuses said that her scholarship requirements for tenure consisted of two book chapters and two book reviews. Another colleague at a state university in the Pacific Northwest received tenure with two book chapters and a few conference presentations to professional societies. Teaching evaluations and availability to students are much more important at regional comprehensives, and tenure standards are relatively clear and straightforward: be a good teacher and a good campus citizen. As a result, Wolf-Wendel and Ward found that women with small children at these universities were relatively satisfied with their jobs and optimistic about their chances for tenure. In our own informal interviews, we found that colleagues working at regional comprehensives were also generally satisfied, although they feared that without time to publish or do research they would not be able to move on to more prestigious institutions in the future, when their children got older.

It can be hard to tell the difference between the regional comprehensive universities and the striving comprehensives. Listen carefully when the chair or the dean tells you about the research expectations. Beware the Research I wannabes. They don't have the resources of a Research I, the teaching loads are greater, and yet they evaluate mainly on research. These can be some of the harshest places to work. A colleague of Rachel's at one of these institutions was told quite explicitly that if she had a child before being tenured she would not get tenure. Rachel suggested that she look for another job, but the woman's husband was happy with his job in the same town, so she stayed. A mentee at a "Women in Economics" session reported pretty much the same story from a different Research I wannabe, despite the fact that this school might well have been categorized as a Research II wannabe.

The irony, of course, is that many women choose a comprehensive university over a Research I because they believe that the tenure standards are lower and more amenable to combining work with family responsibilities. But the Wolf-Wendel and Ward study shows that women at research universities actually believe they have a higher chance of achieving tenure and feel they have less stress than women at striving comprehensives. When you are on the job market and deciding which types of institutions you are going to consider, the key is to do your homework and figure out which of the regional comprehensives are striving comprehensives. Often this is hard to determine unless you get a campus interview and ask specifically about research expectations. But you can also do some calling around, talk to your mentors, talk to other graduate students who were on the job market the year before, or just study the university's website for evidence that it is placing a higher emphasis on research. If you find this to be the case, be careful. If you get a job offer from a university like this, make sure you do your utmost to get a clear sense of what level of research is expected for tenure.

The one possible benefit of the striving comprehensives is that you will have an incentive to keep publishing. You may want to take a job at a comprehensive university when your children are young in the hope that you can move up to a Research I university at a later stage in your career, when your children are older. This will only be possible if you continue with an active research program and establish a name for yourself in your field. And it is possible that your striving comprehensive will make it, earning the sought-after reputation for producing excellent scholars in the future. Either way, one advantage of being in a striving-comprehensive atmosphere is that it might give you greater future flexibility than being at a regional comprehensive and focusing almost exclusively on your teaching. It may be harder to combine motherhood and academia here, but there could be long-term benefits.

Given the wide variety of institutions in this category, always do research before applying to a position at a school that you've never heard of. It's important not only to find out about the tenure expectations (i.e., your teaching load, the amount of service you're expected to do, how much personal interaction you will have with undergraduates, how much social time you will have to spend with your students outside of class), but also to learn what counts as scholarship at your institution. Is it only peer-reviewed journal articles, or will book reviews be included in your research dossier? Obviously the best place to start looking for this information is the Internet, but you can also contact individuals at the institution before accepting a campus interview (after making sure that these individuals have nothing to do with the search committee). Another thing that you can do is find someone who recently left this institution for a job someplace else. A little effort will usually turn someone up who is likely to give you the real scoop about the institution to which you are applying. Always ask about parental-leave policies, tenure clocks, on-campus child care, and so forth, but also think about the type of person you are and what combination of teaching, research, service, and social interaction with students will make you the most satisfied. Place less weight on academic status; at this point just worry about finding a job that will let you do everything you want to do, including starting your family.

In our discussions with colleagues, we asked professor moms to think about how their institutions affected their decisions about family, and what advice they would give to younger scholars hoping to combine an academic career with motherhood. Miriam, an associate professor at a Research I, had this advice to those trying to decide between different types of universities:

> Know your rights and responsibilities up front—get them in writing early on. You will be surprised how many faculty don't know the rules governing their employment and tenure and how departments are footloose and fancy free with the standards. . . . Read your faculty handbook and know the standards for

tenure and promotion. If you are unsure, make sure you get [a letter] in writing early on in your tenure-track years, especially [about] how leave without pay or parental leave is considered in the deliberations. I would recommend that in any such letter the words "leave without pay years may not be considered formally or informally in assessment of tenure and promotion" should appear. There are no absolute standards for tenure because we all can cite cases where the absolute standard has been changed. So know all of the outliers to the "absolute," especially those for the men in your department. You will be surprised how many don't fit into the "absolute."

BACCALAUREATE COLLEGES

There is another category of institution called the *baccalaureate college*. These are four-year institutions that primarily grant bachelor's degrees. These are often referred to as the *liberal arts colleges*, but not all liberal arts colleges are the same. Just as there is a wide variety of institutions in the comprehensive-university category, so too is there a diversity of institutions that fall under the rubric of the baccalaureate colleges. In particular, it is important to distinguish between the top-tier liberal arts colleges and smaller, less well-known colleges. The major difference between them is the level of resources available. Another difference is the selectivity of the admissions policy. These two characteristics are highly correlated. In Howard Greene and Matthew Greene's 2000 book called *The Hidden Ivies*,[13] the authors identify what they call the "Little Ivies": Amherst, Williams, Swarthmore, Bowdoin, Bates, Colby, Hamilton, Middlebury, and Wesleyan colleges. Add to this list Oberlin, Reed, Haverford, Wellesley, Smith, Carleton, Trinity, Pomona, and other colleges like them, and you have the top-tier liberal arts colleges. Top-tier liberal arts colleges can be more family friendly because they are residential colleges and sometimes pride themselves on their family atmosphere. Teaching loads can be relatively low, two to three courses a semester, only somewhat more than what you would have at a Research I university. The difference, of course, is that you are primarily teaching undergraduate students, and you are expected to be available to them in a much more intensive way than at any of the larger universities. However, at many of the top-tier liberal arts colleges, research standards are just as demanding as those at research universities, at least in terms of type and status of the journal or the book press. Absolute quantity may be somewhat lower, but this depends on your discipline. Winning grants and fellowships is also important at top-tier liberal arts schools, especially in the natural sciences.

In a letter published in the *Chronicle of Higher Education*, Daniel Taub reported the results of a comparison of publication rates between faculty at liberal arts colleges and those at universities. He used the National Study of Postsecondary Faculty (2003–2004), which surveyed thirty-five thousand faculty members across the country. He looked at two categories: refereed works and total scholarly works. Overall, Taub found that faculty members at undergraduate institutions generally published less than faculty members at research institutions. What was interesting, however, was that scholars in some disciplines were able to almost match the research output of their colleagues at the research university (despite their more intensive teaching requirements). "Historians at undergraduate institutions published, per capita, 71% of the refereed articles and 95% of the total scholarly works of their colleagues at doctoral universities. Faculty members in Political Science, Communications, English and Literature, Philosophy and Religion and Fine Arts were also able to produce total scholarly or creative work at 70% or more of the rate of their doctoral colleagues."[14] On the other hand, there were other disciplines where research output was far lower at the liberal arts colleges: "In contrast, faculty members in Business, Foreign Languages, Biology, Physical Sciences and Computer Sciences published at less than 30% of the rate of their colleagues at doctoral institutions both for refereed works and for total scholarly works." Of course, one problem with this study is that it only looked at quantity rather than quality, but certainly one can infer that fewer publications are produced in places where fewer publications are required to achieve tenure and promotion. Another problem with this data is that it did not disaggregate between the top-tier liberal arts institutions and the others.

If you take a job at a liberal arts college, you are also expected to be an exceptional teacher, and you do not have graduate students to help you lead discussion sections or grade papers and exams. On top of this, because these college campuses are quite small and there are fewer faculty to share committee work, service commitments can be quite high and will be of a different character from those at research universities. At most liberal arts colleges, for instance, faculty are expected to meet individually with first-year students to advise them on their academic programs or their future choice of major. At larger institutions, staff members rather than faculty usually do this type of advising. There are also a whole host of institutional expectations for faculty to interact with their undergraduate students on a very personal level. Bowdoin, for instance, sent emails out to the student body encouraging first- and second-year students to take their academic advisers out to lunch. Given that individual faculty could have as many as ten pre-major academic advisees, this could result in ten different invitations to lunch. A few weeks later, the Dean of Student Affairs Office sent out a mass email to the entire campus encouraging students to ask their professors out to lunch. Some professors have as many as eighty-five students, and it becomes virtually impossible to eat that many lunches in any given semester. (Luckily for us, our students mostly ignore these emails, but the emails nevertheless show something about the expectations in institutions like this.)

This intense contact with undergraduate students can be a source of pleasure for some faculty, but it can also be draining and time-consuming. What's worse is that the students' expectations in this area are distinctly gendered. Young female faculty, precisely those who are most likely to have young children in the home, are more likely to get asked to lunch by eager undergraduate students than senior male faculty. Students expect more nurturing and attention from young women than they do from young men. This can also cause unevenness in teaching evaluations: "he really knows his topic" for a standoffish male professor is transformed into "she is inaccessible" for a female professor. These differences in student perception happen everywhere, but at liberal arts colleges the student opinion forms matter more for promotion and tenure, and students' claims on their teachers' time are greater. These effects are even more exacerbated at lower-ranked liberal arts colleges, which we will discuss below.

Juliet, the history professor with four children, spent her career at a top-tier liberal arts college and is well aware of the pros and cons of being at a smaller institution.

I work at a small college that is very strong on community, and this has been a great source of support for me in many ways. The college is also fairly "family-friendly"—for example, it is now perfectly fine to leave a meeting at 5:00 or 5:15 in order to pick up children, etc.—although this was not so much the case when I first started twelve years ago. The college has also gone to great lengths to provide and maintain an excellent child care center, which three out of my four children attended from age two until kindergarten—this was a great experience for everyone. In addition to the obvious benefit of good child care, I met a lot of parents through the center. On the negative side, the culture of the college is very demanding in terms of its teaching and advising expectations. As much as I like working with students (and I really do), I sometimes feel that they get a lot more attention from me than my own children. This feeling has increased because new technologies like email have increased the expectation of accessibility.

Helen, who teaches in the natural sciences at a liberal arts college, has also found balancing motherhood with scholarship to be possible, although it gets more complicated at places that also stress excellence in teaching:

This was a decision I made early on—to be at a small liberal arts school instead of at a large university. The stress level of my friends at big places seems outrageous to me (and many of them don't have kids or didn't have kids when they started). Though I am very busy, I feel like the expectations here are a bit more flexible and/or in my control. My job doesn't depend on me getting a huge grant from NIH [the National Institute of Health] (or even two)—an aspect that is in many ways out of my control. It does depend on doing solid research and being productive—something I've found is doable, though the juggling with teaching is tricky.

The good thing about the better-endowed liberal arts colleges is that, along with high expectations for research and publication, they do have funding to support faculty research and are often more generous and flexible with giving junior faculty time off to pursue their research agendas. Several of Kristen's colleagues, and Kristen herself, had two years of junior leave in order to pursue scholarship after they won external fellowships to buy themselves out of teaching. Rachel had a year and a half. Another positive aspect is that liberal arts colleges often tend to hire people that they *want* to tenure, and senior colleagues in your department will help you achieve that goal (if they like you). At an institution like this, moreover, tenure is not a zero-sum game, which makes other junior professors your allies rather than your competitors. Perhaps the most important factor overlooked when thinking about taking a job at a liberal arts college is that you are free from the responsibility of graduate students. On the one hand, good graduate students can be very exciting and intellectually stimulating, but they require a lot of mentoring and hand-holding along the way—much more than just a few friendly lunches. Further-more, if you have graduate students and are advising their dissertations, you are responsible for writing letters on their behalf and trying to find them jobs in the academic world, a time-consuming and sometimes disheartening task. These are the kinds of trade-offs you should keep in mind when comparing institutions of different categories.

Below the top tier of the liberal arts colleges are the rest of the four-year institutions, which focus primarily on teaching and require a considerable amount of service and requisite hand-holding of the undergraduate popula-tion. Back in 2008, Kristen wrote an article for the *Chronicle of Higher Edu-cation* extolling the virtues of the liberal arts college as a place where junior faculty could have productive research careers with lots of support.[15] A slew of emails ensued, mostly from graduate students who were thankful for be-ing tipped off about the possibility of having a research career at a liberal arts institution. Even though Kristen made it clear in the article that she was talk-ing about the top tier of liberal arts colleges, she received several emails from disgruntled colleagues at less well-known liberal arts colleges complaining that their institutions were not at all conducive to research or professional development. One person wrote:

> I teach at a very small and poorly endowed liberal arts college in Tennessee, and can tell you that, for the most part, the stereotypes are true. Without a lot of heavy funding, teaching burdens are profound. Perhaps it is also a lack of insti-tutional self-confidence that leads to a multiplication of committees, and heavy paperwork that people at more mature institutions would find unimaginable. I teach ten courses per year on a twelve-month contract, and have no agreement concerning sabbatical leave at any time. My load is exceptionally heavy, even for liberal arts colleges, but 3-3 to 4-4 is still the typical experience these days. In spite of all this, I do remain active in scholarship; but this is very unusual for people at small liberal arts colleges.

Another newly minted PhD who had just accepted an offer at a Midwest-ern liberal arts college wrote in to say that not all liberal arts colleges were as good as Kristen made them sound. This young tenure-track professor was extremely frustrated with her surroundings.

A 3-3 load came with my January offer from [College X]. I received start-up funds that allowed me to continue my research in the first years here and helped to round out conference presentations, talks, and a chapter of a manuscript. However, the similarities end there. With no pre-tenure leave and a campus climate that encourages dinners with students, attendance at football games, and little real encouragement for intellectual pursuits, it's not perfect. If you squint at my CV, you will see that while I have kept up some kind of research agenda, the list of committee and campus service is ridiculously long. The growth of my CV has been stunted because of it. It's not money that is missing around here, it's time. We don't have enough time to write!

Just as with the comprehensive universities, the lesson here is to do your homework on the institution to which you are applying. The more knowledge you have about the working conditions, the better prepared you will be for the job interview.

ASSOCIATE'S COLLEGES

These are institutions where bachelor's degrees account for no more than 10 percent of undergraduate degrees; most students are earning two-year associate's degrees. They often are called *community colleges*. These can be rural or urban, private or public, not-for-profit or for profit, but what unites them is that they service a more diverse body of students, many of whom are working full-time and trying to earn their degrees simultaneously. Students at a community college may not be very well prepared for advanced academic work, and teaching at an institution like this can feel like teaching high school. Many of the students at these institutions are first-generation college students, and they overwhelmingly come from working-class backgrounds.

There are so many different types of associate's colleges that it is difficult to paint just one picture, even in broad strokes. Generally, however, one could say that research is largely unnecessary to achieve tenure (if tenure is even an option). If you take a job at this type of institution, you are largely expected to be a teacher, and a good teacher, since your student body will present a unique set of challenges very different from the challenges you would face at an elite university or liberal arts college. Service commitments are generally limited, and you are not expected to socialize with your students outside of class; indeed, most of your students will have jobs, and even perhaps families of their own. Many of them will be adults who do not need the kind of hand-holding that eighteen- to twenty-two-year-olds often require.

If your only responsibility is teaching, you will have a lot more time for yourself and for your family, particularly if you do not maintain an active scholarly agenda. But do not forget that you will have to maintain an active scholarly agenda if you ever want to move out from the associate's college. For many women, teaching at this type of institution is satisfying for both personal and political reasons. Where else in the academy might one individual have such an impact on the lives of young people as in the community-college setting? It is hard work, to be sure, but it can also be incredibly rewarding.

According to Wolf-Wendel and Ward, women faculty who teach at these types of institutions have a fairly easy time combining work and family, particularly because many of them have come from industry or from K–12 teaching, where time commitments for workers are higher. Even though community-college professors have much higher teaching loads (up to five courses a semester) and are expected to have office hours to meet with students, community-college faculty reported that they could do all of their grading and class preparation from home during the day. This gave them great flexibility of location and working hours. They could be with their children in the afternoon and early evening and get back to work after the children had gone to bed. Wolf-Wendel and Ward found that many women accepted jobs at community colleges "because they didn't want to deal with what they perceived as the stress associated with working at a more prestigious, research-oriented university."[16]

A WORD ABOUT POSTDOCS

If you are in the sciences, you will very likely have a series of postdoctoral positions after you've earned your PhD. This requires a high degree of mobility. Indeed, the proliferation of postdoctoral positions may be one reason why fewer women take tenure-track jobs in the hard sciences; there is just too much moving around for someone who is trying to find a partner and start a family, or for someone who has a partner and a family already. Postdoctorate fellowships in the sciences also tend to be lab intensive, giving new mothers less flexibility in terms of where and when they work. And it is a lot harder to bring children to the lab than it is to bring them to the office. Still, postdocs are *de rigueur* in most scientific fields, and women in the sciences who want to have children will have to find ways to maintain the balancing act, because waiting until tenure to start a family is even less of an option for them.

Increasingly, there are also postdoctoral positions available in the social sciences and humanities, although these are not required. Some graduate students are faced with a dilemma—take a one-year postdoctoral position at a prestigious Research I university, or take a tenure-track job at a comprehensive university or a liberal arts college. If you take the postdoctoral position, you will have more time to publish and more resources available for your research. You may also have more time to write grants, attend conferences, and network with people in your discipline in a big research-university setting. Do not be fooled, however, into thinking that a postdoctoral position will turn into a tenure-track position. This is exceedingly rare, and you should accept the postdoctoral position with the idea that you will be on the job market again from the minute you get to the university. And please understand that you run the risk of not finding a tenure-track job the following year. Many PhDs hop from postdoc to postdoc for several years before finding a tenure-track position. This means that, in addition to the six years that you will be on the tenure track, you have added another two or three years from your PhD before tenure. While this may give you the opportunity to produce more research and more peer-reviewed publications, be careful that you don't inadvertently increase the amount of scholarship required for you to achieve tenure because you had postdocs before you got on the tenure track. Also keep in mind that you are more likely to achieve tenure in your early forties if you take the postdoctoral route, meaning you will not be able to wait until after tenure to have your first child.

If you are more risk averse, and you are quite sure that you want to be both a professor and a mother, take the tenure-track job. Even if it's not a great job, it is much easier to find a job when you already have one, as long as you maintain an active scholarly agenda. You are also less likely to be moving around from job to job in rapid succession. Yes, it means that you may not end up with the most prestigious position in a research university, but it does mean some semblance of stability for you and your family. You have to keep your own personal goals in mind when making decisions like these, especially when there are apples-and-oranges choices required between two very different types of institutions. As always, we recommend doing as much background research as possible before accepting any position, and be thankful that you even have a choice.

TEXTBOX 5.1. THE PART-TIME ROUTE

In the best of all worlds, parents could all have the option at any college or university of working part-time in a tenure-track position (and then later in a part-time tenured capacity) while their children were young, returning to full-time when and if they chose. Given that most of us teach more than one course at a time and are expected to produce research projects that take substantial amounts of time from conception to completion, there is really no reason why colleges and universities cannot figure out ways to quantitatively divide up the work to create three-quarter-time positions, two-thirds-time positions, or half-time positions. Yet very few universities have done this. Karen Conway, a tenured professor at the University of New Hampshire, was able to broker a reduced teaching load (along with a reduced salary). Her school uses a "pieces of eight" system, where each of one's five classes counts for one eighth of one's duties. The remaining three eighths are research and service. Karen teaches only three classes a year and receives 75 percent of her salary. This allows her to have semesters when she doesn't teach, and these she uses to get her research done. In her article, "One Approach to Balancing Work and Life," she makes a plea for women faculty to bring proposals of this type to the floor for discussion.[1] A few university leaders in this area, such as Berkeley and MIT, are now talking the talk, but whether they are successful at making fundamental changes in the structure of employment remains to be seen. Instead, many academic mothers looking to reduce their work-time commitments have ended up in non-tenure-track part-time positions, the so-called second tier that Mary Ann Mason and Marc Goulden have identified.

As with everything else in life, there are advantages and disadvantages to going down the second-tier path. The advantages are that this might be the only way for you to get enough time to devote to child raising. In addition, if you have strong geographic preferences to stay put, the adjunct track may allow you to stay at the same university where you received your PhD. Staying in the world of academics even as an adjunct has been shown to be a more successful strategy

(continued)

for ultimately landing a tenure-track job than taking a part-time non-academic position. Wolfinger, Mason, and Goulden, in an article called "Staying in the Game: Gender, Family Formation and Alternative Trajectories in the Academic Life Course," found that among recent PhDs whose first postdoctoral position was not tenure track, those taking adjunct or non-teaching academic positions were far more likely to eventually land a tenure-track position than either those who took non-academic positions or those who reported being out of the labor force post-doctorate.[2] The same study showed that married women with children were significantly over-represented in the ranks of the adjunct faculty. A woman with a child under six was found to be 26 percent more likely to be employed as an adjunct compared to a childless woman, and 132 percent more likely to be an adjunct professor compared to a man with a young child.[3]

The disadvantages are mostly financial. Part-time adjunct jobs pay substantially less than full-time tenure-track positions, both absolutely and per hour devoted to the job. James Monks reported that adjunct faculty are paid 26 percent less than comparable tenure-track faculty members.[4] Adjunct jobs almost never include benefits such as health insurance, sick leave, paid parental leave, and so on. With the lower pay you may be tempted to take on additional courses, which leaves you even less time for research. Unless you are certain that your passion is teaching, try to keep your hand in the research pot, no matter how slowly you are proceeding.

Moreover, if you take a non-tenure adjunct position, it is not a given that you will ever be able to return to the tenure track. It will be especially difficult if your ultimate goals are high in terms of the prestige of the institution where you hope to end up. (See the text-box in chapter 6 on how to use your time wisely while you are an adjunct in order to maximize your chances of landing a tenure-track job in the future.) When the time demands at home diminish (and don't be tempted to increase them just to show how important you are at home), you need to think strategically about your next move. It may mean looking for a postdoc or a one-year teaching job somewhere else in order to reestablish your credentials. Still, the article by Wolfinger, Mason, and Goulden is encouraging in showing just how many people were able to make the successful transition back into the tenure track. Ten years after taking an adjunct position as a first postdoctoral position, more than half of 1,444 respondents had tenure-track positions. Slightly more than 40 percent of those who had taken non-teaching academic positions also had transitioned back to the tenure track.

OTHER PATHWAYS

As explained earlier in this chapter, there are not enough academic jobs, particularly good academic jobs, to absorb all of the PhDs granted in the United States and Canada. In European countries, the number of PhDs granted is often restricted to take into account the local job market's ability to employ those with doctoral degrees, but even there the numbers are rising.[17] In the United States, the doctoral degree has become a consumer good, and universities will "sell" as many as people are willing to buy. Having more graduate students provides cheap labor for the university and status for the university's faculty.

The shortage of jobs means that some PhDs will be tempted to try to find employment outside of academia, perhaps in K–12 education. In response to Kristen's article in the *Chronicle of Higher Education*, she received several requests for personal advice about taking jobs outside of university institutions. One person wrote:

I am 100 percent certain that teaching is my calling, but less certain that I want to continue researching and writing. Accordingly, I am applying for both post-secondary and secondary jobs. The thought of a visiting professorship somewhere sounds much less appealing to me than a secure, full-time position at a good high school. I have a family to think about and the insecurity of the visiting/adjunct route that might someday in the future lead to a tenure track position sounds pretty awful right now. Having been surrounded by research professors here at [a Research I university] and at [another Research I] where I earned my MA, I have developed a somewhat cynical view of the academic lifestyle. Most of my professors seem to either be divorced, or to be putting things like family on hold until they secure tenure or full professorship. All of this makes me wonder if academia really is for me, but I'm not yet ready to give up on that dream.

This comment wonderfully demonstrates the impact that a lack of role models can have on young graduate students who are trying to decide whether to pursue careers in academia. It is truly a shame that this person was surrounded by professors who seemed disgruntled and unhappy, and that this graduate student believed all professors to be either divorced or "putting things like family on hold." This is why we think it's essential for there to be more role models of men and women with healthy families and small children in the university setting. But change comes slowly, and inevitably there will be people like this letter writer who decide to take jobs outside of academia.

There are whole books and websites dedicated to alternate pathways and other things to do with your doctoral degree. (One of the best websites is Beyond Academe, at www.beyondacademe.com, although it is targeted primarily at historians.) Since our goal is to convince you that you can be a professor and a parent at the same time, we won't spill much ink on the question of what to do if you fail to get a tenure-track job. But one thing we will say is that once you accept a job at a high school, you are unlikely to ever find your way back into the university system.

There are disciplines where applied research done by consulting firms and government agencies or private industry competes with academics for publications. People in these fields can move in and out of the academy. For example, several of the analysts Rachel knew while she had a fellowship at the U.S. Census Bureau have since moved into academia in sociology. A friend of Rachel's moved from a top-tier liberal arts school to a federal agency, and then just recently accepted a job as a full professor at a Research I university. Scientists in some fields move smoothly between industry and the academy. This is often true for those in fields where there are commercial applications for their research skills. In the humanities it is much harder, unless you are a creative writer or a practicing artist.

As we write this, people are trying very hard to change the academy to create more off and on ramps, particularly because the system does discriminate against people who need to leave the academic labor market for family reasons. But for now, the person quoted above will have to probably give up "the dream" of an academic position in exchange for the stability of a good position in a high school.

We very much hope that you will land a tenure-track job, and you will have to figure out what kind of requirements your institution has for "professional success." Although we know that tenure standards vary considerably across institutions, all schools rely on a mix of excellence in research, teaching, and service to the college and to your profession. In the remaining chapters, we give you concrete tips on how to excel in these professional endeavors and still find time for a family life that includes children.

On the Tenure Track, Part I

Research and Networking

"I wish I could go to the hospital. Just to get some rest."

"Yes, that would be nice. Pneumonia or something, where I would just lie in bed for a few days and watch TV while the nurses feed me."

"No, pneumonia wouldn't be enough. You could probably still work with pneumonia. And the kids would want to visit. It would have to be something contagious, so that I was in quarantine. Like Ebola."

"I don't know about Ebola. . . . That will kill you."

"Well, something like Ebola that wouldn't kill me, but would allow me to have a few peaceful days on my own without having to be mom."

"Where other people were looking after your needs."

"And no grading!"

"No grading? Come to think of it, maybe Ebola wouldn't be so bad . . ."

The exchange recounted above is a rough approximation of about a dozen different conversations that Kristen and Rachel used to have with their fellow junior female colleagues with young children. This particular genre of discussion became known as the "hospital fantasy," and we have always been amazed by the number of young faculty members who daydreamed about being in nonlethal car accidents so that they could get some time off from all of the various obligations they felt pressing down on them. Skiing accidents, head injuries, and rare tropical diseases were among the many calamities new faculty parents wished upon themselves. If you ran into a colleague on campus and she asked how you were, you could simply respond by saying, "I am having hospital fantasies." She would know exactly what you meant.

Both Rachel and Kristen used to have these fantasies too. They both remember thinking at the time that there was no way to survive this period of their lives. In moments of self-reflection, Rachel tried to convince herself that not getting tenure wouldn't be so bad after all. She would open "Connelly's Chinese Cuisine." Kristen told herself that it was not really that hard, and that someday she would look back on that era and realize that a lot of demands that were being made of her as a new mom and a newly minted assistant professor were not as pressing and immediate as she thought them to be. Now that that the time is over for both of us, we feel more comfortable making an objective judgment: *it was hell.* The first five or six years on the tenure track are unequivocally the most difficult and challenging times of any academic career, whether you have kids or not. Having kids just makes it worse. However, we are here to tell you there is light at the end of the tunnel.

In the next two chapters, we will give some very specific guidance on how to survive these first five or six years on the tenure track. While this is not the ideal time in your career to have your first child, it may still be the right time for you. You are not getting any younger, and it is part of your life plan. So whether you had your first child while you were in graduate school (as Kristen did) or while on the tenure track (as Rachel did), you will find yourself with small children during the years when you are striving to be the best scholar and teacher you can possibly be. Even if you have decided to wait until after tenure, most of the advice in this chapter is applicable to all young academics who are trying to navigate their way through the labyrinth of academic politics. In this chapter and the next we provide some practical tips on how to find success and work-family balance in academia in terms of juggling all of your many responsibilities: research, networking, teaching, university service, service to the profession, and finding time to spend for yourself and/or your family. This chapter focuses on research and networking. In chapter 7 we consider teaching, service, and family time.

RESEARCH

There are two key things you need to know about research: (1) at most institutions, you won't get tenure without it; and (2) it is your only portable form of wealth if you ever want to change institutions. No matter what anyone tells you or how much pressure you feel to do other things, research must be a priority. This is true even in institutions that equally value teaching for tenure and those that have high expectations for service and collegiality. This cannot be stressed enough, particularly if you find yourself at a college or university where some senior faculty members have very little research to show for their many years at the institution. Their tenure standards were not your tenure standards, and, no matter how unfair it may feel, it is a reality that you must face. The job market has become a lot more competitive in the last two decades, with the academy being one of the few professions that offers lifetime job security. This means that institutions can demand a lot more from younger faculty than they were able to demand in the past. More importantly, with people like Steven Levitt and Francis Fukuyama calling for the abolition of tenure and the complete marketization of the professoriate, and with increasing cost pressures faced by all institutions, there is now a rise in adjunct and part-time positions that are unstable and insecure, making it even harder to find a tenure-track job. All of these factors mean that the stakes are much higher than they have ever been in the past, and universities have good financial incentives to deny tenure if there is even the slightest doubt that you will continue to be productive.

Producing quality publications based on original research is one of the most demanding tasks for a young scholar, and it is also a task that can feel frustratingly out of your control. The journal article that you sent out six months ago could be sitting under a stack of coffee-stained newspapers on some senior professor's desk while you wait desperately for a decision. Landing a first book contract for your revised dissertation may be imperative, but it often depends on the mood of some mercurial and faceless editor at a struggling university press who is underpaid and underappreciated. On the other hand, doing research is what you love to do. It is the reason you went to graduate school in the first place. It makes the job that you are striving to keep worth keeping. Why do senior faculty continue to publish long after the last promotion? Because they enjoy it—it is personally satisfying, and it allows them to travel to exciting places and to meet interesting people.

There is some degree of luck in early publishing endeavors. The solution to this uncertainty is having the right mentors, having enough output so that some of it can sit on an editor's desk without bringing down the entire house of cards, and getting yourself out there so the editor and reviewer know you (and feel guilty about taking so long). Remember that merely being smart is seldom enough. Networking (which we will discuss in the next section) matters a great deal. In the sciences and engineering, developing good working relationships with your lab mates and co-authors is essential to publishing and grant-writing success.

More difficult even than producing the scholarship is dealing with the inevitable rejection letter. As we have already mentioned, the whole publishing process can be a brutal hammering on your ego. Even if you are thick-skinned, there is so much at stake when you are pre-tenure that it is easy to succumb to a crisis of self-confidence. No one likes rejection, and yet rejection is a constant and enduring part of every academic career. It is easy to understand why so many new professors find time spent teaching more rewarding than trying to get their work published.

It is essential that your work be peer-reviewed often through a double-blind process. This means that you prepare a manuscript with no identifying information, and it gets sent out to two or more anonymous reviewers. You don't know them, and they don't know you. The theory behind this arrangement is that it ensures that only the highest quality work gets published and that there is no question of professors favoring their graduate students, nor are there senior scholars resting on their laurels to publish substandard work. In reality, the peer-review process is often a mechanism to ensure that younger scholars cite the appropriate senior scholars in their fields and that established authors have veto power over what newbies can say about them in print.

Despite some shortcomings in the review process, the peer-reviewed article or sole-authored book is what you must prioritize, no matter how many invitations you receive to write encyclopedia entries or book reviews. Yes, these are publications, but, no, they do not count for much on your road to tenure and promotion. Although there are some exceptions, which will be detailed below, you should use your time strategically, initially turning your dissertation into the basis for your first publications.

Chapters in edited volumes should also be avoided, unless you want to do the editor a favor or there are several established scholars contributing to the book. Too many junior scholars bury their best research in book chapters for edited collections and then have nothing left for peer-reviewed journals. However, a chapter may make a good companion piece to a more rigorous analysis. It may be the place for the more descriptive part of your dissertation. The most important thing is to think about the time cost versus the benefit of any collected-volume invitation. Furthermore, only agree to review books that you are going to read anyway, and then only agree to write reviews for the top journals in your field. Kristen was a book-review editor for an international journal and was always astounded at how few senior people agreed to write book reviews. It was mostly junior faculty hungry for publications who accepted these assignments, and it was precisely these young scholars who should not have been doing them. Another reason not to do book reviews when you are junior is that you might end up offending someone important in your field and thereby making an enemy you cannot afford to have made come tenure time. If you read a really awful book, it is best not to write the review at all; the book-review editor will understand. Encyclopedia entries are similarly thankless; so unless the editor is someone you really want to help out for other reasons, the best thing to do is politely decline. This is also true for refereeing journal articles or book manuscripts; these endeavors are best saved until after you have tenure—unless it is a piece of scholarship directly in your field that you think you can learn from, or it is in a journal or press in which you hope to publish.

It is not only quantity of publications that matters; quality is equally important. Your external reviewers at reappointment and tenure time will be looking at which university press you were published and in which journals your articles appeared. You need to be very strategic in choosing where to submit your work, given that the best journals are also the most competitive and therefore have a higher rate of rejection. Journals also differ in turnaround time, and that should certainly be a criterion of where to send your work. Some journals publish the date submitted and the date accepted, but not all do that. Ask your senior colleagues about the reputation of the journal and expected turnaround time for submissions.

If you are in the humanities or in one of the more humanistic social sciences (anthropology, for instance), a sole-authored book of original scholarship will most likely be expected for tenure, although some institutions will accept a series of well-placed journal articles. When books matter, there are three things that you should pay attention to: (1) original scholarship, (2) sole authorship, and (3) finding the best university press you can. You are on your own, and you must prove your own talents to the larger academic world. To do this you must have something interesting and new to say, something that contributes to the academic debates in your field or subfield. This is often the easiest part to figure out, and for many of us the most exciting and enjoyable. Dissertations in the humanities are not co-authored, and neither should your first book be; the early years on the tenure track are not the ideal years to collaborate if you are in the humanities.

In psychology and the natural sciences, co-authorship is a given, and you should try to get your name on as many papers as possible. In large scientific collaborations, where authors are listed in order of their contribution, do the extra work necessary to get your name high up on the list. In economics, where co-authors' names are listed alphabetically, two scholars have even gone as far as suggesting that a scholar change her name if it is a surname that starts with a letter later in the alphabet. In 2006, Liran Einav and Leeat Yariv published a paper called "What's in a Surname? The Effects of Surname Initials on Academic Success," which found that economists with last names that started with letters earlier in the alphabet achieved tenure at higher rates and were more likely to be fellows of the Econometric Society.[1] Publishing journal articles is important, but getting your work cited and having your name associated with certain ideas is just as essential. If you do publish with a co-author, you may want to trade off being the first author on your joint papers.

If you go the book route, the hardest part is finding a press that will publish your work, and here there is definitely an important hierarchy. Publishing in a little-known press can mean both that your book will not be read and that it will not count as much for your tenure case as your efforts warrant. Once again, each discipline is very different, but there will always be a handful of top university presses in your field. There are several ways to figure out what they are, but the three easiest are (1) to look on your own bookshelves and figure out which presses have published the majority of books that you read, (2) to go to the book exhibit of your discipline's national conference and see which presses have the biggest booths and the most traffic, and (3) to ask someone senior in your discipline the top three or four presses that they would consider sending their next book to (more on the politics of asking for advice below). Once you have this information, make a list, and begin sending your proposal out as soon as you think you have a good working manuscript.

There are many good books about academic publishing (particularly *Getting It Published* by William Germano),[2] so we will not delve into the nitty-gritty of publishing your dissertation here. The important thing to realize is that it is better to send your manuscript or your articles out sooner rather than later. Many new professors want to do extensive revisions to their dissertations before they consider approaching a press, but this is often a mistake. If you land your manuscript with readers at a good university press, you can expect to receive detailed reports, and these will be useful even if the press ultimately passes on the book project. The same goes for referee reports from good-quality journals. You will have to revise in light of these reports either way, so use the reports to improve the manuscript and submit it to your second-choice presses. Remember what we said about rejection, and give yourself ample time to submit the book or article to several presses or journals before it finds a good home. Do not get bogged down by extensive revisions if you get an outright rejection from a journal or press. Unless the comments are truly constructive and you agree with their general thrust, it is not worth rewriting a piece unless it has been rejected from two journals or two presses for similar reasons. Reviewers can be grouchy and territorial, and as a young scholar it is important to have some faith in your own ideas. Once a manuscript is accepted, it often takes several months before it goes into production and up to a year before it is published. With tenure clocks ticking, it is essential to start this process as early as possible.

In all of the sciences, and many of the social sciences, the goal of pre-tenure scholarship should be well-placed refereed journal articles with your name as first or second author (or the last author, if it is your lab). Co-authorship is accepted, but you should be careful about continuing to publish exclusively with your dissertation-committee members. Daniel Hamermesh, in "An Old Male Economist's Advice to Young Female Economists," explains it this way:

> Readers and tenure referees tend to assume that a young economist who co-authors with a more senior economist, especially a thesis advisor, is doing the dirty work rather than providing the central innovation of the study. This is regrettably especially true when the junior person is a woman and the senior economist is male. It is important to become an independent researcher—to leave the nest of one's dissertation advisor's ideas and co-authorships—well before tenure time, and that is particularly so for women.[3]

Whether you are solely authoring or co-authoring papers, you should try to place them in journals with the best reputations. One way to figure out which are the best journals in your field is by using Thompson's Journal Citation Reports or other ranking indexes like Scimago (www.scimagojr.com) or Eigenfactor (www.eigenfactor.org). In the sciences, being a principal investigator in a successful grant application also matters, as is being the supervisor in a lab. Tenure committees are looking for evidence of substantial scholarship beyond the dissertation and evidence of independent contributions. The best way in any discipline of judging the expectations for tenure is to look at the vitae of those in your department most recently tenured and talk to as many people as possible about expectations.

Books, peer-reviewed journal articles, and grant applications: trying to get this all done can be incredibly time-consuming, especially if there are children around. Both Kristen and Rachel had one child through all or almost all of their pre-tenure years. As we have said, it might be better to wait from a "how to increase the chances that you get tenure" point of view, but there are many good reasons not to wait, especially if having children is one of your life goals. Having children around can bring joy and meaning to daily life and is a good distraction from the pressures of publishing and teaching. If you can be disciplined with your time, having a child before tenure can be a very positive thing.

What do we mean "being disciplined with your time"? Like dieting, it is easy to understand what needs to be done, but much harder to do it. You need to figure out when you are most productive in research and then use that time optimally. For Rachel, it is in the morning (but not too early), or whenever she can get long, uninterrupted periods of research time. Kristen's most productive time is usually in the middle of the night. Because Kristen was a single mom for much of her time on the tenure track, she rarely had long chunks of time to really concentrate on research (except when on leave). When she did extended writing, Kristen sometimes worked between the hours of 2:00 a.m. and 5:00 a.m., when the house was quiet, her daughter was asleep, and there were no distractions. She tried to make up the sleep by taking power naps during the day, or by going to bed really early with her daughter at 8:00 p.m. (easy to do if you do not have a partner). The key was that she used her most productive brain time for the thing that required the most extended concentration.

Another strategy that Kristen still uses is the topic-sentence outline. Once she has an idea for an article, she will sit down and do a detailed outline that includes the topic sentence of each paragraph that she needs to write. Then she uses the little bits of time she manages to scrounge throughout the day—the hour between classes, the bus ride, and the twenty minutes in the morning while her daughter gets ready for school—to write one paragraph at a time. The first draft of a paper written in this haphazard way is usually a mess, but it does give Kristen a starting place. This is a great strategy if you have kids around because there are always little snatches of time that you can use. This is why one respondent, Sonia, believes that mothers are more efficient with their time. They have far less of it, and they have to make the most of what they do have.

Once you figure out when your most productive time is, guard it. Use it for research. Don't use it to make phone calls for your child's soccer team or even meetings with students. It should not be the time that you use to schedule doctor appointments and cable-guy visits. You will not be able to guard thirty hours a week between the hours of 9 and 5 Monday through Friday, but you should be able to safeguard some research time every week. Even at a small liberal arts college, where teaching demands are high, you can carve out some research time for yourself every week. Rachel and Kristen have a colleague who tries regularly to secure the entire day of Friday for her research. This means she arranges her teaching schedule and committee meetings so that she keeps Friday free. Whatever you have to do, your research time must be sacrosanct.

Be particularly vigilant about email. Yes, we know that it is an essential part of our modern lives, but it can also be an incredible time sink. If there is one thing that you can do to increase your productivity, spend more time on your teaching, and spend more time with your family, it is to drastically reduce the amount of time spent writing and responding to email. Most of us don't realize that we spend about two hours a day dealing with email. This is particularly problematic because it is often the first thing we do in the morning, when our brains are fresh and we should be thinking about our research. All sorts of administrative stuff comes over email, and it's the kind of thing we should wait to deal with until our brains are already tired and working at half capacity anyway. (Be careful about actually answering email when you are tired. If it is important or delicate, answer it the next day.)

Another thing about email is that it is very distracting. You could be writing all day if not for the constant mail notifications that a new message has appeared in your inbox. Most of the time it's just spam anyway. It may be very difficult for you to switch off the grid, especially in this day of ubiquitous iPhones and Blackberries but it is worth doing some of the time. Email is a distraction and one that you can and should control. Once you get tenure you can spend five hours a day on email if you choose. But until then, try to check it only once or twice a day. Also get in the habit of never responding to an email until a few hours have passed. You can train your students and colleagues to accept the fact that you are not always instantly available. Finally, use the auto-response vacation messages on your email program to occasionally buy yourself a few email-free days. A lot of professors use these when they are traveling, but they can also be used when you want to have a few uninterrupted days of writing or even just a weekend to yourself.

In addition to email, identify the other things that you do to fritter away time, and try to limit them. Web surfing and online shopping are two common time suckers for the busy mom who is trying to read the news, order her nonperishable goods from an online grocer, and find a new pair of rain boots at Zappos.com while scarfing down a sandwich at her desk. Web surfing is usually just procrastination and you must guard against it, even if it means finding a coffee shop with no wireless so that you won't be tempted. If you work at home, the impulse to tidy up or do a load of laundry can also be a big distraction. Whatever it is for you, try to discipline yourself. Maryellen Giger, a professor of radiology at the University of Chicago and mother of four, suggests that we need to establish a finely tuned on/off switch, turning off home life when we're at work and vice versa. "You have to be able to turn the switch so you can focus on where you're at."[4]

Also, do whatever it takes to create deadlines for yourself. Find a junior colleague and set deadlines for each other. Type into your calendar the things you hope to get done in a given week, or set it up so that you get daily calendar alerts about what you should be accomplishing each day. Committing to a conference paper can play a valuable role in creating a meaningful deadline. Teaching, service, and family obligations can feel so pressing and immediate that it is easy to let the research agenda fall to the bottom of your to-do list. But with tenure clocks ticking, you must compel yourself to work on research by sticking to your own personal deadlines. You also need to limit the number of extra things you agree to do: small service-related tasks that seem insignificant when you say yes can then pile up and eat away your research time.

TEXTBOX 6.1. TIPS FOR SURVIVING THE ADJUNCT TRACK

For many recent PhDs, spending some time on the adjunct track is inevitable because the number of tenure-track positions is limited and the competition is fierce. Also, unlike other professions that hire throughout the year, academia has a distinct hiring season in the fall for most tenure-track assistant professorships and postdoctoral fellowships. If you are not lucky enough to get an offer by late February or early March, then you will have to go back to H-NET, *Inside Higher Ed*, the *Chronicle of Higher Education*, or wherever your discipline posts its job ads and start looking more closely for all of those positions listed as "visiting assistant professor" or "lecturer." Although the pay and benefits of these jobs is often quite pitiful, it is perhaps the best way to warehouse yourself until the next cycle of the job market comes around.

Much has been written about the so-called silent revolution in the American university system, which has witnessed a steep rise in the number of contingent faculty since the 1960s. In 1960, 75 percent of faculty were full-time tenure-track or tenured professors. By 2009, this percentage had fallen by more than half to only 27 percent.[1] The economic reason behind this is that adjuncts are much cheaper than full-time faculty, and there are a myriad of circumstances that require universities and colleges to hire instructors on a short-term basis. Full-time faculty members go on sabbatical, take parental or medical leave, win grants to buy themselves out of teaching courses, or get poached away to another institution before the home institution can organize a tenure-track search. In some cases, there are classes that senior faculty simply do not want to teach, such as large survey or introductory "101" courses or basic language-instruction classes. No matter what the circumstance, adjuncts pick up the slack when full-time faculty members exercise their various privileges, and today they make up the backbone of the American university system (together with graduate-student instructors).

(continued)

While still finishing up her dissertation, Kristen taught as an adjunct instructor both at Berkeley and at San Francisco State University, in order to get some teaching experience before heading onto the job market. She taught one regular-semester course and one summer-school course at Berkeley and one regular-term academic course at SFSU, and she was paid on a per-course basis. In all three cases, the salary was extremely low. Admittedly, however, the demands were also low compared to the demands made on her when she became a tenure-track assistant professor. Outside of preparing and delivering lectures, Kristen had few obligations either to her students or to the institutions, and she was given complete freedom to design her courses as she wished. Given that she was pregnant and suffering from ongoing fatigue during two of these classes, the adjunct position was perfect for her. She could muster enough energy to teach for a few hours a week and then spend the rest of the time at home alternating between napping and writing her dissertation. In a wonderful advice column in the *Chronicle of Higher Education*, Gerardo Marti discusses the important differences between being an adjunct lecturer and an assistant professor, with the latter being better paid but completely overwhelmed.[2] Indeed, in their recent book *The American Faculty*, Martin J. Finkelstein and Jack H. Schuster find that many women, who make up the majority of adjunct laborers in the academy, report that they are quite satisfied with their jobs. Finkelstein and Schuster hypothesize that adjunct positions give women the flexibility that they need to stay in the academic labor market while their children are young,[3] and Kristen agrees that adjunct teaching is a lot less demanding than being an assistant professor, as long as you have a partner who can financially support you.

The truth is that it is difficult to live on a per-course salary unless you are working at multiple institutions or teaching online distance courses. But if you have a partner who can help pay the bills, adjuncting can be a viable part-time option in the short term if you want to eventually end up on the tenure track, as long as you continue to publish. In addition, there are some PhDs who think of adjuncting as a longer-term strategy; they are happy to fill in as a sabbatical replacement occasionally in order to keep their foot in the academic game, but just as happy not to have all of the service and research obligations of full-time faculty. Finkelstein and Schuster confirm that adjunct faculty are far less involved in institutional governance and curricular decision making than are their tenure-track colleagues. Additionally, contingent faculty members are far less burdened with professional obligations such as writing book and journal manuscript reviews, letters of recommendation, reports, and so on. So there are real benefits to being an adjunct. On the downside, full-time faculty are less likely to befriend you because they know that you are temporary, and some might even resent you because they fear that your willingness to work for such paltry wages threatens to undermine the tenure system.

Whether you have chosen to become an adjunct for work/family reasons, or whether you are adjuncting because you had a bad year on the job market, we assume that someday you will want to find yourself a tenure-track position. If this is the case, then most of the advice in this chapter and chapter 7 still applies to you. In addition to being a good teacher, you should concentrate on getting your work published and getting your name out there to scholars in your field. By all means, continue to attend the national conventions in your discipline (no matter what the expense), and attend faculty colloquia and lectures at your institution so people get used to seeing you around.

In addition, you want to make your presence known on campus. Of course, if there is an opening for a tenure-track position at your current institution, you want to be a known quantity on campus so that you have a leg up in the search. More importantly, when there is a position at another institution, you need to be able to ask one or two of the permanent faculty members at your current institution to write letters of recommendation. Many adjuncts do not think about this until it is too late. Since they are poorly paid and have few obligations on campus, they rarely take the time to develop professional relationships with permanent faculty. But when job time comes around again, adjuncts need letters of recommendation because prospective employers will want to hear about their teaching from someone at their current institution. We can think of countless colleagues who have grumbled about having to write a letter of recommendation for

(continued)

a visiting assistant professor whom they hardly ever saw and about whom they knew very little. Take the time to at least cultivate a positive relationship with the person who hired you, so that when you have to ask for a letter, it will be a good one.

Another important thing to do if you are an adjunct is develop an academic website hosted by the institution where you are teaching. Having a web presence is really important. Take the time to develop a scholarly home page, and make sure that you include its URL in the signature of all of your professional emails. You want people to be able to find you when they type your name into Google. It's best to have a website at an official .edu address; if you can't manage that, make sure you maintain a steady web presence some other way. If your current institution will not allow you to have a website, then you can create one at Academia.edu or a similar web host.

Also, have all of your professional correspondence come from your institutional email account with a .edu suffix, even if this means that you have to change email accounts every year. Sending emails from your Gmail or Yahoo! account not only looks unprofessional but your messages might also end up caught in spam filters. It may seem like a small thing, but when people are sifting through piles of application materials or grant proposals, even tiny things like not having a "real" email address might get you tossed into the reject bin.

A common mistake that some on the adjunct track make is to call themselves "independent scholars," because they do not have a permanent institutional affiliation. Many permanent faculty have an inherent suspicion of those calling themselves "independent scholars," assuming that either they were denied tenure somewhere or they left academia for a long period of time and are now trying to reestablish themselves. Many fellowships and grants require that you have an institutional affiliation, no matter how temporary, and journal editors will often look askance at articles submitted with cover letters not on institutional letterhead. Similarly, unless you can organize a panel, submitting paper proposals to national conventions may also be tricky, as conference organizers also tend to prefer people with professional affiliations. This is terribly unfair, particularly to women who take time off to stay at home with their kids for a few years, but this is the current reality whether we like it or not, and you should avoid this title if possible. "Visiting assistant professor," "instructor," "lecturer," "fellow," or even "researcher" are all better titles if you can arrange them.

Finally, remember that many adjunct faculty members do eventually find themselves on the tenure track, and some of the faculty at your current institution may have been adjunct professors themselves for a while. Scrutinize the CVs of your colleagues on campus, and seek out those who list "visiting assistant professor" under their professional experience. These will be your natural allies on campus, and they may be able to offer you valuable advice. Make an effort to cultivate these relationships. If you really want that tenure-track position, don't let yourself get discouraged. Many adjunct careers work out quite happily in the end.

One question we hear a lot from junior faculty is, how do you say no? This is a topic that will come up again in the university-service section in the next chapter, but it is worth touching on here since you will have to say no to some publication opportunities if you are going to get your book and/or articles done on time. There are two key rules about saying no. First, always be prompt and very specific about the other research obligations you have to meet rather than just saying that you are too busy. Say something like, "This is a wonderful opportunity for me, but I have a 'revise and resubmit' on my desk that needs to be back to the journal by May 15"; or something like, "Thanks so much for thinking of me. I would love to contribute, but it is absolutely essential that I concentrate all of my efforts on my own book right now since I will be coming up for tenure in two years." The second thing to do is always offer at least two names of other people who might be able to write a chapter instead of you, even if you have to resort to Google to find names. A relatively new website, Academia.edu, makes it easy to find people by research topic, and an editor will be very thankful if you can throw in a couple of names with your polite refusal. Of course, you do not want to say no to everything. There will inevitably be articles or books to review that will be exactly in your field and may help you with your own scholarship. But if it is not of direct benefit to your research, then the most prudent thing to do is decline at this stage in your career.

NETWORKING: TALKS, CONFERENCES, SOCIAL MEDIA, AND SHAMELESS SELF-PROMOTION

Although this section should really be a part of the "research" section above, we have decided to bracket it out because of its independent importance to your academic career. As we discussed in chapter 2, one of the biggest myths of academia is that you only have to be smart enough and have good ideas to succeed. Nothing could be further from the truth. For better or worse, the marketization of academia and the persistence of "old boys' clubs" in universities around the world means that who you know is just as important as what you know. In one study in economics, researchers found that manuscript ratings and acceptance rates were unaffected by the gender of the author, but were affected by "mutual affiliations" of author and journal editors and co-editors.[5]

This is one of lesser-known aspects of the academic world, because so much of your graduate-school training will have been about attaining the appropriate knowledge rather than the appropriate contacts. Indeed, some professors will insist that nothing but merit counts, even if they are well aware of realities to the contrary. We believe that it is a cruel disservice to graduate students for advisers not to prepare them for the realities of academia, no matter how much they might wish things were otherwise.

When you do finally get something published (and it does happen eventually), one of the most important things that you can do is send offprints of the article or copies of the book to the senior colleagues in your field. It used to be that when you had an article appear, the journal would send you free copies of the article in its published format, but today most journals just send you a .pdf of your article. You can send this .pdf as an attachment via email to your friends and other junior colleagues, but if you really want someone senior to read your work (and then possibility cite it), it is best to print it and send it as a hard copy, with a handwritten note saying something like this: "I am sending you a copy of my latest article. I found your work really helpful while writing this, and I would appreciate any ideas you might have on how to improve my arguments."

This strategy works really well if the senior colleague is someone you have cited in your bibliography, and you should be citing *all* of the senior people in your field, even if their work is tangential to your own. Citation is a way of demonstrating that you know your field and you know who the key thinkers are. It is amazing how often the same person will be asked to referee your work. Rachel was annoyed with a junior faculty member at another institution who works in the same field but seldom cites Rachel's work, or, if cited, it is only disparagingly. Rachel was asked to referee three or four papers for this young woman before tenure. This woman's university then asked Rachel to be one of the woman's external reviewers for tenure. Luckily for this young woman, Rachel didn't hold a grudge. Don't count on that.

Another way to get your work read and cited is to make sure that you keep your faculty website up-to-date, and always ask the journals in which you publish if you can "self-archive" your article, which means posting the .pdfs on your own website. Some journals won't allow you to do this with their formatted text, but you can do this with the document you submitted to them as long as you cite where and when the final article was published. A lot of websites also allow you to upload citations to your own work so that it will be easier for other academics to find. One site is Academia.edu, which is like Facebook for academics. Others include Getcited.org, Citeulike.org in the United Kingdom, and ResearcherID.org, which is specifically for the natural sciences. The benefit of these websites is that they provide an easy way to get your articles and books listed on the web in large, searchable databases. Some academics also have their own personal websites, but your faculty page should be sufficient as long as you keep it current and always have the latest version of your CV available for download. You also want to have a short paragraph on your research interests, so that Google will find your page if someone is looking for an expert in a particular field. Of course, the World Wide Web is constantly changing, and it is not always easy to stay on top of all of the new academic sites, but it is worth your time to make sure that your hard-won publication gets out there and read as much as possible. This means promoting your research (and yourself) by going to conferences, giving talks, and writing grants.

Writing grants is one of the most important things you can do when you are starting out on the tenure track. Even if you have plenty of internal funding, grant writing is one of the best ways to put your name in front of the senior colleagues in your discipline. No matter what discipline you are in (yes, even those of you in the humanities), there are always grants out there for research funds, summer salaries, summer workshops, conference travel, and so on. It is great if you get the grants, but it is worthwhile even if you don't, as long as you have written a clear and concise grant proposal that describes your current research and scholarly goals. Grant-review committees are made up of senior professors, and they often read the grant proposals of their younger colleagues with great interest. Indeed, many overworked senior faculty agree to sit on grant committees because they want to keep up with the "cutting edge" of research in their fields. (For a great book on the internal logic of grant review committees, see Michèle Lamont's *How Professors Think.*[6])

Also, it is important to always, always, always accept every invitation you get in your junior years to give a seminar or public talk. No matter how difficult the logistical or child care arrangements are, you should try to give as many public talks as you can. If someone goes to the trouble of finding the money to invite you, you should be hugely flattered that he or she has taken an interest in your work. Indeed, giving talks, both before and after tenure, is one of the most rewarding things you can do in terms of creating a community of scholarly colleagues.

One reason grant writing and giving talks are so important is that when you come up for tenure, anywhere from four to twenty-two scholars external to your institution will be asked to read your file and comment on your scholarship and the contribution it makes to your field. The more these people have heard your name before, the better the chances that they will be favorably disposed toward your work. But another key thing that very few junior faculty members are aware of is the process through which external reviewers are chosen.

There are several things that you can do to help stack the deck in your favor if you understand the rules of collaboration and acknowledgments. Normally, you are asked to propose a certain number of names for your external reviewers, and your tenure committee will come up with their own list of names. You usually have at least one veto of someone who is known to be hostile to your work or to your particular point of view, or someone whose work your own research revolves around challenging or undermining. Academic egos are sometimes fragile, and reviewers who should be objective can sometimes let worries about being usurped by a young researcher cloud their judgment about your tenure case. Tenure committees know this and will be sympathetic if there is someone who should absolutely not review your file. But after that, you have little say over who will ultimately be chosen to write your external letters.

The first thing to know is that anyone you openly and officially collaborate with will be excluded from your list of reviewers. This means co-authoring papers or co-writing grants will keep your collaborators off the list of potential external reviewers, and the same may even apply when you contribute to a collection edited by a senior scholar in your field (another reason to say no to those edited volumes). So even if a very well-meaning mentor or superstar in your field wants to work with you while you are still junior, you should think twice about whether the collaboration is worth excluding this person from your potential pool of external tenure reviewers. In some cases, it will be more valuable to you to have that publication with a senior colleague; in other cases, it might be best to politely decline by explaining that you do not want to exclude the scholar from your potential list of external reviewers, particularly if he or she likes you and your work well enough to collaborate with you. You can always explain that you would be delighted to work together after you get tenure; since most senior faculty have a longer time horizon than those on the tenure track, they will understand and will likely wait for you to join the hallowed ranks of the employed for life. In fact, the worst thing you can do is work with all of the people who like your work. You may think you are being proactive, but it would mean that the only people left to write your external letters are those who do not like your work.

Another thing to be careful about is how you write your acknowledgments for any book or article you publish. It is natural for junior scholars to want to thank all who have helped them in their research and writing, and certainly you should always thank your home institution and any external agencies from which you have received funding. But be careful not to thank too many of your senior colleagues, because tenure reviewers will carefully scrutinize your published acknowledgments to see if there is anyone who should be excluded from your list of potential external reviewers. (This is also true of editors looking for potential referees for your article. If you don't want someone to referee the paper, thank him or her in the acknowledgments. If you want someone to be a referee, don't thank that person, but be sure to cite him or her in your bibliography.) In most cases, it is better to cite your colleagues than to thank them in print, and you can certainly call them and let them know how much you appreciated any assistance that they might have given. Again, you only have a limited time to get tenure, and you must always think ahead to the time when you will be putting your file together and sending it out for review.

Another important thing to effect success is to go to conferences. Conferences cost money, often a lot of money when you consider registration fees, professional-association membership fees, air travel, hotels, meals, and other incidental expenses. But they are among the most important investments that you can make with your time and money when you are pre-tenure. Going to conferences and presenting papers there is the best way to get to know people in your field. Knowing people in your field and, more importantly, having people in your field know you, is essential if you want to establish a reputation as a serious and committed scholar worthy of permanent employment. Email and social media are never enough; you need face-to-face contact with those people who will ultimately review you. They will want to see you in action, and perhaps meet with you individually if they have the time, to hear about your current and future projects. Meetings are invaluable because these people will be the same people who will review your grant applications, your articles, your book manuscripts, and ultimately your tenure file. Indeed, in two short articles for the *Chronicle of Higher Education*, Saranna Thornton and Pat Phelps argue that networking provides the most bang for your buck when it came to allocation of time resources.[7] Be proactive and put together a panel, so that you can increase your chances of being on the program. Submit paper proposals to your professional association's national convention every year, and always attend if you are accepted.

This doesn't mean that it is easy, especially if you have children. Most of the larger meetings offer some kind of child care, and, if they don't, you can try to coordinate child care with other parents attending the meetings. In terms of financial support, your institution usually has some amount of travel funding available to you if you give a paper. If not, then use your credit cards; this is an investment in your future, not pure consumption. You don't have to stay at the conference hotel, and you can certainly skimp on your travel options, but take every opportunity to go out for dinner or drinks with your colleagues, even if this means going out to a place you wouldn't usually choose. If you do find yourself in a large group of people having dinner, you should know that the common practice is to split the bill evenly among everyone. This can be a considerable expense. If money is really a problem, discreetly inquire with the waitperson if you can have a separate check, and then only order a small appetizer, explaining to the party that you already ate in your room earlier or that you had a big lunch. But by all means, always take every opportunity to socialize; this is where a lot of scholarship gets done, and you do not want to exclude yourself from this process.

In addition to attending panels, make coffee dates or lunch dates with senior colleagues, journal editors, and book editors in advance. (In fact, acquisitions editors at all of the major university presses go to conferences precisely to meet with prospective authors, but are booked up months ahead of time.) If you are confident of which press you would like to send your book manuscript to, contact the acquisitions editor in your discipline and ask for a coffee date at the national meeting. If articles are the primary research output in your discipline, try to make meetings with the editors of the journals to which you hope to submit your research. Ask about putting together a special issue, or ask for specific advice on getting journal articles published. Remember that if the journal editor knows you, he or she may be more likely to send your paper out to review.

One thing to watch out for, however, is going to too many small regional conferences. Yes, it is easier to get papers accepted here, and they will be listed on your CV and will demonstrate to your department that you are being active in your discipline, but they will not give you the same networking opportunities as the big national (or international) conferences. Do some research on who the keynote speaker will be at the small conference. Email senior colleagues at neighboring institutions and ask which conferences they plan to attend. Think strategically about how you spend the time away from your family, and allocate your resources to maximize the value of the networking opportunities that you will have.

In addition to networking with people in your discipline, it is also important to network with people on your campus, some of whom will ultimately be judging you for tenure. Certain institutions are more conducive to collegiality than others, and different institutional cultures place differential weights on collegiality. If you are at a top Research I, you can be a complete jerk and still get tenure if you have the publication record to warrant it. But at most places, even if not officially admitted, collegiality counts for a great deal. Recall the quote from chapter 2 about Louis XIV not rewarding some-one whom he did not see at court. Daniel Hamermesh argues that you need to engage in "activities that generate the 'bonding' that is crucial in any work environment."[8] Thus, it is a good idea to be strategically visible on campus before you come up for tenure. By "strategically visible" we mean that you should be visible at faculty meetings, colloquia, invited lectures, search-committee dinners, and other professional events requiring your physical presence, and less visible, say, at the gym, or practicing your tacks and jibes with the sailing club. If you can help it, the only time you should be seen on campus is when you are working, particularly if you are on a campus that places more weight on research than teaching. One exception is faculty re-ceptions or socials, where you can informally chat with senior colleagues and talk about your research.

This strategic visibility is also true of social-networking sites. Avoid Face-book altogether, as you don't have total control of the content. Someone might write something on your "wall" that you don't want broadcast to the world. The video link you thought was amusing might offend someone else. In addition, it is awkward to decline "friend" invitations from colleagues once they've seen you on their university or college network. If you do use Facebook, set your privacy settings so tightly that no one can find you other than those you invite.

Another core element of networking on campus is finding mentors who can help you understand the institutional culture in which you are operat-ing. Finding mentors can be a difficult task because people are very busy, and many senior faculty are hesitant to sink too much of their time into junior faculty who may only be around for a few years. The best way to approach senior faculty is to meet them casually at a faculty social of some kind or in-vite them to have coffee, and to ask how they dealt with a particular issue at an earlier career stage. Make it about them and not about you, and you will be on your way to establishing healthy relationships with senior colleagues. Certainly, there could be a lot more mentoring in academia, but no one is entitled to a mentor, and the last thing you want to do is demand that your senior colleagues give you special attention. You should make your own con-certed efforts to seek out guidance in a polite and politic manner. Of course, you can always fall back on your dissertation adviser in a pinch, but it is best to cultivate at least one senior colleague on campus who knows the peculiarities of your particular institution.

Institutions differ on the extent to which faculty socialize with each other outside of work hours. At Bowdoin, faculty members often invite each other to each other's houses. It is a very vibrant social community, partially because Brunswick is a relatively small town. When Kristen celebrated her fortieth birthday with a large group of fellow faculty members, a colleague from an Ivy League school who happened to be visiting for the weekend was astounded that faculty would voluntarily socialize with each other off campus. Figure out what the norms are at your institution, and organize your social life appropriately, but be careful. One too many drinks, and a careless comment about a senior colleague (or, worse, your dean) can come back to haunt you. Remember that until you get tenure, you are always "on."

Another thing to think about is how much you should or should not talk about your child (or children) to your colleagues before you have tenure. Opinions vastly differ on this, and certainly it will vary greatly from institution to institution and department to department, but as a general rule it is best to be careful until you get tenure. No matter what your parental obligations or how demanding your child care schedule becomes, spare your colleagues the details and try not to use your kids as an excuse to miss meetings or deadlines or other departmental obligations. If you must miss something, say as little as possible about why. The truth is that when your baby is sick, it is often Mommy who is most wanted and who must then rearrange her schedule without any notice, meaning missed meetings and canceled classes. It is best to keep these dramas to yourself, no matter how comforting it might be to have someone to listen to your frustrations.

Depending on your institution, you may want to limit the number of pictures of your offspring in your office, or on your computer's screen saver, until after tenure. Unless your department is really family friendly, it's also best to keep the child art at home on the refrigerator, not on your office wall. You want your colleagues to think of you as a scholar, you want your students to think of you as a professor, and you want everyone on campus to think of you as a young professional who is organized, in control, and worthy of tenure. Senior members of your department may have pictures of their children in their offices, but colleagues and students will not perceive them as being less committed to their work if they have kids. Until you have tenure, image control remains important.

Finally, it is important to note that things are always changing and that universities in general are trying to make it easier for faculty to achieve a decent work-family balance. There are certainly many policies and programs that can be put into place to help junior faculty who are parents, and there may be those on your campus who want to recruit you to fight for this cause. While it is absolutely essential that parents on campus place pressure on their respective administrations to put more family-friendly policies in place, *this is not your main responsibility at this stage in your career.* Leave most of this work to your senior colleagues, and commit yourself to joining the cause when you are safely ensconced in the ranks of the senior faculty. Right now, you must get on with the other important things that you have to do beyond research and networking: spending time with your family, honoring your service commitments, and becoming a better teacher.

On the Tenure Track, Part II

Teaching, Service, and
Finding Time for Your Family

TEACHING

It is very difficult for us to speak generally about teaching because teaching expectations vary so widely from institution to institution. It is absolutely true that there are some universities that care almost nothing about how good you are in a classroom, and will only evaluate you on your scholarship. If this is the situation that you are in,[1] then there is no need to read this section; just skip to the section on university service. For most tenure-track faculty, however, teaching will factor into the tenure case, and at some institutions it is the most important factor. The other key variable is *teaching load*, or how many classes you have to teach in a given semester or quarter. Generally, the higher your teaching load, the less scholarship you are expected to produce for tenure. The lower the teaching load, the more publications you will be expected to have when you come up for review. Finally, there is a huge variability in class size and the availability of teaching assistants and graders to assist junior faculty. Unlike scholarship, where external reviewers do the evaluation, teaching is reviewed internally and is very institution-specific. This is part of the reason why being a good teacher is less of a portable asset than one might think.

The thing about teaching is that most institutions want you to be a good teacher even if they will not grant you tenure for it. At all but the top research universities, when you are a junior faculty member, it is hard to gauge how much time you should be putting into your teaching because the administration wants to keep this ambiguous. Teaching obligations can easily expand to fill all of your available time, at the expense of your research. Preparing lectures, meeting with students, and grading papers can all feel like immediate and instantly achievable goals, whereas scholarship requires a ton of patience because of the long delay before any form of professional gratification can be derived from the activity. Students are also in your office asking you pressing questions, and many people truly enjoy the time they spend in the classroom sharing their knowledge with young adults. All of this can become a trap for the junior faculty member who is unsure about how to allocate her time, and uncertain how "good" her teaching needs to be in order to be acceptable.

The quality of teaching is usually determined by three methods: evaluation of your teaching by students in the classroom, evaluation of your teaching by colleagues who visit your classroom, and retrospective letters (i.e., letters written by students *after* they have taken your class). In addition, most tenure committees will ask to review teaching materials such as syllabi, exams, and writing assignments. All of these methods of evaluation have their drawbacks, and tenure committees do try to take this into account. What they don't always take into account, however, is the substantial literature showing that teaching evaluations are incredibly subjective and biased against women.[2] One study demonstrated that more "feminine" professors tend to be more harshly judged on teaching evaluations than more "masculine" ones (meaning that men generally do better than women, and women who are more "masculine" in their demeanor do better than those who are more "feminine"). "Good-looking" teachers also seem to get better evaluations.[3] Students often imagine that the ideal professor is an older bearded man with a pipe and elbow patches on a corduroy jacket; so the further an actual professor deviates from this stereotype, the harsher he or she will be evaluated. This creates a particular problem for young, female faculty mothers who are already feeling the stress of trying to balance scholarship with family demands.

One piece of advice we can give you is to think about being more dynamic in the classroom. A study conducted in 1973 found evidence for what the authors call the "Dr. Fox Effect."[4] This was a controlled study where professors wrote lectures with varying degrees of content coverage, from high-content coverage to low-content coverage. These lectures were then variously delivered by a real professor and a professional actor referred to in the study as "Dr. Fox." This actor had no academic training and knew nothing about the subject matter, but simply memorized the text of the lectures verbatim. One fascinating finding of the study (which has been widely used to critique teaching evaluations) was that the professional actor scored higher on student teaching evaluations when delivering a low-content-coverage lecture, even when the students performed better on achievement tests taken after the high-content lecture with the real professor. A trait called "expressiveness" seemed to make up completely for lack of content when it came to student evaluations. Three key factors were gesticulation, voice modulation, and movement about the classroom. Apparently, students prefer dynamic professors to knowledgeable ones, and it certainly cannot hurt to try to vary the tone of your voice a bit and try to make your subject matter a little bit more interesting (particularly when you are less prepared for class than you would have liked to be).

Aside from taking voice lessons, you might screw up your courage and have someone videotape you while you are teaching. A lot of schools have teaching centers that employ someone to help with teaching. No one likes to watch herself on videotape, but it does help. In addition, try to teach classes that you are passionate about or with content that overlaps with your research interests. Your excitement for the subject matter will come through. If this is not possible, then try to teach multiple sections of the same class, so that you minimize your prep time. If you teach multiple sections, you may worry less about getting every fact exactly right and allow yourself to relax in the classroom.

Finally, do not try to teach your undergraduates at the graduate level, a mistake that almost all new professors make. Always show your syllabi to your colleagues and ask if you are assigning too much reading and whether your expectations for assignments are too high. The last thing you want to become is the hardest professor on campus if teaching evaluations are going to be a part of your tenure dossier. Interestingly, however, there is no evidence that being an easy grader increases your chances of getting better evaluations.[5] On the contrary, some students will feel like they are wasting their time with you. Most students like to be challenged, but they also like to be made to feel that the goals and requirements of a particular class are reasonable and attainable. To have struggled and then succeeded is the most positive learning experience. Be the best professor you can be in terms of being prepared for your classes, but also be aware of the performance aspects of teaching.

There are quite a few good books available with teaching advice for new faculty (among the best is *Quick Hits for New Faculty*),[6] and it can be a worthwhile investment to read some of these books to help hone your teaching skills. You can also ask senior colleagues in your department, many of whom will be more willing to give teaching advice than share research strategies. You can also read pedagogy Listservs such as Hastac (www.hastac.org) or specific Listservs and/or blogs in your discipline. You should do research on teaching the way you would do research on any other topic; a great deal has been written about teaching in various disciplines, and it behooves you to read at least some of this literature. If nothing else, you will be able to cite it when you are writing your self-evaluation for tenure, to demonstrate that you have put some effort into becoming a good teacher. Certainly, beginning your career with good teaching evaluations is not a bad thing. But if your teaching evaluations are less than stellar in your first year or two, it is not a disaster, but an opportunity for you to show steady improvement over time. You want to get better, not worse, over the course of the years leading to your tenure evaluation; while it would be good for your evaluations to start out very positive and stay that way, starting out low allows you to demonstrate that you have learned to be a better instructor.

Unfortunately, teaching is not only delivering lectures, but it is also about designing assignments and then assessing them. If there is one universal truth in academia, it is that grading is the pits. That is all you need to know, because there is little that you can do about it. There is an apocryphal story that J. R. R. Tolkien, an English professor, started writing *The Hobbit* on the back of a student paper that he was supposed to be grading. If someone would go as far as to invent an entire world called Middle Earth, complete with its own fully developed languages, to avoid grading, then it is abundantly clear that this is the worst part of a professor's job, and perhaps the least rewarding. Just hold your nose and do it. Babies generate dirty diapers. Students generate material that needs to be graded.

The small bit of good news is that there are a few things you can do to shorten the time grading takes or at least reduce the unpleasantness of grading. A well-thought-out writing assignment is easier to grade than a poorly formulated one. The teaching center on your campus may be able to help you improve your writing assignments. You don't have to grade everything you assign. Assign some low-stakes writing to help students keep up with the readings or process the information. Low-stakes writing can just be glanced at or graded with a check/check-plus approach. Terra McKinnish, in "A Survival Guide to Having Children While on Tenure Track," writes that she replaced homework and papers with ungraded in-class exercises. "I found that not only did this save me time grading: students enjoyed the break from lecture and retained more of the day's material."[7] Finally, you don't have to edit your students' papers word for word. There are lots of suggestions out there on how to spend a bit less time on each paper.

There are a few simple, low-time-cost things you can do that may help your student teaching evaluations a bit. Never hand back assignments on the same day that you are doing your evaluations, and, if you have a choice, distribute evaluations at the beginning rather than the end of class. Some institutions allow you to pick the day that you hand out the teaching evaluations, and you can carry them with you until you teach a class where the student who you know likes you the least is absent. Passing out your evaluations on a sunny day is usually better than giving them out on a gray, rainy day. Some of your senior colleagues will also have advice on this, and it is best to solicit their expertise on how to get the best evaluations that you can. They will be the ones judging you, after all.

Finally, be careful that you do not become too open and available to your students in the hopes that they will give you better evaluations if you are chummy with them. Students will feel more comfortable approaching a young female professor with their personal and academic problems and will subsequently expect you to be more lenient with them if they blow a paper or an exam. If you are not, they will judge you more harshly than a young male professor who refused to be swayed by a particular sob story. Draw a firm line in the sand about what students can and cannot seek your counsel for, and if they come to you with relationship problems immediately refer them to the counseling center. In his advice to young women academics, Daniel Hamermesh writes:

> Many students apparently believe that you are there to nurture them, but you are not their mother. Seeing them outside of a restricted set of office hours; devoting excessive amounts of time to substantive questions by one or a few students, and dealing with their personal problems (a job best left to your institution's counseling service) all do a disservice to other students and to yourself. I have seen male students attempt to bully young professors, especially women, into allowing more points on exams, providing extra exam time, postponing exams, and other grade-badgering. This subtle, and often less subtle coercion does not belong in a university. Giving in to such requests often means more work for you and gives the student the idea that he (once in a while she) can

play the system. You are the authority, and erring on the side of toughness with such students will save you further troubles.[8]

You also don't want to become the one person in your department who is known, for instance, for teaching basic English composition skills. If you do, all of your colleagues will begin sending their remedial writers to you for help, no matter how many other obligations you may already have. Students may also begin seeking you out on their own. Kristen once made the mistake of hosting a small workshop on how to work and travel abroad after graduation, providing specific examples of different programs and opportunities in various foreign countries. Although this session was meant for a handful of gender and women's studies majors and minors, for years afterward Kristen had random students on campus (many of whom she had never even met before) showing up at her office to ask for advice on how to find a job or internship abroad. Remember, your pre-tenure time is precious, and you have to allocate it strategically, particularly since research, teaching, and family are not your only obligations.

Another downside of being too friendly with your students is being asked to write countless letters of recommendation. While it is true that writing letters is an important duty for professors, and you certainly should write letters for the students of whom you think highly, letters of recommendation can be extremely time-consuming, particularly if you are trying to finesse a letter for a marginal student. We've all been in that situation before: we get asked to write a letter for someone we barely remember, and then try to use a few kind words and hope that the letter will suffice. Make a firm rule and say you will only write letters for students you have had in two or more classes, and who come to talk to you in person about their graduate-school plans. Furthermore, don't be fooled into thinking that students don't talk to each other; if you get a reputation on campus as someone who will write letters for weaker students, then year after year you will have a barrage of seniors hammering down your door. At Bowdoin, students who are applying to medical school are encouraged to get one letter of recommendation from a non-science professor. Kristen made the mistake of writing such a letter for a student whom she had in only one class. She broke her own rule because the student in question had done quite well in the class, and had made the effort to come to office hours on several occasions. Once Kristen wrote the letter, however, about six other pre-med students who had taken just one class with her, in some cases two years previously, suddenly asked for letters as well.

SERVICE

Service commitments vary from institution to institution, but one thing is generally true throughout academia: service officially counts for almost nothing. You will be assigned to a committee or two and you will have department meetings, which you must attend. This is part of your job. Your colleagues will develop grudges against you if you try to avoid the service that you are assigned to do. You must carry your fair share of the burden of university administration, but not more than your fair share. Service also gives you the opportunity to meet senior faculty members, and, especially on a small campus, these people may turn out to be your allies if you are a borderline tenure case. Service will not get you tenure, but a service deficiency could be counted against you, so it is something that needs to be done and shared equally.

The important thing is not to volunteer, or allow yourself to be volunteered, for anything beyond what is required of you by the faculty senate or the dean's office. Normally, first-year professors are not given service obligations, and you must protect yourself at all costs. Junior faculty get dumped on all the time, and it is difficult to say no to your senior colleagues. The mantra you should learn and repeat to yourself ad nauseam is this: "I have to publish to get tenure, and I cannot focus on scholarship and take on these extra obligations at the same time." If your colleagues press you, politely list all of your service obligations and ask to be excused from some other service obligation in exchange for the new task. If all else fails, ask them honestly if doing this service will make up for not having as many publications, and no senior colleague should be able to look you in the eye and say yes.

There is admittedly a lot of work that needs to be done on campus, but this is not the time for you to be doing it. You don't want to commit yourself to creating a more family-friendly environment on campus if you are not going to be around to enjoy it because you were denied tenure for not having done enough research. No matter how hard or awkward it may seem, you must say no to as much as you can. Just make sure that you do so in a polite and politic way, by promising, for instance, that you would be happy to serve on a search committee, curriculum-review board, or other body after getting tenure.

TEXTBOX 7.1.   PUTTING TOGETHER YOUR
TENURE DOSSIER

Putting together your tenure dossier is more than just compiling all of your research into a file; it is a narrative about who you are and an explanation of why you are worthy of being offered lifetime employment. This is the document that will represent you to your external reviewers and your senior colleagues from your institution, and it must convince them that you have been a thoughtful and productive academic who should be counted as a full member of their discipline and their institution. As with so much in this book, the standards for your dossier will vary by discipline and by institution. It is best to ask your senior colleagues for guidance or to ask a colleague who has recently been tenured to share his or her tenure dossier with you. What is most important is that you know the standards for your institution in specific and your discipline in general, and have a clear sense of what constitutes enough for tenure. At most institutions, tenure standards are deliberately kept vague, but you need to try to get a sense of what other faculty members who recently achieved tenure at your institution had in terms of research when they came up for tenure. This is important because putting together your tenure dossier requires some delicate decisions. Do you include everything you've ever written? Do you include manuscripts in progress? Should everything be in chronological order or should you put your best pieces first? These are tricky issues, and much will depend on standards in your field. Here, we try to give you some general guidelines, or at least some things to take into consideration as you are compiling your materials for external review.

Almost all tenure dossiers require a self-evaluation of some sort. This is a very difficult document to write because you must walk the line between sounding too confident in your research qualifications and not sounding confident enough. It is very important not to sell yourself short. This is definitely the time to toot your own horn. But unfortunately, even this is quite gendered. Men can easily talk with confidence about their research without sounding arrogant. But women must find the right balance between confidence and self-deprecation, or else they run the risk of sounding overbearing and/or obnoxious to most external reviewers. One thing to think about in your early career is whether to use your full name or just your initials. It is rumored that J. K. Rowling, the author of the Harry Potter series of books, was told to use her initials rather than her full name so that young boys would not be put off by books written by a female author. In the British system, it is most often the case that academic authors use their initials and thus avoid "outing" their gender. In the United States, however, authors are expected to use their full names unless they specifically decide otherwise. Depending on your field, you may wish to only use your initials, but the lack of a gender-neutral pronoun in English makes it difficult to hide your gender to your external reviewers in the long run. Besides, if you have followed our advice about going to lots of conferences and giving lots of talks, your external reviewers should already know who you are.

The key thing about your self-evaluation is to clearly discuss your scholarly contributions to your discipline and to let the external reviewers know the extent to which you have engaged with the scholarship in your field. If you are in an interdisciplinary field, it is extremely important to explain in detail why you published in the journals that you chose. In some cases you will want to list the impact factors for each of the journals in which your articles appeared, and you will certainly want to discuss the appropriateness of the university press that published your book. So, for instance, if you published a book with Ashgate or Westview because they had the best list for your scholarship, you should clearly explain that it was your decision to go with this publisher rather than a traditional academic university press. The self-evaluation is your chance to explain your decisions and to champion the importance of your scholarship. Do not downplay your achievements in this letter, no matter how tempted you might be to be humble.

When writing your self-evaluation statement it's best to solicit examples from your colleagues, particularly senior colleagues at your institution, to get a sense of the tone, content, and length of their letters. The biggest mistake that young faculty make is to ignore the importance of the self-evaluation and carelessly dash off a quick

(*continued*)

document. Make sure you have several friends and colleagues read your self-evaluation before you turn it in. This is not the time for careless typos or bad grammar. You want to present yourself in the best possible light. Focus specifically on your accomplishments, and then talk eagerly about your research that is in process and the new research that you hope to do in the future. You don't want to have just finished up a book based on your dissertation with no current project to describe. However great that book is, tenure evaluators are looking for evidence that you will be a productive scholar well into the future. If all you have accomplished is publishing your PhD dissertation, the fear is that you need the help of your adviser to produce publishable research.

If you have co-authored pieces in your dossier, then you need to tell the reader what the nature of that collaboration is. Was it a 100-percent-we-do-everything-together collaboration, or were you in charge of all the statistical work (which is the heart of the paper), or did you simply have to list another author in order to be able to use his or her data? Your description of your work should be accurate. (Someone out there is going to know someone who will be asked to corroborate.) Also, this is where you need to tell the reader that you spent two years in the field collecting these data, or that the time involved in a single experiment was two months, or that you needed to learn Bulgarian before you could do your fieldwork.

If you are at an institution that values teaching, you may also be asked to discuss that in your evaluation. It is important to talk about improvements in your pedagogy over the time that you have spent while on the tenure track. If there are courses where you received particularly poor evaluations, here is the place to justify them. The most important thing is to demonstrate that you are responsive to criticism and that you are willing and able to put time and energy into your teaching to make it better. If you are teaching a particularly demanding subject, this is also the place to suggest gently to your colleagues that they consider the subject matter as well as the pedagogy. English professors will usually have higher teaching evaluations than physics professors because of the nature of the subject matter. But be careful to think about who your readers are. Are they other physics teachers? They will be comparing your evaluations to theirs. Do not say anything that can be construed as criticizing your departmental colleagues. You should also talk about the improvements you hope to make in your teaching in the future. If you are planning to assign more writing, or if you are going to start teaching service-learning courses, this is the place to discuss your plans. As in the research section, evaluators are looking for someone who will be a thoughtful teacher well into the future, not someone who has prepared six courses and will rotate through them with no changes for the rest of her working life.

If you have had children on the tenure track, you should also explicitly state in this letter that a one- or two-year extension on your tenure clock should not be included as time when you should have been producing scholarship. While it should be the university's job to inform the reviewers about how tenure-clock-stopping leaves are handled, Saranna Thornton's research shows that this is not always the case. Half of the seventy-six colleges and universities in her sample reported that they let the tenure reviewers use their own judgment about number of years in rank.[1] Thus, you need to make it crystal clear to the external reviewers that the clock stopped because of parental leave. One way to address this is to constantly use sentences like the following: "In the six years that I have been on the tenure track at my institution, I have published x, y, and z." Even if it has been eight years since your PhD, using phrases that repeat the number of years that should count will emphasize in the reviewers' minds that they should not be counting the two years that you were home after the births of your children. Unfortunately, too many external reviewers believe that scholarship can be done with small children at home. No one would expect anyone to be doing scholarship while undergoing chemotherapy, but somehow childbirth and the months of early infancy are considered more compatible with primary research and writing. Your self-evaluation document is the place to clearly state that due to the birth/adoption of your child (or children), you took leave from both teaching and research, which at your institution means that you were not responsible for producing scholarship during this period. Emphasize this at several places in your self-evaluation if you have to, lest you risk raising the bar for yourself.

(continued)

Should you mention the fact that you threw up for six months prior to the birth of your child, or the fact that your child is a special-needs child, or other facts of this type? These are very difficult questions. In general, we would say the answer is no. Too much information about parenting demands makes you look like you are making excuses: "The lady doth protest too much." Only include this information if you are trying to explain a semester of poor student-opinion forms or a glaring hole in your research agenda. If you do need to include personal information, then be sure to put it in context.

In addition to your self-evaluation, you will have to provide copies of all of your scholarly production for the years that you have been on the tenure track. This will include your book, your articles, book chapters and other published articles, reviews, encyclopedia entries, and anything else you have produced in the last six or seven years. Do not merely organize these materials in chronological order, unless you are explicitly told to do so by your department. Instead, always put the most important of these articles (most likely the peer-reviewed articles in the best journals) in the front of your packet. If there are things that you are not particularly proud of, exclude them. They may be listed on your CV, but there is no reason you have to include them in your tenure dossier, unless they are a major piece of your scholarship. Think carefully about the order in which you are going to present your research; most reviewers will read your file from start to finish, carefully reading those articles at the beginning and then most likely skimming those articles toward the end. Their first impression of you will be made by those articles that you put at the front of your tenure dossier. Make sure your best work is the first thing they see.

It is also worth clearly stating in your table of contents the order of the articles as they appear. If they are not in chronological order or reverse chronological order, make some notation as to which order they are in. You may simply say by "order of importance," or by order of "scholarly significance." Either way, this is a subjective decision and puts the reviewers on notice that these are the articles that they should pay the most attention to. Most reviewers are busy. They receive very little if any compensation for reviewing your file. You want to make their experience in reading your research as painless as possible. This means that you should also take care to make your file neat and easily navigable. You may choose to use a three-ring binder, or you may choose to have your materials bound into a course-packet-type booklet or something like a spiral notebook. Kristen's tenure materials were organized and bound as a course packet, and she later ran into one of her tenure reviewers who admitted that the neatness and organization of the materials made an incredibly favorable impression on her. This reviewer was able to take the bound packet with her on a plane to review Kristen's tenure case while on a transcontinental flight.

Another tip is that sometimes tenure reviewers will consider the weight and/or thickness of a tenure file before they even consider the content. It is not easy to pad a sparse research record, but, for instance, if you have had an article reprinted or translated into another language, it is worth including the reprint or translation in your tenure file, even if it is already listed on your CV. A little extra thickness never hurts. All book reviews, encyclopedia entries, newsletter articles, and so on should also be included if you are proud of them. They may not count for much toward your tenure case, but once again they will add thickness and weight to your file. One question that arises is whether or not you should include manuscripts of works in progress. In general, if your case is borderline, you should include everything you have, even those things that are still in preparation (as long as you make it clear that these are, in fact, works in progress). If you are fairly confident, however, that you have enough to meet your institution's research standards for tenure, leave the manuscripts of works in progress out of your file. They will not be nearly as polished as your published work, and they might damage your scholarly reputation. More importantly, these are the manuscripts that will constitute your dossier for promotion to full professor after six years (assuming you get tenure, of course). Once again, tenure standards will vary from institution to institution and from discipline to discipline, so it's best to have a clear idea of what is needed for your promotion and then do the best you can to put together a strong dossier of your work. Before you turn it in, make sure you show it to some senior colleagues to get their feedback. Once you are satisfied that you have presented yourself in the best

(continued)

possible way, hand your file over to your chair or dean, take a deep breath, and focus on what's important to you. That may be looking for another job, trying to get pregnant, spending time with your family, or spending some time on yourself. Once you have turned in your tenure dossier, the whole process is out of your hands. Try to relax and recognize that you have little control over your future for now. It is unlikely that you will know anything definitive for the next six to twelve months. Yes, the time lag can be infuriating, but it can also be quite liberating. Regardless of the decision on tenure, you still need to be looking ahead.

FAMILY

When talking about research in the previous chapter, we urged you to be disciplined with your time. The same goes for family. Family time should be a top priority of yours. Reserve some time each day as family time. When it is family time, don't check your email or try to read an article for class. Let yourself just be mom and partner for a while. The more time you earmark as family time and research time, the less time disappears into the world of "I have no idea what I just did with that hour" time. Rachel has a rule that she does not work on anything college related on Friday nights and all day Saturdays. She finds it essential for her mental health. She reports that the few times she worked straight through a two- or three-week period, she spent as much time moping and feeling sorry for herself as she had gained from the Saturday work time.

Your children don't need you there twenty-four hours a day, but they do need you there consistently, especially young children. An hour daily at bedtime delivered unfailingly is better than a seven-hour stretch on Saturday. When her first child was an infant, Rachel spent an hour with him every morning while her husband was taking a class. Then she went to her office and didn't do parenting things again until 5:30 p.m., when she returned home and took over the child care duties until bedtime (except for breastfeeding at lunch time when he was less than six months old). This schedule allowed her to spend at least four hours a day with her son, at times when he was awake and playful. In addition, they had cuddle time at the end of every day. After he went to bed, Rachel graded papers or prepared for the next day's classes. This allowed her to use her most productive hours in the morning for research.

Another important rule of busy parenting is "no guilt." It is not useful to always wish you were somewhere else. If you miss a child's first steps, you will see the second steps the same evening. If you don't read that chapter tonight, you can read the next chapter tomorrow night. We enjoy our kids and want to spend time with them. But they also benefit from time with Dad or Grandma or the babysitter. Engaging high-quality day care is important, and once you have secured it, use it. Once Rachel succumbed to maternal guilt and picked up two of her children early from summer camp. After all, she thought, they had been there from 9:00 a.m. to 3:30 p.m. When she arrived the children were angry. "We don't want to leave—after this comes snack and then dodge-ball." In addition, children are amazingly forgiving. They take each person for who they are. When Rachel's children were young, they received lots of attention from one of their grandmothers and very little from the other. But they never compared them or asked, "Why don't we get presents from this grandma?" It is an important lesson that we as parents can learn from our children. We are by no means child-development experts, but we do observe that our children have strong, healthy relationships with us as well as with their fathers, their grandparents, and an extraordinary range of relatives and adult friends. Our children are also very open to new places and new people, the result of many work-related relocations over the years.

Don't be afraid to take your children with you to a conference or while going on leave, but remember that when your children are young you cannot watch them and attend a conference session at the same time. Use the conference day care center, share caregiving with another faculty parent, or pick conferences near Grandma and Grandpa. Rachel attended a conference in Madison, Wisconsin, when her first child was seven months old. Since he was still nursing, Rachel asked her mom and dad to accompany her to the conference. Grandma, Grandpa, and her son had a good time during the days, going to the zoo and feeding the birds, and Rachel was more comfortable not having to pump all the time. It certainly was a win-win-win situation. On the other hand, there was the time when Rachel and a colleague went to a national conference, each with her third baby. They agreed to share child care so each of them could go to sessions while the other looked after the two babies. The problem was that the colleague's baby cried the entire time her mother was gone. It was not as successful a trade as one would have hoped for.

Going somewhere else while on leave with a young child in tow is a challenge, but going away while on leave may be something you need to do to get the research done. In some cases, the only grants you can get are residential fellowships that require you to move to a new place. There is certainly extra work needed to move away and then move back, but the relief you get from teaching can be shared between more research time and more family time. Both Rachel and Kristen spent some leave time in Washington, DC. It is a good city for a leave since it is relatively easy to find short-term housing, and there are lots of fun things for families to do. Kristen has also taken one-year residential fellowships in Princeton, New Jersey, and Cambridge, Massachusetts, and done extended fieldwork in Eastern Europe. Rachel spent two separate sabbatical years in Beijing. Although the logistical hurdles are considerable, most of the residential-fellowship programs have staff members who will help you organize housing and schools for your kids. The Institute for Population Research at Peking University helped Rachel arrange visas, housing, and schooling for her children. At the Institute for Advanced Study, fellows are guaranteed a spot in the on-site day care center (which is a dream), and the bus for the Princeton public school system picks up and drops off right at the fellows' housing complex. Conditions were not so easy at Harvard, but for Kristen, getting a year off of teaching was worth considerable inconvenience.

There are hundreds of books about parenting, but don't read too many of them. Many of them are hostile to employed mothers. Instead, trust yourself, and remember the no-guilt mantra. Of course, it is also important to find time for yourself and your partner. The no-guilt mantra and the disciplined approach to time use work in these arenas as well. You need to get some exercise, but you don't need to be running marathons. Prioritize your leisure time use like any other time use. You and your partner need some time to be alone, so figure out what time works best for that and stick to it, whether it's a "date night" every other week or an hour in the evenings after the children are asleep.

TEXTBOX 7.2.   TRAVELING WITH KIDS OVERSEAS

In our experience, children are flexible and forgiving beings. But they also are amazingly perceptive. If you are nervous about something or if you feel guilty, they will pick up on that and run with it. And they never seem to miss an opportunity to push that newfound button. So if you feel guilty about missing their school field trip, they will definitely whine and moan about why you weren't there. Our advice is to exorcise that guilt. You will all be happier to enjoy the time you have together instead of always wishing you were doing something else.

Taking children traveling is a great way to expose them to different cultures and encourage flexibility. When Rachel and her husband traveled abroad for the first time with their first child (he was just under two), he cried at bedtime the first few nights about wanting to go home. Their response was "Mama is here and Da is here, so we are home." After about four weeks of traveling, as they were wandering down the street in yet another new city, Martin, getting a bit tired, chirped up from his stroller, "Let's go find home for tonight."

Traveling with one child and two adults certainly is easier than traveling with four children and one adult, but even that can be done once the older ones can help carry. In 1992, Rachel and her husband moved with their then two children, a six-year-old and a one-year-old, to Beijing for a year. Six years later, they moved with their then four children to Beijing for another year. That second time they lived in a two-room apartment in the university section of the city (not two bedrooms—two rooms). The oldest child (age thirteen) studied at home with a combination of parental tutoring, hired tutors, and lots of quiet reading and writing time. The middle two children went to local schools: the old sink-or-swim approach to language learning, which works great up to about age eight or nine. The youngest one was home with a Chinese-speaking babysitter. It was a tight squeeze with all four children sleeping in one room—three in one bed, in fact—but it was lots of fun. Rachel was able to get plenty of

(continued)

work done, and there was still extra family time because she wasn't teaching. Since then the family has graduated to a three-bedroom apartment in the same neighborhood in Beijing, and the children and their father return twice a year to reimmerse themselves in Chinese-language learning.

People always ask about what happens to their schooling in the United States when they are in Beijing. They simply miss three to four weeks at a time, twice a year. The trips are timed to coincide with school vacations so that the number of days missed in the United States is minimized, but they still miss a bunch of school. Some of the schoolwork missed is made up, but much of it is adapted to fit with their Chinese experience. They have written papers on ancient Chinese astronomical devices for science class, researched religion in China for humanities class, done photo essays for language arts, and so on. Not every teacher is understanding, but most are, and the children have had to learn early on about trade-offs. Rachel's advice regarding the school system is not to ask permission; instead, politely tell them what you plan to do.

If you are doing extended fieldwork, then you do need to think about how it overlays with your children's schooling. In many cases, staying for an entire school year is a better option than staying for one semester. International schools are expensive, so consider the alternatives. Home-schooling with tutors is the option Rachel used for her teenager. Local schools work well for younger children. High-school students can enroll in correspondence courses, college distance-learning courses, or college-age study-abroad courses taught in the city where you are staying. One of Rachel's professor mom friends taught a semester course in China for her university when her daughter was in ninth grade. Her daughter studied Chinese along with the college students and then worked on her own on the other high-school subjects with materials supplied by her hometown high school. The widespread availability of the Internet, even in developing countries, has made all of this easier. When they went to China in 1998, Rachel brought along reference books as well as reading material for four children at different reading levels. Now everything is there for the Googling or can be loaded onto the iPad or Kindle before you leave.

Kristen is more respectful of the school calendar than Rachel (or maybe it is just that she did her first extended stint of fieldwork as a mother when her daughter was still preschool age).[1] Kristen continues to do fieldwork in Bulgaria every summer, and does one shorter trip during the winter months every other year. Kristen's daughter is remarkably adaptable and good-natured, and feels as at home in airports as she does on playgrounds. She knows the TSA security procedures as well as she knows her spelling lists these days, and she's now old enough to accompany her mom to conferences and invited lectures, often sitting in the back of the room with a portable DVD player while Kristen talks about "boring stuff." Other academic moms are always asking Kristen how she manages to travel so much with her daughter, but she always answers the same way: "I don't have a choice." Starting early and being clear that this is ordinary also helps.

One consequence of all this travel is that all of Rachel's children are fluent Mandarin Chinese speakers and feel comfortable not only in their hometown of twenty thousand in Maine, but also in a city with a population nearing twenty million, where their mere presence on the street is often cause for remark. For Kristen's daughter, extensive travel time in Europe has resulted in Bulgarian language skills, familiarity prior to first grade with the pantheon of Greek gods, and an exceptionally catholic approach when it comes to cuisine. This seems to us to be a very good trade-off for a few missed days of school.

The hardest thing about traveling is actually getting there. Our advice here is to use a stroller for much longer than you think you should. Strollers are great luggage carts. You can also send books ahead if you are staying long enough. Buy cheap toys where you are and leave them there when you leave. Kindles and iPads have made the how-to-bring-enough-books-for-the-kids problem a lot easier. Expect to buy some T-shirts and cheap kids' clothes where you are going. Use the extra room you have saved in the suitcase for the beloved blanket or stuffed animal that will make any bed feel like home. Rachel's son Louis took his down blanket and pillow back and forth to Beijing twice a year for ten years, which seemed silly to some, but was necessary for his sense of well-being. Louis's French horn, Patrick's violin, and

(continued)

four very full backpacks made quite a scene in the airport, but once they got to Beijing they were home. The French-horn teacher and the violin teacher were called, the children called their Beijing friends, and they started up exactly where they had left off.

What about all the other things that fill a day? Here is where you are going to find the time to devote to research, teaching, and your family. The message here is the same as in the service section of this chapter—figure out ways to say no. If it is important to you or your partner to have a clean house, pay someone else to clean it; otherwise let it be dirty. Having an untidy house is one of the realities of being a working mom. This perpetual untidiness frustrated Helen, the tenured natural scientist and mother of three, but she accepted it as a reality and focused on the things that needed to get done:

I wish I had a wife. Seriously! If I had someone at home who could keep the house cleaned up, deal with all the home crap that piles up (broken window, calling about furnace repairs or leaky faucets), do laundry, cook meals, do grocery shopping, etc., I would be in heaven. I love my husband, but it doesn't bother him when the house gets messy or when the kids don't have any clean underwear. If I had a wife, I bet it would bother her!! (Incidentally, we've never hired anyone to clean the house—for a couple of reasons, it seems like more work than it is worth sometimes, plus I think ethically, we both have a problem with hiring someone to clean up for us—something we think our whole family should be capable of doing for ourselves.) I do believe that maintaining a nice, tidy house and feeding a family in a healthy manner is a nearly full-time job (ok, a nearly half-time job). [But] with both parents working there are many things that just don't get done. Those evenings after dinner when I'm tired already, and I realize that I could clean up for a bit or I could start working on whatever deadline I have coming up, I opt for working towards the deadline, leaving the cleanup for another time.

Like Helen, we also suggest that you lower your standards when it comes to cleanliness and doing those traditional-mom-type things that you always feel guilty for not doing. Do not iron anything, period. Don't make handmade Halloween costumes unless you find sewing therapeutic. Don't volunteer to make cookies for the bake sale. Send a check to the food bank instead of contributing food to the food drive. You can give up matched socks—time spent matching socks can be a waste of time. If you care whether socks match, buy one kind. If you don't care, as is the case in Rachel's family, then just put all socks, unmatched, in the sock drawer. Letting go of small tasks like these can make your life feel less hurried and disorganized. Embrace chaos.

Rachel has a rule that she does not attend any meeting or college event that begins after 5:00 p.m. Of course, once in a while, she breaks this rule if it is important, but an easy-to-articulate rule goes a long way toward reducing time demands. After 5:00 is family time in Rachel's house, and family time requires that you be there (and not be trying to write a book at the same time). You don't need to go on school field trips (yes, you want to and your child wants you to, but that is work time). Rachel's children understood that Mom worked while she was on campus, but when she got home she was totally there for them. A side benefit of having this disciplined approach to time is that when you violate your own rules it gets noticed. For example, Rachel wanted to impress upon her children that Hebrew school was important, so she violated her own rule and volunteered at Hebrew school every Wednesday afternoon (post-tenure). The children got the message that Mom thought that Hebrew school was worthy of an exception.

Kristen is exponentially less disciplined than Rachel is, but she was a single mom for a long time and only has one child. There are no boundaries between work and home for Kristen. She prefers to grade at the kitchen table in her pajamas, reads in bed, and thrives on the flexibility of being able to write whenever she is feeling in the "zone" (even if that means working in the middle of the night and sleeping during the day). This always worked well for Kristen when she was on her own with her daughter, because outside of the predictable child-related obligations, her time was completely her own. Her daughter, Kristiana, is very easygoing and has always enjoyed playing (and now reading) alone. Although Kristiana needs her mom's attention like any normal kid, she is also used to seeing Kristen working at home and has accepted that there are times when Mom has to be marking papers or working at the computer. Things get more complicated when there is another adult in the picture, and it is important to remember that partners need attention, too.

Finally, with all of these responsibilities, it is inevitable that you will forget about yourself. This is what you need to do. It stinks. Get over it. You can go shopping and get manicures galore after tenure. Until then, buckle down and just try to get enough sleep.

8

So You Made It
The Early Years after Tenure

Congratulations! You did it! The trustees have awarded you tenure. You are now an associate professor. This is what you have been working for, worrying over, obsessing about for the last seven or eight years. Often there is a post-tenure let down where you look around and say, "Now what?" But things don't magically change after tenure. Your job is still your job. You still need to teach, edit that paper that came back "revise and resubmit," write new grant applications, and meet with your students. There are hills and valleys, just as there were before tenure. But the good news is that the valleys are less low. The consequences of the most recent rejection letter are clearly not as dire as they were before. So yes, it was worth the battle, but if you expected to feel totally different post-tenure, or if you expected that the weight of the world would be gone, you will be disappointed and a bit disoriented.

When we asked her about the myths prevalent among young assistant professors today, Miriam, an associate professor of history, wrote:

[There is a myth] that life is easier after tenure. In many universities now, there are provisions for a "research semester," support for research, etc. to get women tenured and promoted to associate. Also, most academics utilize their PhD work for their first substantial research project, which gives them an available body of research. Having the research down and partially digested is a huge leg up in terms of publications. No one talks about the second research project and how difficult finding funding and time might be. This is, of course, paired with increased responsibilities and duties that were not part of most non-tenured faculty workload before. Additional professional obligations and familial circumstance make it harder to do research in blocks of time. Fellowship monies are oriented to those early in career and not to mid-career. Also, if academics delay having families until tenure, the midyears of a career are then the years that balancing family and work are most difficult.

Do you have kids yet? If not, you need to get going on that front. Clearly you are a one-thing-at-a-time person, so put as much effort into getting pregnant as you did into getting tenure. But many of you already have one or two children. For you it is time to ask the question, do you want more? While one might have been your pre-tenure limit, post-tenure you might consider another one (or two or three). You wouldn't be the first newly minted associate professor to throw away the birth-control at news of your successful promotion. Indeed, tenure babies are very common in the academy, and you have every right to indulge in the possibility of enlarging your family. Go back and reread chapter 4, which discussed family size in more depth.

In all areas of your life and work, the years immediately post-tenure are a time for regrouping and reflection. For most of us, however, tenure can feel like a bit of an anticlimax. We got good grades in high school so that we could get into a good university so that we could get into a top graduate program. We excelled in graduate school so that we could write an excellent dissertation that would land us a tenure-track job at a good institution that suited us. We worked like hell to get our research done, persevered through the countless rejection letters and disappointing teaching evaluations, and hunkered down to do all of the university service that was required of us to finally attain the hallowed status of a tenured associate professor. Lifetime employment guaranteed, with a good retirement fund and health insurance, plus getting paid to set our own schedules and research agendas and studying the things that we really want to study. There it is. You made it. What comes next?

Tenure is a time to celebrate your successes but also a time to make adjustments, some modest, some major, on those aspects of your life that come up short in your estimation. There are now several questions that you will want to seriously consider. Are you at the right institution? Are you doing the type of research you intended to do? Are you spending the right amount of time on teaching? (Remember that you could as easily be spending too much time on teaching as too little.) What about your other professional time? Again, you need to assess whether you are doing enough of that which you want to and not too much of that which you would rather not do. The aim, of course, is to increase the amount of time and effort put into all the various aspects of your job and your family life that bring you pleasure and help you achieve your professional and domestic goals. Reduce the amount of time and effort you put into those aspects of your job and your family life that merely annoy and aggravate and which do not serve any of your personal goals. But don't push this too far. The reality of our bundled lives is that we don't simply get to stop doing things we don't like. We don't like grading, and yet we grade. Rachel does not like attending school chorus concerts, and yet she continues to attend them (and recognizes that as the children get older, the concerts *do* get better). Kristen dislikes committee meetings that convene with no agenda, but she goes to them nonetheless. An active imagination helps here; you can always try to think of ways to reduce grading time without compromising too many of your other pedagogical goals, just as you can use the "space out" time in committee meetings to think about your next project or a fun activity that you might be doing with your kids on the weekend. The point is, a heck of a lot less is on the line now that you have tenure, but you still want to do your best to be a decent campus citizen. In this chapter, we consider research, teaching, service to your department and institution, service to your profession, and family issues separately.

RESEARCH: TIME TO THINK BIGGER AND WITH LONGER HORIZONS

We know that different disciplines have different expectations for tenure. We spent a lot of time earlier in the book urging you to be strategic about your research time. All of us share the constraints of the tenure clock. Pre-tenure you need to wrap things up quickly so you will have results to show the tenure committee. Post-tenure you can think a little bigger and a little broader. It is okay if the projects take a little longer. Now is the time to jump into that big messy problem that you have been skirting around for the last six years, collect all your articles into a book, or look into an entirely new area of research. But before you do anything else, take some time to think about the big picture. (When was the last time you had a moment to do that?) Explore funding opportunities, and consider going somewhere else for a year to get reinvigorated or retooled. Not going anywhere because of family considerations? Then bring the world to you. Organize a symposium, and invite some scholars at the same stage in their careers to join you for a weekend. Look beyond your friends from graduate school, and make some new research connections.

This is a time to launch yourself into the big world of academia. Having tenure changes your status in your discipline, and suddenly you will be asked to review more articles, book manuscripts, tenure-promotion files, grant proposals, and so on than before. This allows you to suddenly have a larger stake in shaping the intellectual contours of your field. For Rachel, the years immediately post-tenure meant reconnecting with graduate-school friends who were now out of graduate school and ready to collaborate on research projects. Pre-tenure, all her articles were single authored. Post-tenure, almost all her articles have been co-authored. Rachel finds co-authoring more enjoyable as it is less isolating, there is someone to turn to when she gets stuck, and someone else cares about the outcome of the endeavor. When she is tired and fed up, she keeps going because her co-author may need the article for tenure or promotion.

Kristen also started co-authoring after receiving tenure, but still does most of her work on her own. (It's hard to be collaborative when writing ethnography.) Once Kristen got over the post-tenure anticlimax, tenure meant being able to really widen her intellectual horizons. She applied for and won a National Science Foundation cultural-anthropology grant for methodological retooling, and did a two-summer fellowship at the Max Planck Institute for Demographic Research in Germany, learning the tools of demography with an Italian collaborator. After finishing her second book, Kristen also started experimenting with ethnographic essays and ethnographic fiction, two genres that were quite different from her more social-theory-driven earlier research. Because she no longer had to worry about tenure and already had two serious academic books behind her, Kristen decided to publish a collection of these essays and stories as her third book, something written specifically to be accessible to a wider audience, including not only scholars interested in the material, but also undergraduate students and the general public as well. It is not uncommon for established scholars to try new things. Since academia is a career for the long term, you want to maintain passion and interest in your own research, even if that means changing fields, experimenting with different genres, or writing for different audiences.

With all this talk of change, we don't want to leave you with the sense that there is a tremendous break between the pre- and post-tenure years. Mostly life goes on pretty much like before. If you have been self-reflective from the beginning, there is no reason to expect a major change in research behavior post-tenure. Just enjoy the new freedom it brings to take some risks, either in topic or approach. Your goal has always been more than tenure. It is a continued life as a producer of knowledge; you are at the beginning of the rest of your career. So keep it up. We think you will find it gets easier and more enjoyable over time. The rejection letters and failed grant proposals certainly impart less of a sting than they did before. Furthermore, you probably have quite a number of things still in the pipeline from your frantic pre-tenure years. So it is perfectly reasonable to take a year to rethink and reassess where you are and where you want to go. You are now paid to think and read and write—that is your job. Enjoy the pleasures that this brings, because not that many people are in your position. You worked really hard to get where you are.

TEACHING: TIME TO EXPERIMENT WITH NEW COURSES AND NEW PEDAGOGY

Whether you are at a Research I institution or a school with a high teaching load, you will still spend some part of your work life teaching. Now is the time to make teaching more enjoyable as well. Even if no one cares about the quality of your teaching, you do, because it is more fun to do if you know you are getting through to the students. You have the opportunity to change the lives of young people in your classes, to open their eyes to new ways of seeing the world, to new ways of thinking, to new ways of questioning previously held beliefs. Both Kristen and Rachel are always pleased when they receive emails from their former students expressing appreciation for how much their undergraduate experiences were enhanced by being in their classes.

At Bowdoin, tenure decisions rest squarely on the quality of teaching (or at least on student opinions of teaching), so by tenure time Rachel was considered a good teacher. But she was unhappy with certain aspects of her teaching and with one course in particular: her senior seminar. It was difficult to get the students to talk in class, and their research papers were frequently mediocre. Based on their responses to the student-opinion form, the students liked the course, but she was not happy teaching it. So in that period of post-tenure reflection, Rachel decided to revamp the entire course. Before tenure she had been afraid to make too many changes, since she wasn't sure the changes would work and the students were not unhappy with the course. Once she had tenure, she realized she was going to be teaching the course for the foreseeable future and decided that she might as well take a stab at making it better. She thought long and hard about what she could do to get the students engaged in the material and reorganized the assignments to a set of problem sets that forced the students to think about the material before coming to class. The change worked very well for the students but created too much grading for Rachel. So she revamped the course yet again so that students worked in groups. This produced almost the same positive effect for the students, but with substantially less grading. This is a good example of the importance of thinking about time trade-offs in decision making. You should not be after the best pedagogy (or the best research paper for that matter), but rather the best pedagogy within reasonable time limits. The same can be said for every aspect of one's life, especially raising one's children.

A philosophy professor we know at a small liberal arts college also made substantial changes in her teaching post-tenure. She was tired of reading terrible papers with epidemic plagiarism. She also struggled with students unprepared for class, and realized that they were having trouble reading the material, so she decided to concentrate on working through the readings before allowing the students to write. She dropped the research-paper requirement and added a lot more structure to the course. She reports that it is working: "The hardest thing for me," she writes, "was giving in to using a teaching style that I would have hated as an undergraduate. But that is what I needed to do and there is much more learning going on in my classes now than there was before. I am less frustrated and so are they."

Post-tenure is also a time to think about increasing the connection between your research and your teaching. It can be very gratifying to bring your research and teaching lives together, and for students to see you in your role as researcher and producer of knowledge. Add a section to your course on your research topic. Give it two or three weeks instead of the one week you used to allocate. In general, consider covering less material more thoroughly. Thinking of a new research project? Try it out as a course topic first. This will allow you to read the necessary background materials on your teaching clock instead of your research clock. In every course, assign something you have been meaning to read. Yes, that means that sometimes you make a mistake and assign a reading that really wasn't what you thought it would be, but your students will learn as much from your critique of the article as they would have from the old standby.

If you have the opportunity, why not build an entire course around your research interests? Rachel has taught courses on the economics of the family, and Kristen developed a senior seminar called "Gender and Sexuality in Contemporary Eastern Europe." When Kristen found herself interested in questions of secularization and women's rights, she developed a course called "Gender and Secularisms" that allowed her to familiarize herself with an entirely new field of critical scholarship. While it is true that the liberal arts environment allows more flexibility in creating your own courses, anyone who is past the tenure hurdle should be able to find ways to integrate her teaching obligations with scholarly interests.

Finally, and perhaps most importantly, feel free not to read your teaching evaluations for a few semesters. Different people have different reactions to course opinion forms; Kristen has a colleague who will not read them until she has had three margaritas. Whatever your proclivities, teaching evaluations can be very informative and can help you improve your teaching, or they can just get you down and make you feel antagonistic toward your students. If you are at an institution where teaching matters, then allow yourself the luxury of not caring for a semester or two. If you are in an institution where no one has ever really cared about your teaching, then allow yourself to care for a semester or two. Either way, feel free to experiment with new ideas and pedagogy so that you enjoy your time in the classroom.

SERVICE TO YOUR DEPARTMENT AND INSTITUTION: BEWARE, THIS WAY MADNESS LIES

It is an unfortunate truth that as soon as you achieve tenure at your institution, you become eligible for a whole world of service commitments that you did not previously know existed. Suddenly, you become fair game for labor-intensive committees that no one would think of putting you on before tenure. This is also the time when you could be tapped to be chair of your department or to assume some other senior administrative post at your institution. In essence, you will be dumped on, massively. Just when things seem to be settling down and you feel like you've achieved a modicum of professional success, your dean or your chair will come after you to do some horrible, boring, and probably thankless job in your department that nobody else wants to do. We have heard it said that some senior faculty are desperate to tenure junior faculty members in a department because then all of the onerous service commitments can be dumped on the newbie. There is also the (probably apocryphal) story of the itinerant assistant professor who has way more research than necessary to achieve tenure, but who deliberately changes institutions every six years in order to reset his tenure clock and thereby avoid the service commitments of senior faculty, so he will have more time for his research.

This is a very difficult thing to protect yourself against. In some ways, there really isn't much you can do. You will have to serve on the tenure committees of the junior faculty in your department; there's no way around that. In smaller departments, you will eventually have to chair your department as well; there's probably no way around that either. But if the dean is looking for you to chair some new appeals committee or some campuswide diversity initiative, be careful: this way lies madness. Indeed, it seems that if you say yes to too many things in your first year as an associate professor, your colleagues and the administrators at your institution will collectively place you on the mental list of people on campus who like to do service. Alternatively, if you tactfully say no to as many things as you can in that first year past tenure, you will be more or less scratched off the list in people's minds. This doesn't mean that you should shirk all responsibilities, but it does mean that you should not become a service "chump" or someone who always gets dumped on when no one else wants to step up to the plate.

Watch out for being too "good" at doing service. Some of us, especially the working mothers among us, are very competent and organized people whom everyone wants to have on their committee. Then there are people no one wants to have because they are disorganized, scatterbrained, chronically late, or simply unpleasant people. If you are on a committee with these people it can be extremely frustrating, but they count on someone else to step up and do the work of the entire committee for them. While you don't want to become one of those people, neither do you want to do everyone else's work for them (even if they are truly incompetent). Never do the work of an entire committee, even if you are the chair of that committee. We know that sometimes it is easier to do the work yourself than to wait for the consensus of the committee, but this means that you are micromanaging, and unless this is a committee that you really care about, don't do it. This is the time in your career when you should have some more time for your family; don't let that be robbed from you through an increase in service commitments.

So what kinds of service are we talking about? Well, as with everything else, that depends on your institution. There are many tasks on campus that the faculty are expected to do. Some examples are graduate admissions, chairing search committees, advising graduate students, advising undergraduate students, overseeing the choice of a "first-year book," and staffing any number of campus committees concerned with the status of women, the status of minorities, the status of disabled persons, the status of the future of the humanities, or the status of resident megalomaniacs. Then there are an endless variety of student organizations and student initiatives that are always looking for faculty sponsorship. There are the trustees who want to interface with faculty or the development office that wants to use faculty to connect with alumni. There are events for prospective students, as well as an endless succession of talks, seminars, colloquia, and lectures that require your attendance or your supervision.

It is entirely possible that you could work fifty hours a week and do nothing but your teaching and service work. For some people who are happy to have achieved tenure and are not worried about the prospect of remaining associate professors for the remainder of their professional lives, these endless service commitments provide the perfect excuse for deferring research, sometimes to the point of research extinction. But be careful. Giving up on your research means that you will no longer be able to leave your institution for another academic position. It may also mean that you will be less satisfied with your work life, which would be a shame after all you did to get where you are.

In human-capital theory there are two types of investments. The first category, called *general human capital*, consists of investments in the individual—that is, investments in an individual's base of knowledge that are essentially portable. In academia, these include your education and degrees, your publications, your research experiences and expertise in certain fields, and your awards and fellowships, as well as your syllabi and your ability to teach certain subjects at different levels. The other type of investment is called *firm-specific investment*, and this is the kind of investment that is not portable, consisting primarily of service to your institution that does not increase your competitiveness on the job market. Use this distinction to consider the nature of a task you have been asked to do and whether it is something that increases your portable human capital or something that is only of value to the particular institution where you are currently employed. For instance, chairing an institutional-research board that oversees human-subjects research at your institution is something that will probably be seen as valuable on the broader job market. Overseeing a very specific plan for changing the college-level distribution requirements, however, will not be seen as valuable to an institution that may have a very different set of norms and standards for undergraduate education.

After tenure, your institution will want you to do as much firm-specific service as they can get you to do. They may have invested a lot in you to get tenure, and would be loathe to lose you if you are planning to leave for a better or better-paid position at another institution. It may sound slightly conspiratorial to say that institutions overburden tenured faculty with so much service that they don't have time to think about the job market or to pursue further research that will make them attractive to other employers, but many associate professors have felt these pressures. In order to protect yourself you should try to steer as much of your service for the institution toward the type that simultaneously increases your individual (portable) human capital. Examples of this might be chairing your department (administrative experience is always valuable), overseeing the graduate admissions process, or chairing a particular search committee in a particular field that is related to your research interests. Service on the college-wide promotions-and-tenure committee is also not a bad idea, or any committee that allows you to gain a better understanding of the internal mechanisms of academia as a profession. Things that will not increase your portable human capital are things like serving on the committee to discuss the architectural redesign of the campus art museum (unless you are an architect), working on the committee to discuss how to make pre-major academic advising more effective for first-year students at your specific institution, or sleeping through the faculty committee meetings called to rethink your campus's recycling plan. These are real committees on which our colleagues and friends have been asked to serve.

In addition to trying to direct your service to portable human-capital-enhancing committees, you can try to focus your service hours on causes you care about. Rachel has done considerable service work at Bowdoin over the years. There were so few women on campus when she arrived that all women were overburdened with committee work. There was no getting out of it.

Instead, Rachel decided to employ the strategy of volunteering for committees working on matters she cared about, instead of waiting to be assigned committees on a hit-or-miss basis. A bad experience she had as the faculty member assigned to the student judiciary board reinforced this strategy for her. If you follow this strategy, the time you spend on committee work will not be as unpleasant and may even bring with it the pleasure of having made a difference. After all, the origins of this book are the result of Rachel's term as director of the gender and women's studies program, which involved two years of chairing a large search committee, but which, in the end, led to the hiring of Kristen.

So, how do you say no? We discussed this briefly in the pre-tenure chapter, but now the stakes are a little different because they can't fire you. You have tenure. You have the right to say no to things that are above and beyond what you think you should be doing, and certainly to things that require you to work in the evenings or on weekends or during summer break. Remember how Rachel categorically refuses to do anything after 5:00, and doesn't do anything work related on Friday nights and Saturdays? Too bad the trustees always meet on Saturdays. Sorry. This is a good rule to have in place once you are tenured, if you can stick to it. Of course, the ability to say no will vary from institution to institution, but we encourage you to get out of the habit of trying to please everyone. Do your fair share of service, but *never* do more than your fair share unless you are strategically angling to move out of scholarship and into a permanent administrative position. Psychologically, people are more comfortable asking women to do things because women are less likely to say no than men. Even if you risk getting a reputation as being "cold" or "uncollegial," it is worth standing up for your rights. Do not let the senior male faculty in your department take advantage of the fact that you are newly tenured and afraid to say no.

SERVICE TO THE PROFESSION: TIME TO STEP IT UP AND GET YOUR NAME OUT THERE

Service to the profession, unlike service to your institution, is inherently portable. Academia thrives on the volunteer labor of tenured professors; this is a time-honored truth. Many people— people you may never know or meet—read your articles, your book manuscripts, your grant proposals, and your tenure file, all out of duty to the profession that they have joined. Once you earn tenure, you are now a bona fide member of this profession, and with that membership come certain responsibilities. It is essential that you take on some of these responsibilities, but only those that will be interesting to you and will help you keep current with scholarship in your field and make a difference in the shaping of your discipline. In other words, just as we argued in the sections on research, teaching, and service to the university, you should do things for your profession that you think are important.

There are a whole host of things that will be coming your way. You will be asked to write more book reviews, to review more article and book manuscripts, to sit on grant-review committees, to read tenure files for scholars from other institutions, to do external departmental reviews of similar institutions or programs, to run for office in your professional society, to organize symposia and lecture series, and to engage in other types of activities that enhance knowledge production in your discipline. It can be incredibly frustrating when you are sent three book manuscripts to review in the same month, but sometimes these are books that you would like to read anyway, and reading new book manuscripts is a great way to keep on top of the most recent literature in your field. More importantly, if these are books directly related to your previous work, you also have the opportunity to help shape the thinking of younger scholars about key issues and debates in the discipline. Although this labor often seems thankless (most presses offer only a token amount of money to review a book manuscript), it's important to keep in mind that someone has reviewed your book (or will review it when you finally get it written and off to a press). Whenever Kristen has a pile of manuscripts on her desk waiting to be reviewed, she tries to remember her own frustration at waiting for a reader's report when she was pre-tenure. This motivates her to get her reports done more quickly, even if there are fifteen other things she should be doing as well, not the least of which is spending time with her daughter.

Another thing you may be asked to do is become an editor of a journal in your field or serve on an editorial board. The latter is much less work than the former, but they are both big responsibilities, and you should be sure that you are ready to take them on. This is also true of running for president of your professional organization or agreeing to write a textbook. No matter how research-intensive these activities may be, most campus promotion committees will not consider them as part of your scholarly dossier for promotion to full professor. These things fall under the category of service to the profession.

Being a book-review editor pre-tenure might score you some points in the research column, but the rules change after tenure. The promotion committee is looking for publications, and publications only. Kristen had a colleague who spent many years editing a new international journal that gave voice to scholars from a non-English-speaking part of the world. This colleague, who had two young children, devoted many hours working through convoluted language trying to salvage good ideas from bad prose, and shaping an entire field of thought emerging from this region. When she came up for full professor, she hoped to include her work as an editor on this journal as part of her research. Her institution insisted that it was only service. Think about the kinds of new projects you are willing to take on, and how they will reflect on your ability to be promoted to full professor within the next seven or eight years. You don't want to overload yourself so that you are as stressed as you were before tenure.

FAMILY: SLOW DOWN A BIT AND MAKE MORE TIME FOR THE ONES YOU LOVE

As we said at the beginning of this chapter, if you haven't already had a baby, now is certainly the time. If you've already had one, or even two, you may want to try to get pregnant again. But remember that getting tenure does not mean that life gets less busy. As detailed above, service commitments can increase considerably at your institution, as can service commitments to your discipline. Our message about family life post-tenure is very similar to that about research post-tenure. Take the time to reevaluate. Spend more time on family-related things that you enjoy or that you think are important, and reduce the time you spend on things that are less important or that get in the way of spending more family-oriented time. Family has always been important to you, otherwise you wouldn't be reading this book. To the extent that tenure provides you more time or at least less high-stress time, spend some of your extra time with the people that you love: children, extended family, and friends. Continue to invest your time wisely. Going to the playground with your daughter is more important than cleaning the garage. Invite friends over for dinner, and linger after dinner while the children play in the next room. Give some of your time to a good cause or to a friend who could use it. Be as strategic with your home time as you are with your work time. You still don't have any time to waste.

You can do more combining of work and family than you did pre-tenure. Put up those pictures of your children in your office. Choose conferences based on where they are—a fun place to take the family, or a place for a romantic weekend getaway after the conference. Rachel sometimes volunteers to do the hotel-room interviews at the national meetings in exchange for staying in the interview suite. Her children get a huge kick out of staying on the thirtieth floor in a magnificent hotel room looking out over San Francisco Bay (even if they do have to vacate the room by 8:30 a.m.). Kristen always accepts talk invitations from colleagues who have young children; she pulls her daughter out of school for a few days and brings her along for the trip. The plane ride is a great time for them to connect, and her daughter gets the feeling that she is getting to do something really special.

While it is okay to slow your research pace when the children are young, don't let the scholarship stop altogether. It's much harder to reboot a scholarly agenda from scratch than it is to speed up an agenda that has been temporarily slowed down. The mistake a lot of people make immediately after tenure is to just throw up their arms and give up on research for a couple of years. This is a bad idea, and in the long run it can hurt you. So while we certainly recommend carving out more time for yourself and your family when your children are young—don't just turn to deadwood at your institution. The university is still paying you to work full-time, after all.

Coming Up for Full Professor

Your Last Promotion

You have been doing your thing for a while. You have gotten better at the juggling act that is your life: research, teaching, and hanging out with your children. The children mostly get to school on time and to the dentist twice a year. You are even managing to get to the gym yourself on a semi-regular basis. Research is going well—you put in a bit less time, but you're actually better at it so your success rate is higher. People ask you to give talks which lead to papers which lead to publications in a way you only dreamed about before tenure. Teaching is less stressful and, if you followed our advice from the previous chapter, more enjoyable for you. The kids are older and more independent. Oh, they still need you, no doubt about that—they need you to drive them hither and yon, then to make yourself scarce while they do their thing. They need you to watch them at sporting events, plays, and musical performances, they need help with their homework, and they need you for those important but impossible-to-predict-when-they-will-happen conversations, like the one at bedtime when your ten-year-old was wondering about the existence of God, or the one after your thirteen-year-old got dumped by his first-ever girlfriend. Even though things are easier, the three important components of your life—research, teaching, and family—are still there, and they still take up most of your time. So why would you want to add more stress to your life by coming up for full professor?

Let's be real. The most important reason for becoming a full professor is that it almost always means a raise. Those braces on your child's teeth are not cheap. Summer camp costs a small fortune. And then there is college tuition looming in the increasingly near future. In addition, on the plus side of the equation, it feels good. Being a full professor is the definition of having made it in the world in which you live. It is hard to explain to parents and friends not in that world, but after doing this for fifteen years or more, admit it. It matters to you. It is a celebration of your achievements, and it will feel good when it is over. That is all well and good, says the pragmatist you have become from the constant juggling you do, but it is a lot of extra work and aggravation in the short run. You need to prepare your dossier and you need to present yourself to your department. Why not just take off your clothes and prance around the hallway near your chair's office? Because that is what it feels like (again). Didn't I already do this once, you ask yourself? Surely, the tenure process was enough self-exposure.

The good news is that the stakes are not as high this time, and as a result the dynamics are different. Don't forget, you have tenure. They are stuck with you. So they are going to think thrice before really disparaging your work and accomplishments. Yes, there are standards to maintain, and that jerk who voted against you for tenure will still vote against you because he doesn't think what you do is actually real scholarship, despite your new book coming out at a top university press. Forget about him, think of the orthodontist bills, pick a relatively good time (like having a baby, there is really no good time to add extra work and stress into your life), hold your nose, and send that letter to the dean or your chair announcing your intention to stand for promotion.

Rachel delayed and delayed this moment. In addition to the two children she had prior to coming up for tenure, she had two more children posttenure. And there were some bad feelings in her department, the residue from an ugly departmental battle, so she mostly wanted to be left alone to concentrate on her juggling. (If you stop concentrating, all the balls do actually seem to fall to the ground at once.) But also, more than anything, she wanted to be asked. She wanted someone in her department to notice that her vita looked very healthy and her student-evaluation numbers were up. "I see you just published your fourth paper this year and all my students can't wait to take your course. I wonder why you haven't come up for full?" That was what she was hoping to hear from her senior colleagues. Forget it. That is not a good enough reason to wait for a raise. Luckily for Rachel, one of her co-authors badgered her into it. "Too many women are not coming up for full. You need to do it for all womankind." Why was "for all womankind" a good enough reason, but enough money for a nice week's vacation with the children was not? (Actually, we know the answer to that one. If it were just about money, you would have found another job long ago.)

Once Rachel started the process, it turned out to be almost fun. Writing the self-evaluation was a nice opportunity for self-reflection. A couple of the external reviewers let slip that they had been asked and told her how impressed they were with the sum of her work. Former students and fellow faculty members shared the letters they had written on her behalf. Her department was equally complimentary, and the promotion sailed through. As things were wrapping up, one of the members of her department said to her, "I always wondered why you hadn't come up yet." The lesson again is, don't wait to be asked.

Since you are not going to wait to be asked, when is the right time? Just as you did before tenure, look around your institution and get a feel for the process. Do most people come up for promotion like clockwork six years after their promotion to associate? Or is promotion to full professor based on a certain threshold of achievement? Is there pressure to come up for full on some sort of schedule, or are there a large number of long-term associate professors on your campus? At many institutions, the threshold for promotion is a second book or a second body of work approximately of the same quantity and quality as that which was needed for tenure. Of course, this differs substantially by institution, so we can't provide specific advice on this issue—you have to discern the institution-specific norm where you work.

If you are having trouble picking up the clues as to what the criteria are, don't be afraid to ask senior colleagues on campus. They should be more forthcoming with you about this promotion than they were about tenure. (Since they are now stuck with you, it is in their interest to push and prod you in the direction they want.) Of course, you may not get the same answer from all your colleagues. Listen carefully to the tenure discussions in which you now take part for others. The closed-door discussions for promotion to full are almost identical. If Professor Y doesn't approve of co-authored work for tenure, he most likely doesn't approve of it for promotion either. But if he is outvoted by the other senior members of the department, then don't worry about it—go ahead and co-author away.

If teaching mattered at tenure time, it most likely matters at promotion time as well. Be especially conscious of your last few semesters of teaching before promotion. Do the student-opinion forms indicate largely satisfied students? If so, then you should be fine in that department. If not, decide that this year is going to be the year of the student: make some real changes in your courses, and see how it goes.

Don't expect excellence in one area to substitute for a weak performance in another. If your school values research, being a top teacher will not be enough. Likewise, if your school values teaching, your teaching performance must be good enough. Yes, you could go to a place where teaching matters less, and certainly you should consider that, but just because some other institution would take you doesn't mean that your institution will make you a full professor. Reread textbox 7.1 on preparing your tenure dossier. All that advice also applies to preparing your promotion dossier. Once you decide to apply for promotion, you need to take the process seriously and give it your best shot. A sloppy, halfhearted application is not going to make anyone happy.

Finally, don't get yourself into a game of chicken that you don't want to see to the end. A friend of Rachel's got so angry at her department over their delay of her promotion that she left academia altogether and went to a consulting firm. It was her department's loss, and she is happy with the change in jobs—so we are not saying never do this, just make sure you are comfortable with either potential outcome before you begin an all-out battle.

The rest of this chapter assumes you have taken the plunge, put yourself forward for promotion to full professor, and were successful (since you had done your homework ahead of time about knowing what was necessary to be successful). What will life be like as a full professor?

WORK LIFE: RESEARCH, SERVICE, AND TEACHING

Just as you did after you were promoted to associate professor, use the time directly after promotion to full professor to do another check-in with yourself. Are you doing the kind of work you value? Are there things you care about that you put aside before, when the kids were younger and your ladder climbing was more important? Now might be the time to try your hand at writing for a more general audience, if that is something you have considered. You can write a column, a blog, or a trade book. Now is the time to say yes more often, to give back to a community of scholars who understood why you said no before. Now is the time to advocate for tenure-clock-stopping leave and paid parental leave that actually work. Now is the time to start that mentoring program that you wished had been in place when you were just starting out.

What if you decide that you are not where you want to be? Perhaps your partner has never warmed to the town in which your university is located. Or the past transgressions of your department members are not fading in your memory. Or you are not happy with the mix of teaching and research time that your college's teaching-load policy imposes on you. This might be a good time to look for another job. Unless you want to leave so badly that you would take any other job, be very selective in your applications. You should never apply for a job at this point that you would not consider taking. It should be in a place you want to live or at an institution that has the teaching load you are looking for or that admits the sort of students you would like to be teaching. Again, as with all the advice in this book, a good dose of self-reflection goes a long way to making this a smoother process. Like the application for promotion to full professor, applying for a senior job is a time-consuming process and emotionally draining. It should not be entered into lightly. On the other hand, good things can come from putting your CV out there.

Going out on the job market is a good way to assess your market value and to experiment with different professional options. Although there are some job ads for senior positions, usually you will be invited to apply for an open position. Many senior hires take place when one department poaches a professor from another. Usually, you will be invited to give a talk without even knowing that you are being considered for a job. If you have been publishing consistently and have made a name for yourself in your field, it is not uncommon for you to be courted by different schools. You may decide that you are happy where you are, or you may take the opportunity to shift gears and explore other options.

Several years after taking the plunge to become a full professor, after a very rejuvenating and productive sabbatical, Rachel was asked to apply for an endowed chair at a research university. It was tempting in so many ways. The teaching load was lower than at Bowdoin, and the location was in a bigger city with many more universities in the area, a necessary ingredient for a vibrant research community. The children were older, and their college tuition bills were imminent. After much soul-searching and discussions with her husband and a few trusted colleagues, she submitted her application.

The interview process was a lot more fun than it had been when she was a graduate student. After all, she could very easily stay where she was. She was not unhappy at Bowdoin or in midcoast Maine. Similarly, the campus visit, while as exhausting as she had remembered it, was enjoyable. Rachel presented a new paper that was at the stage at which it would benefit from comments anyway. She met nice people who had interests similar to her own.

When the offer did come, then it was not so much fun. Yes, it is very nice to be wanted and courted, and she would have been disappointed to not be wanted, but it is very difficult to make big, life-changing decisions. Each job had its advantages, and it was difficult to compare those advantages given an uncertain future. Rachel let her dean at Bowdoin know as soon as she received the other offer. It is important to give your dean enough time to make a counteroffer (only if you would entertain a counteroffer). Perhaps a better time to have let her know would have been when she went for the on-campus interview. Deans like to know this sort of thing, and it is nothing to be embarrassed about. It is not showing disloyalty to your job, just an openness to explore other options (unless you do it all the time, then it probably gets old). Bowdoin did make a nice counteroffer, including pulling an endowed chair out of its back pocket. (Yes, it would have been nice to be given the endowed chair without an outside offer, but it is like waiting to be asked—don't dwell on that.)

Again, never make an ultimatum in a negotiating process unless you are willing to follow through. But you can go back to both parties with a conversation about what else you might like. Be realistic about what wiggle room the dean or the chair has. Sometimes thinking a bit out of the box will work. Is your concern college tuition for your children? Can you be vested early in their college tuition program? Do you need travel funds or start-up funds to enhance your research? Can you take your years of credit toward your next sabbatical with you so that you would be eligible for sabbatical at the new university sooner? If you are ready to take the new job, then negotiate for moving costs, but not before that.

On Wednesday, Rachel was sure she was going to take the other job, but by Friday, more soul-searching and spreadsheet gazing had convinced her to stay at Bowdoin. It was a tough decision, since in the hierarchy of our profession, the research university was certainly the "better job." But, in the end, quality-of-life issues won out. The price of housing was so high in the university city that Rachel could not have afforded a house big enough for her family in a school district where she was willing to reside. The teaching load was lighter, but class sizes were bigger, and Rachel does enjoy the interaction she has with Bowdoin's undergraduates. The salary was higher, but the contribution to the pension was lower and required a co-pay on Rachel's part. It would have been exciting and challenging to join the research community in the city, but Rachel knew that there are other ways to do that. Conferences have always played that role for Rachel, and Bowdoin has a generous travel allowance for conferences, and competitive funds available if you go over your annual allotment.

After her decision was made, Rachel thanked the many people she had consulted along the way. Most were surprised by her decision, but one of her co-authors summed it up: "Just because you can do it, doesn't mean you have to do it." A former professor said he wasn't surprised. "You have always done it your own way," he said. Rachel knew he was right, and was happy that she had stayed true to her own modus operandi. If you are following the advice in this book, then you, too, should be doing it your own way, even if that means making decisions that your colleagues do not always understand.

If looking for another job does not suit you or your family's needs, another common move at this stage of your career is a move into administration. As with any thoughts of changing jobs, you need to think about what parts of your job you like and which parts you would rather not do. Then find out as much about the new job as possible. What parts of the new job do you think you would like, and which parts would you find disagreeable?

There may be opportunities to try out administrative jobs without having to give up your tenured position. While temporary administrative jobs are good ways to explore these possibilities, remember that everyone knows it is temporary, and so the dynamics of that job if it were permanent might be different. But most temporary administrative jobs put you in close contact with full-time administrators, so watch and learn from them.

One reason for thinking about moving to administration is that those jobs usually pay more than teaching-faculty positions. This might be a good reason for taking an administrative job temporarily, to amass a college tuition fund for your child. But there might be other ways to get that one-time extra salary infusion that would be less disruptive to your research and family time. Consider teaching a summer-school course at your institution, or somewhere else more exotic. Rachel taught one summer in Beijing. It was not a wonderful experience, and she found herself tired when the fall semester began, but it did pay well. One of our colleagues at Bowdoin has taught summer school at Harvard, and another has taught in a Middlebury summer-language program. Alternatively, apply for summer fellowship money or a grant that offers summer support. This is certainly a way to have your cake and eat it too, although one must always remember that when one accepts the grant money, one has to actually do the project. Sometimes what seemed like a good idea when you wrote the grant turns into more of a burden after you get the grant. Never submit a grant for a project you are not interested in doing. Finally, if the grants don't come through and summer-school pay is too low to bother with, then propose an administrative project to the dean for one summer. Don't undersell your time. If the dean would have had to pay a consultant to do the project, you could be saving the university a substantial amount of money while you help rethink a campus diversity initiative or spearhead the effort to make the campus more family friendly.

FAMILY LIFE

During this time of reflection, you will undoubtedly be thinking about your family life as well as your work life. As your children age, they need different inputs of parental time. When they are young, they need you there at least an hour every single night before bed. They are constantly interrupting you throughout the day, demanding your attention. As they become teenagers, the roles reverse. We find ourselves thinking of ways to demand their attention. "Can't you have dinner home tonight?" "Can't, Mom. I need to be at rehearsal at 6:00." "How about going to the cabin this weekend?" "Sorry, you know I'm going out on Saturday night." They just don't need us in the same way anymore.

Don't give up. You are still their parent, and, yes, they still need you—just more unpredictably, and in bigger chunks. Create family traditions that demand respect above and beyond you just asking them to join you. Rachel and her children have an annual August camping trip with a group of friends. The children think twice about missing that annual event. When the conversation with your child turns serious, make sure you take the time to finish it. This summer while they were camping, Rachel and her third child were discussing college. It was not the first conversation (or the last), but it was the one that mattered. Rachel was trying to tell this middle child that he didn't need to do something just because his older brothers had done it. It is hard being in the middle. It was not the first time she had said this, but it might have been the first time he heard it. The problem with teenagers is that you don't know when these conversations are going to happen. So you need to put in the time to have lots of encounters, so that when the time is right, you are there.

Lots of conversations with older children happen in the car. It is a safe place somehow. So think about driving them to school once in a while. Be sure you are there when they come home from the school dance or the SAT test. These are the moments of transition when they are likely to be open to conversation. Take them with you to conferences. They don't need day care anymore. You can point them to a museum or tourist site if they are old enough, but just hanging out in an expensive hotel room in a big city can also be fun.

Make use of the resources your university offers for your children. Rachel's children have each audited Bowdoin classes, and Rachel has taught Economics 101 to quite a few of her colleagues' children over the years. Some of the resources on campus may also be open to them—the radio station, the media lab, some of the club sports. Kristen and her daughter make good use of the campus swimming pool, the field house, and the library. Kristen's daughter is also a regular visitor to the campus art museum, where they have a children's program one Saturday every month.

Your university has experts on financial aid and the college admission process. Take an admission counselor to lunch and pick his or her brain about the process when your oldest child enters high school. There are also experts around on all sorts of learning issues, which may help you as a parent. You have tenure; it is okay to admit you have children. Look around and see what resources are out there. Let your children be proud of the fact that their mom is a university professor. Campus may also be a good place for your children to come after school when they are old enough to be left alone but you want them working on their homework. When one of Rachel's children was having trouble in high-school algebra Rachel hired a student to tutor her son on campus. The school bus dropped him off on campus. He made his way to the tutoring session on his own and then spent the hour after tutoring doing his homework and playing on the computer before Rachel and he drove home together.

While our advice to you when the children were young was to be fairly rigid with your time, our advice at this stage is to be more flexible. If they are all at soccer practice on Sunday afternoon, then that is a good time to work on that new grant application. Always have an article in your bag for the inevitable wait in the parking lot when your daughter said she would be done with rehearsal at 6:00 p.m. but it didn't finish until 6:30. A tenured professor Rachel knows at a Research I university uses time spent waiting in the car at soccer practice to return phone calls and answer emails. You certainly don't have to watch every practice. Even during games, Rachel has been known to ask the person in front of her for a summary of the game right before the game ends. "Hey, that was a great goal you made in the second half," she says, hoping she is not pressed for more information. The basic principle of time use, though, is still the same. Save your best uninterrupted time for research since there are plenty of other things you do that can be done in fits and starts. But when you do have your child's attention, it is time to put down the article, turn off the email, and just "hang out."

Finally, take some time for yourself. Whatever it is that you always wanted to do, you don't have to wait until the kids are out of the house before you do it. Although that time will come soon enough, if you wait until then to learn how to treat yourself well every now and again, you may simply forget how.

Conclusion

When we began thinking about writing this book, we sent out questionnaires to other academic moms, soliciting opinions, ideas, and advice. One of the things we hoped to find was a set of commonalities about what it takes to be able to find work-family balance in this most demanding of professions—something like "the eight secrets to successful hamster breeding" or "the six pitfalls of investment banking." We hoped the result of our questionnaires would be "the five habits of relatively sane academic mothers." Well, we didn't come up with five, but we did come up with one. One thing that the vast majority of women we surveyed have in common is this: they are very careful with their time. They don't do anything that doesn't directly benefit their scholarship, teaching, or family life. Unsurprisingly, this particular rule includes not filling out seven-question email surveys on how to combine motherhood with academia.

We sent out more than eighty surveys to our friends and colleagues (mostly friends), and the response rate was truly abysmal. Most of the women just ignored the emails, while others sent short notes promising that they would do the survey in the next week or two and then never sent us anything. So ubiquitous was this result that we believe we found a truly general characteristic. The truth is that there is a lot of voluntary labor in academia, and one has to protect oneself from doing too many things that are not directly related to one's specific goals. There are always surveys to be completed; letters of recommendation to write; extra meetings to go to; professional newsletters to read; tenure files, articles, and book manuscripts to review; email correspondence to stay on top of; phone messages to return; books to order; syllabi to prepare; and a million other small tasks that can eat up one's work time and cut into family life. In our crazed and bifurcated lives as mothers and professors, there are just not enough hours in the day for all of the things we *should* be doing. You have to be able to say no to the things that are not important, to know your priorities and to observe firm and fast rules about how you will and will not spend your time. A short email survey may seem like nothing, but our lives are full of short, seemingly insignificant tasks that can absorb our entire working day if we are not constantly on guard. So work hard, but be careful and protective of your time—use it wisely, exorcise the accompanying guilt, and you will do fine. That is the advice the many people who didn't respond sent us.

Given the time crunch in our lives, we guess that only a few of you have gotten to this page by starting at page 1 and reading all the way through the book. Many others of you came to these concluding pages first, a strategy we learned in high school that still works for getting a quick overview of the general argument or main point of a book. In recognition of the fact that you are busy, we have decided to present our conclusion in outline form, giving you our main theses and some discussion questions for you to review. There is much advice contained within these pages, and not all of it will apply to everyone. It is our hope that this book will continue to be a resource to you no matter where you are in your academic career or how many children you already have or want to have in the future. We know that it can be done, and that it can be done well if you are disciplined about your time and accept without regret the consequences of your own decisions.

We start with five main points to remember:

1. Academia is hard.
2. Academia is hard for everyone, both men and women, with or without children.
3. Although times have changed considerably and things are improving, it is still a proven empirical reality that it is harder for women with children to achieve tenure compared to men and women without children and men with children.

4. Although it is difficult to be both a successful academic and a mother, it is absolutely possible. Knowing what you are getting into will help you beat the odds.

5. Although it will require a lot of hard work, it is worth it. You get to read what you want, write about what interests you, and influence a new generation of students and scholars. And then you come home to someone who calls you Mommy.

Keeping these points in mind, answer the following questions, and be honest with yourself. Not all questions will apply to every individual because you may be past a certain stage in your career, but it might be helpful to think back and consider how you might have answered them if you had been asked in graduate school.

1. Are you sure you want to be a professor? Be sure. It is not a part-time job, and it takes years of work to even be in the running. Know what the sacrifices are, and be willing to accept them. There are many.

2. Do you want to have children? How many? There is no such thing as a good time to have them, but they are fun to have. They put work in its proper place—it shouldn't be the only thing you do. If you do want children, don't wait too long. Infertility is unpleasant.

3. Are you aware of the challenges you will face? Know that it is not going to be easy to be both a mother and an academic, but that there are things you can do to make it possible. You are not alone; there are successful role models to observe. Watch and learn from them (but don't pester them too much—they are busy too).

4. Have you done research about where you want to work? There is considerable variation in expectations, resources, and working environments among schools, even those in a given tier. Don't rule out Research Is. There are some Research Is that are making an effort to be more family friendly, and they have the resources to buy you some time. Don't only look at Research Is, despite what your advisers tell you. You can "do it all" at any university or college. But it helps a great deal to know what your definition of doing it all is.

5. What is your time worth? Be disciplined with your time—use it for important things, and try not to interrupt yourself. Try to save your best

time for research. You can't do a full-time academic job in twenty hours a week. Make sure you devote enough time to be successful. Try to provide consistent predictable time to your children. When they are young they need to know that there is a time each day when your attention is on them. When they are older they need you to be able to drop everything and seize the moment once in a while.

6. What parts of your life can you outsource? Don't waste your time on unimportant things (the things you know to be unimportant). Either let someone else do them, pay someone else to do them, or do without them. Buy the highest quality child care you can afford when your children are young, and use it without feeling guilty—high-quality child care is good for children.

7. What are the work-family balance policies available at your institution? If you are eligible for a paid parental leave, take it. If you are eligible for an unpaid leave, take it if you can afford it. Do not, however, expect your parental leave to be a research leave. You will be busy doing what you need to do at that moment—recovering from childbirth, generating quarts of breast milk every day, and hanging with your newborn baby. That *is* doing something.

8. Are you schmoozing enough? Networking is important to your success in academia. Take it as seriously as the rest of your job. Go to conferences, give talks, attend symposia, and send offprints of your work. It is not only *what* you know, but *who* you know, who knows you, and how they can help you.

9. Are you saying no often enough? Learn to say no politely, but often. There is a time and a place for everything. When you are pre-tenure you will feel a lot of pressure to say yes, but say no anyway.

10. Are you ready to make a move? You don't need to stay at your first institution. If it is not a good match for your aspirations pre-tenure, go back on the job market and look for a better fit. If you want to speed it up or slow it down post-tenure, you can venture out on the market again. Never go on the job market cavalierly, but it is not something to be reluctant to do either.

11. Are you ready to start changing things for the better? Once your kids are older, it is time to give back and make the academy a better place for work-family balance. After you have achieved tenure, lobby for changes

at your institution. Institutional changes are essential, but they take time
and sustained effort.

Finally, remember that academia starts out as a sprint but then turns into
a marathon. If you achieve tenure by your late thirties, you will still have a
good thirty years' worth of a career ahead of you. Your career will outlast
your parental responsibilities. Your books and articles and your students may
be as much a part of your legacy as your children. Celebrate them all. Both
motherhood and academia can be incredibly fulfilling vocations despite the
many challenges you will face in trying to combine the two of them. Know
the realities, but don't be discouraged. There are plenty of women who have
done this, and it is our sincere hope that there will be plenty more of them in
the future. Good luck!

Afterword

Reflections on Institutional Change

Since the fall of 2011 when we wrote *Professor Mommy*, we have received some terrific feedback from readers. It has been wonderful to get emails and even handwritten notes of thanks from those who found the book personally helpful to them. In addition, we received notes from tenured faculty at research universities saying that they were recommending the book as a "must read" to their students. But they also wondered what else could they do to make the path easier for their newly minted Ph.D. students. This afterword is for them, and all those convinced by Anne-Marie Slaughter's argument (among the many other voices) that self help is not enough to address the problems facing mothers in the labor market.

In our first edition of *Professor Mommy*, we did not intend to give short shrift to the cause of institutional change. The high work hours requirement and inflexibility of the tenure clock are the main demons of the academic workplace. In its demand for long work hours, the academy is not much different from other jobs with comparable levels of education. But the inflexibility of the tenure clock is a special feature of the academic landscape, which makes combining parenting and full time employment an additional challenge for women. If we value having both men and women as faculty in the academy, we (collectively) need to work to make the academy more welcoming for aspiring academics who also want to raise children.

Of course, one of the problems with giving specific prescriptions for change is that institutional contexts vary widely. What is possible at a small liberal arts college will be very different from what is possible at a large state university. Some universities have unions and collective bargaining, while at others it is left up to the individual to negotiate for specific benefits like parental leave and/or sabbatical leave. On some campuses, department chairs have substantial power over class schedules, leaves, and salaries; at others, one must negotiate with the provost or the dean. Some departments enjoy easy camaraderie among colleagues, while others are snake pits where one faculty member's gain is always considered a loss for the others. Thus, it is impossible to have a one-size-fits-all set of solutions or policy recommendations for institutional change.

With this caveat in mind, we have some advice and thoughts about things that may be possible across different institutional contexts. There are some policies that cost the institution very little. In addition, there are national trends that administrators can be convinced will be of good PR value for your campus or are good for recruiting new faculty members. At the very least, initiating a discussion about work/family balance at your institution might spark new interest and ideas for incremental change.

As we already emphasized in the book, you should be especially careful about advocating for change before you have tenure. Even if you already have tenure, you need to spend some time identifying likely allies. There is power in numbers—always go out in groups. A well-thought-out proposal supported by multiple faculty members will have a better chance of success than a lone voice, no matter how impassioned it is.

Also, be sure you know your institution, including the institutional history of family policies. Do your research! Have there been previous committees empowered to look at issues of work-family balance on your campus? If so, find their reports and read their recommendations. What policies have been proposed in the past? If there were successful changes made, how were they achieved? If they were shot down, what about the institutional context has changed that makes it worth trying again? You may not want to push for a major overhaul of the parental leave policy when there is a dean or president who is known to be hostile or unsupportive. Also, make sure you have done your homework on what your peer institutions have done for families. If a comparable college has recently instituted a spousal hiring policy, then it might be worth trying to push for a similar policy on your campus. If there has not been a committee to look at these issues, see if there is enough interest among your colleagues to form one. Committees to study a problem cost nothing, and are often a good place to start.

If you are senior enough, you might consider moving into administration, either temporarily or permanently. Many schools offer limited term administrative positions for faculty. (As always, if it is temporary, don't totally abandon your research agenda during your tenure in this position. You want to keep your hand in your research so it will be easier to return to full strength when the time comes.) If you are in a position of power you can more easily advocate for institutional change. When Mary Ann Mason became the dean of graduate studies at Berkeley, she was able to push through major changes throughout the entire UC system. Drew Faust's presidency at Harvard has coincided with a better climate for achieving work/family balance. Administration is admittedly not for everyone, but if you are truly committed to institutional change, the best way might be to put yourself on the inside. If you are not yet advanced enough in your career to become an administrator, you might consider encouraging one of your more senior colleagues to step up for dean or provost. At the very least, you should be paying attention to who is being appointed to these positions.

So what kinds of policies can be advocated for? Once again, everything depends on your institutional context. But there are plenty of examples of things that other campuses have done to make it easier to combine a career in academia with parenting. The following list is not exhaustive, but intended to give a broad outline of what is possible.

1: TENURE CLOCK STOPPAGES AND EXTENSIONS

We put this policy at the top of the list for a number of reasons. As we mentioned above, the inflexibility of the tenure clock is one of the primary obstacles to sane professor mommying. In addition, this policy costs the institution almost nothing in direct costs. It can and should be implemented without the requirement that one take a parental leave. (Parental leave is another important policy, but it is separable from policies to stop the tenure clock for childbirth or adoption of a young child.)

Push for a policy that does not limit the number of times one can stop the clock. Why is one child okay and not two? Why is two okay, but not three? In advocating for the policy, emphasize that it still does not cost the institution anything and that in the context of a thirty to forty year career, another year delay does not matter all that much.

An important concern with the implementation of a tenure clock policy is to make sure that those who avail themselves of it are not held to a higher standard than those who come up for tenure on time. Whether intentionally or not, some external reviewers and tenure committee members will look at the date of the Ph.D. and judge a candidate's scholarly productivity based on how much time has elapsed. This can actually put parents at a disadvantage vis-à-vis their childless colleagues. Proper language needs to be inserted into instructions for both external and internal reviewers, which clarifies the exact number of years being evaluated.

2: PARENTAL LEAVE
In the United States, the Family and Medical Leave Act (FMLA) guarantees 12 weeks of unpaid leave with some caveats (one needs to have been employed for more than one year with one's current employer, have worked more than 1250 hours the previous year, and have been employed at an employer with more than 50 employees). Unfortunately, most semesters are longer than 12 weeks and babies don't always come at the beginning of a semester, making the FMLA provision confusing in an academic context. All faculty parents will benefit from negotiations for a specific unpaid parental leave policy for faculty members, which clearly defines the beginning and ending dates of a semester and gives provision for periods that may cut across two semesters. It is best to define a leave policy in the currency of the academic workload: how many courses off, provisions for replacement teachers for leaves of less than a full term, and so on. But do not forget that universities are bound by FMLA. They MUST give you at least 12 weeks off and allow you to return to your former position. This is not a gift or a concession on their part; it is federal law. You can negotiate up from FMLA, giving special consideration to the needs of the administration to plan ahead, to the needs of the students to have a coherent course, as well as to the needs of the faculty parent recovering from the birth and/or settling in to life with an infant (and all the sleep deprivation that this inevitably requires).

Beyond instituting a special policy that works with the academic calendar, it is also important to consider how the policy is implemented. Junior faculty need to feel safe taking the leave. Too often, there is a policy in place, but pre-tenure parents are afraid to make use of it. This is especially true if your institution does not replace faculty members taking parental leave. Other members of the department will have to work more to cover a leave, so it is important to make sure that there is no resentment against new parents, especially against those who have more than one child while on the tenure track.

Obviously, a policy of paid parental leave is much better than unpaid parental leave, but harder to get. Paid leave is usually for a term and junior faculty should be encouraged to take it even if their children come during the summer months. As with unpaid leave, tenured faculty should ensure that junior faculty feel comfortable asking for and taking this leave.

Paid leave for graduate student TAs is something that Mary Ann Mason advocated for while she was dean of the Graduate Division at the University of California, Berkeley. In their new book, *Do Babies Matter? Gender and Family in the Ivory Tower (Families in Focus)*, she and coauthors Nicholas H. Wolfinger and Marc Goulden argue that the lack of maternity leave for graduate students is part of the remaining gender divide in the sciences and partly to blame for the differential outcomes for men and women academics upon the birth of a child. Thus, it is important to think about implementing policies that will help support parents at all stages of their academic careers.

3: SPOUSAL HIRING

One of the biggest challenges in academia is the so-called two-body problem. Many academics are partnered to other academics, and finding two jobs at the same institution is difficult. It used to be that spousal offers were only available to faculty being poached away from other institutions. Some campuses, however, now have policies in place to extend at least half time faculty appointments to spouses and domestic partners in order to promote faculty stability and continuity. Although on the surface this seems an expensive policy, it can be cost effective for the institution. Recruiting costs are reduced as the percent of offers taken will increase. Spouses are already covered by their partner's health insurance plan. Given the difficultly in finding two jobs at the same institution, couples are also more likely to stay at the institution in the long run. Furthermore, when one partner is only teaching half time, but has full time research and service obligations, the institution benefits from having an extra faculty member available for committee work and student advising.

And as long as spousal hires do not detract from the possibility of future lines within a department, they are helpful for "leave-proofing" departments against curricular holes cause by sabbatical and parental leaves.

4: PROVIDING CHILDCARE FOR ALL CAMPUS EVENTS

Since collegiality is such an important component of tenure and promotion, faculty with young children are often at a disadvantage when it comes to attending receptions or other social events held in the evenings or on the weekends. Organizers of these events can hire some students to provide child care in a nearby room. Once again, this costs very little, but it sends a clear message that a campus is inclusive of those professors with family responsibilities. When Kristen's daughter was a toddler, she loved going to all of the campus events because there was always pizza and there were new toys and other children to play with.

5: ON-CAMPUS CHILDCARE

The real gold standard for work-family balance is an on-campus child care center with preferences given to graduate school TAs and junior faculty members. If the institutional conditions are right, administrators and university presidents can be convinced that it is a worthwhile investment. On-site child care centers are very useful in recruiting new faculty members, and fees charged usually cover operating expenses. If the college does not want to employ the center's teachers, they can contract with one of several national firms that provide employer-sponsored child care centers just as colleges contract with outside food service providers.

There can also be compelling curricular reasons to build a child care facility on campus. Many universities have lab schools for their education departments, and child psychology classes often utilize children's centers as a place where students may do observations or internships. In addition, on-site child care centers help to create a supportive community for graduate student and faculty parents on campus. Having a community of parents helps with sick days and snow days and information sharing. Beware of advocating for centers that are too small and/or too expensive for graduate school and junior faculty members. Centers with long waiting lists or centers which are too expensive can create more ill will than good will.

6: OTHER FAMILY FRIENDLY POLICIES

There are many other policies that also support work family balance, and there is always room for creativity. Consider after school care, summer day camp, sick child care, assistance for child care costs related to conference travel, spousal employment help, work/family counseling, etc. Think about the extra constraints that parents face, and then think about policies that could lessen the severity of the constraint.

Research facilitating policies also support work-family balance as they provide more time for research. Sabbaticals or course reductions are good examples of this type of policy. At one state university Rachel visited recently, the faculty wanted to know about how they could institute a sabbatical policy. Their institution had no provision for regular sabbaticals. If your institution does not have sabbaticals this is certainly a good place to start. At some schools sabbaticals are competitive, but even that would be better than nothing as long as the selection process is above board and based on objective criteria. At other schools, faculty can take sabbatical if they win external research grants. Grant writing workshops, therefore, can be one way to help parents increase their chances of taking research leave.

In terms of course reductions, consider the university's formula for buying out of a course. If your teaching load is 5 courses per year the "price" of a course should be less than 1/5 of your salary. Faculty members do much more than just teach. What about all of the advising and committee work we do, to say nothing of the research? In addition, consider compensation schemes for extra advising, chairing, or thesis supervision. These things all take time away from basic research and teaching. Faculty members can advocate for additional compensation for the extra responsibilities they take on. These can be a course reduction either at the time of the service or banked to supplement a sabbatical leave.

BEYOND THE UNIVERSITY

On a supra-institutional level, there are many things that the federal government could do to support families as well. To start with, the United States is one of the few countries in the world that does not have a national paid parental leave policy. Furthermore, the government should do more to support public preschools and to subsidize child care.

In addition, we need to change the twin cultures of overwork and superparenting so endemic to our contemporary society. At the top end of the education spectrum, parents of young children both work longer hours and spend more time on child caregiving than others in our society, and both numbers have been increasing over the last forty years. As we have pointed out throughout our book, it is important to make choices for yourself and not allow your life to be ruled by the unreasonable expectations of others. You cannot be everything to everyone at all times. While it would be wonderful if our society could embrace the idea that having and raising children is a public service that benefits everyone, the reality is that it is still very much seen as an individual choice for private benefit. Junior faculty are often made to feel like they are selfish to have had children. As a senior faculty member with a family, you should be open about your own experiences and make your department and institution a place where it feels safe to talk about your kids. For instance, Carol Colbeck and Robert Drago argue that campus climate really matters in their 2005 article "Accept, Avoid, Resist: How Faculty Members Respond to Bias against Caregiving . . . and How Departments Can Help." Thus, making an institution family friendly is not only about implementing policies, it is also about creating an atmosphere that accepts people as full human beings.

We have only covered a few basic ideas here, and there are plenty of places to look for information about best practices. Both the *Chronicle of Higher Education* and *Inside Higher Ed* regularly run features on work-family balance. The AAUP website has a whole section dedicated to "Balancing Family & Academic Work" (http://www.aaup.org/issues/balancing-family-academic-work), including a section where you can compare your institution's parental leave policy and its policy on stopping the tenure clock with model policies at other institutions. Harvard University has an Office of Work/Life resources and their website is another great place to look at best practices (http://employment.harvard.edu/benefits/worklife/). The Berkeley Parents Network has suggestions for navigating institutional cultures (http://parents.berkeley.edu/) as does the 2013 book *Do Babies Matter? Gender and Family in the Ivory Tower*. This is, of course, only a limited list; there are many other excellent resources available for you to bone up on what other colleges and universities are doing.

Finally, we invite all of you readers to give us comments and suggestions via our Facebook page for Professor Mommy (www.facebook.com/professor-mommy). We are always happy to hear from readers and would love to have you share your own thoughts about how to make academia a more hospitable place for professor parents.

Appendix 1

Association of American Universities—Members

Note: Dates in parentheses indicate the year each institution joined.

Brandeis University (1985)

Brown University (1933)

California Institute of Technology (1934)

Carnegie Mellon University (1982)

Case Western Reserve University (1969)

Columbia University (1900)

Cornell University (1900)

Duke University (1938)

Emory University (1995)

Georgia Institute of Technology (2010)

Harvard University (1900)

Indiana University (1909)

Iowa State University (1958)

Johns Hopkins University (1900)

Massachusetts Institute of Technology (1934)

McGill University (1926)

Michigan State University (1964)

New York University (1950)

Northwestern University (1917)

The Ohio State University (1916)

The Pennsylvania State University (1958)

Princeton University (1900)

Purdue University (1958)

Rice University (1985)

Rutgers, The State University of New Jersey (1989)

Stanford University (1900)

Stony Brook University, The State University of New York (2001)

Syracuse University (1966)

Texas A&M University (2001)

Tulane University (1958)

The University of Arizona (1985)

University at Buffalo, The State University of New York (1989)

University of California, Berkeley (1900)

University of California, Davis (1996)

University of California, Irvine (1996)

University of California, Los Angeles (1974)

University of California, San Diego (1982)

University of California, Santa Barbara (1995)

The University of Chicago (1900)

University of Colorado Boulder (1966)

University of Florida (1985)

University of Illinois at Urbana-Champaign (1908)

The University of Iowa (1909)

The University of Kansas (1909)

University of Maryland, College Park (1969)

University of Michigan (1900)

University of Minnesota, Twin Cities (1908)

University of Missouri–Columbia (1908)

University of Nebraska–Lincoln (1909)

The University of North Carolina at Chapel Hill (1922)

University of Oregon (1969)

University of Pennsylvania (1900)

University of Pittsburgh (1974)

University of Rochester (1941)

University of Southern California (1969)

The University of Texas at Austin (1929)

University of Toronto (1926)

University of Virginia (1904)

University of Washington (1950)

The University of Wisconsin–Madison (1900)

Vanderbilt University (1950)

Washington University in St. Louis (1923)

Yale University (1900)

Appendix 2

The Other Perspective
Words from Our Children

William Connelly (at age six, in answer to the question, "What does your mom do for work?"): "She grades papers."

Patrick Connelly (at age twelve, during a walk on campus): "How is it that you know EVERYONE?"

Louis Connelly (at age five): "Mama, I WANT YOU TO COME HOME!"
(At age nineteen): "Mom, what kind of research do the big-shot economists do? What statistical software packages do you use? What do research assistants do? Who do you know who can help me get a job?"

Martin Connelly (at age seventeen, in a discussion about his American history paper): "How did I end up studying exactly what you study—the economics of women's employment?" (He was writing a paper about the young women who worked in the Lowell, Massachusetts, mills in the 1830s.)

Kristiana Ghodsee Filipov (at age eight, when asked to say something about her mom's job): "My mother, Kristen Ghodsee, is a professor at Bowdoin College, and sometimes it is very annoying that she can't be free for a lot of the time. It's very sad that I don't have much time to play with my mom. But I like the fact that I get to go around the world because of her job. She is a beautiful, tall woman, and I love her."

Notes

INTRODUCTION

1. Division of Science Resources Statistics, National Science Foundation, *Women, Minorities, and Persons with Disabilities in Science and Engineering: 2011*, Special Report NSF 11-309, figure F-1 (Arlington, VA: National Science Foundation), at www.nsf.gov/statistics/wmpd/.

2. U.S. Education Department, "Number of Full-Time Faculty Members by Sex, Rank, and Racial and Ethnic Group," Fall 1995; U.S. Education Department, "Number of Full-Time Faculty Members by Sex, Rank, and Racial and Ethnic Group," Fall 2005.

3. Mary Ann Mason and Marc Goulden, "Do Babies Matter? The Effect of Family Formation on the Lifelong Careers of Academic Men and Women," *Academe* 88, no. 6 (November–December 2002): 21-27, at www.aaup.org/AAUP/pubsres/academe/2002/ND/Feat/Maso.htm?PF=1.

4. Sylvia Ann Hewlett, "Executive Women and the Myth of Having It All," *Harvard Business Review* 80, no. 4 (April 2002): 69.

5. Hewlett, "Executive Women and the Myth of Having It All," 66.

6. Elrena Evans and Caroline Grant, eds., *Mama, PhD: Women Write about Motherhood and Academic Life* (Piscataway, NJ: Rutgers University Press, 2008). The blog is available at www.insidehighered.com/blogs/mama_phd.

7. Emily Monosson, *Motherhood, the Elephant in the Laboratory: Women Scientists Speak Out* (New York: ILR Press, 2010).

8. See, for example, JoAnn Miller and Marilyn Chamberlin, "Women Are Teachers, Men Are Professors: A Study of Student Perceptions," *Teaching Sociology* 28, no. 4 (October 2000): 283–98; Susan A. Basow, "Student Evaluations: Gender Bias and Teaching Styles," in *Career Strategies for Women in Academe: Arming Athena*, ed. Lynn H. Collins, Joan C. Chrisler, and Kathryn Quina (Thousand Oaks, CA: Sage, 1998), 135–56; and Kenneth A. Feldman, "College Students' Views of Male and Female College Teachers: Part II—Evidence from Students' Evaluations of Their Classroom Teachers," *Research in Higher Learning* 34, no. 2 (April 1993): 151–211.

9. Mary Marotte, Paige Reynolds, and Ralph Savarese, eds., *Papa, PhD: Essays on Fatherhood by Men in the Academy* (Piscataway, NJ: Rutgers University Press, 2010).

10. And we are not as far from this as you think. See Scott Gelfand and John R. Shook, eds., *Ectogenesis: Artificial Womb Technology and the Future of Human Reproduction* (New York: Rodopi, 2006).

11. While we don't want to come across as stodgy and traditional second-wave feminists who have never heard of things like intersex people or think that biological sex is not also a product of social construction, for the sake of this book, and for the sake of speaking to a whole world of young women out there who are considering academic careers and who may not know all the fine intricacies of feminist theory, we will focus our analysis primarily on boring old biologically determined female-bodied individuals, called "women" by most laypeople.

CHAPTER 1

1. Joan C. Williams, "The Glass Ceiling and the Maternal Wall in Academia," *New Directions for Higher Education* 130 (Summer 2005): 91–105.

2. Particularly insidious is the phenomenon of women being penalized for being too accomplished. Williams gives the example of when a leading journal decides to publish a woman's article "and some of her colleagues begin talking about her arrogance rather than her accomplishments." "The Glass Ceiling and the Maternal Wall in Academia," 93.

3. Mary Ann Mason and Marc Goulden, "Marriage and Baby Blues: Redefining Gender Equity in the Academy," *Annals of the American Academy of Political and Social Science* 596 (November 2004): 86–103.

4. Second-tier positions referred to adjunct teaching, lab instructors, administrators, and so on. Basically, this category included all positions that were not tenured or tenure track.

5. Mason and Goulden, "Marriage and Baby Blues," 93.

6. See, for instance, Belle Rose Ragins and John L. Cotton, "Easier Said Than Done: Gender Differences in Perceived Barriers to Gaining a Mentor," *Academy of Management Journal* 34, no. 4 (December 1991): 939–51.

CHAPTER 2

1. Mason and Goulden, "Marriage and Baby Blues," 86–103; Mason and Goulden, "Do Babies Matter?" 21–27.

2. Mason and Goulden, "Marriage and Baby Blues," 99.

3. Daniel S. Hamermesh, "An Old Male Economist's Advice to Young Female Economists," *Newsletter of the Committee on the Status of Women in the Economics Profession*, Winter 2005, 12.

4. See, for example, Miller and Chamberlin, "Women Are Teachers, Men Are Professors"; Basow, "Student Evaluations"; and Feldman, "College Students' Views of Male and Female College Teachers: Part II."

5. See, for instance, Williams, "The Glass Ceiling and the Maternal Wall in Academia."

6. Martin J. Finkelstein and Jack H. Schuster, "Assessing the Silent Revolution: How Changing Demographics Are Reshaping the Academic Profession," *American Association for Higher Education and Accreditation Bulletin* 54, no. 2 (October 2001): 3–7, at www.aahea.org/bulletins/articles/silentrevolution.htm.

7. Finkelstein and Schuster, "Assessing the Silent Revolution."

8. See, for instance. Steven Levitt, "Let's Just Get Rid of Tenure (Including Mine)," *New York Times*, March 3, 2007, at freakonomics.blogs.nytimes.com/2007/03/03/lets-just-get-rid-of-tenure/; and Francis Fukuyama, "Why We Should Get Rid of Tenure," *Washington Post*, April 6, 2009, at www.washingtonpost.com/wp-dyn/content/article/2009/04/16/AR2009041603466.html.

9. See, for instance, Nancy Fraser, "Feminism, Capitalism and the Cunning of History," *New Left Review* 56 (March–April 2009): 97–117, at newleftreview.org/?view=2772.

10. A good book that every pregnant woman should read is Vicki Iovine, *The Girlfriends' Guide to Pregnancy*, 2nd ed. (New York: Pocket, 2007). Iovine dispels many myths and gives you the real deal about how difficult and uncomfortable pregnancy really is.

11. Frank Gilbreth and Ernestine Gilbreth Carey, *Cheaper by the Dozen* (New York: Harper Perennial, 2002).

12. Susan Douglas and Meredith Michaels, *The Mommy Myth: The Idealization of Motherhood and How It Has Undermined All Women* (New York: Free Press, 2005).

13. Judith Werner, *Perfect Madness: Motherhood in the Age of Anxiety* (New York: Riverhead, 2005).

TEXTBOX 2.1

1. Rachel Connelly and Jean Kimmel, "The Importance of College for Child Care Worker Wages and Turnover," unpublished paper, 2005.

2. Deborah Lowe Vandell and Barbara Wolfe, "Child Care Quality: Does It Matter and Does It Need to Be Improved?" report prepared for the Office of the Assistant Secretary for Planning and Evaluation, U.S. Department of Health and Human Services, 2000, at www.aspe.hhs.gov/hsp/ccquality00/ccqual.htm#outcomes.

3. Vandell and Wolfe, "Child Care Quality."

4. Ellen S. Peisner-Feinberg and others, *The Children of the Cost, Quality, and Outcomes Study Go to School*, Executive Summary (Chapel Hill: University of North Carolina, 1999), 2–3.

5. Peisner-Feinberg and others, *The Children of the Cost, Quality, and Outcomes Study Go to School*, Executive Summary, 3.

CHAPTER 3

1. Hewlett, "Executive Women and the Myth of Having It All," 5.

2. Jane Waldfogel, "The Effect of Children on Women's Wages," *American Sociological Review* 62, no. 2 (April 1997): 209–17.

3. Susan Moller Okin, *Justice, Gender, and the Family* (New York: Basic Books, 1989).

4. Naomi Granville, "Have No Illusions: Dual Academic Careers Require Luck," *Chronicle of Higher Education* 57, no. 18 (January 7, 2011): D17–18.

5. Leslie Bennetts, *The Feminine Mistake: Are We Giving Up Too Much?* (New York: Voice, 2007).

6. Susan Athey, interview by Rachel Croson, *Newsletter of the Committee on the Status of Women in the Economics Profession*, Spring–Summer 2001, 7.

CHAPTER 4

1. Mary Ann Mason, "A Look at the PhD Problem," *Daily Californian Online*, January 22, 2010, at www.dailycal.org/printable.php?id=107911.

2. Jane Leber Herr and Catherine Wolfram, "Work Environment and 'Opt-Out' Rates at Motherhood across High-Education Career Paths" (NBER Working Paper 14717, National Bureau of Economic Research, February 2009).

3. Herr and Wolfram, "Work Environment and 'Opt-Out' Rates at Motherhood across High-Education Career Paths," 17.

4. Kristen Springer, Brenda Parker, and Catherine Leviten-Reid, "Making Space for Graduate Student Parents: Practices and Politics," *Journal of Family Issues* 30, no. 4 (April 2009): 435–57; Arielle Kuperberg, "Motherhood and Graduate Education: 1970–2000," *Population Research and Policy Review* 28, no. 4 (August 2009): 473–504. See also Roberta Spalter-Roth and Ivy Kennelly, "The Best Time to Have a Baby: Institutional Resources and Family Strategies among Early Career Sociologists," *ASA Research Brief*, July 2004.

5. Carmen Armenti's qualitative study of Canadian academics concluded that faculty members who were childless were worried about the effect children might have on their careers—as reported in Kelly Ward and Lisa Wolf-Wendel, "Academic Motherhood: Managing Complex Roles in Research Universities," *Review of Higher Education* 27, no. 2 (Winter 2004): 235. Also see Carol Colbeck and Robert Drago, "Accept, Avoid, Resist: How Faculty Members Respond to Bias against Caregiving . . . and How Departments Can Help," *Change* 37, no. 6 (November–December 2005): 10–17. Colbeck and Drago found in the survey of 4,188 chemistry and English faculty in 2001 that 16.1 percent of the women reported staying single because they did not believe they had time for both family and a successful academic career. They reported that 25.5 percent had fewer children than they wanted, and 12.7 percent had delayed having a second child until after tenure. Finkel and Olswang (1996), in a survey of women faculty at a research university, found that almost half the participants in their sample were childless as a result of their careers, and that 34 percent of those who delayed having children reported doing so because of the careers (Ward and Wolf-Wendel, 236).

6. Monosson, *Motherhood, the Elephant in the Laboratory.*

7. Steven Stack, "Gender, Children and Research Productivity," *Research in Higher Education* 45, no. 8 (December 2004): 891–920.

8. Springer, Parker, and Leviten-Reid, "Making Space for Graduate Student Parents."

9. Carmen Armenti, "May Babies and Posttenure Babies: Maternal Decisions of Women Professors," *Review of Higher Education* 27, no. 2 (Winter 2004): 211–31.

10. Lisa Wolf-Wendel and Kelly Ward, "Managing to Have Children on the Tenure Track: A Qualitative Study," *Newsletter of the Committee on the Status of Women in the Economics Profession,* Summer 2007, 8.

11. Mason and Goulden, "Do Babies Matter?"

12. Beth Ingram, "Combining Childbearing with a Career," *Newsletter of the Committee on the Status of Women in the Economics Profession,* Summer 1993, 8.

13. This can still be found at parents.berkeley.edu/advice/allkinds/compatible.html.

14. Karen Conway, "One Approach to Balancing Work and Family," *Newsletter of the Committee on the Status of Women in the Economics Profession,* Spring–Summer 2001, 4.

15. Robin Wilson, "Is Having More Than Two Children an Unspoken Taboo?" *Chronicle of Higher Education* 55, no. 41 (July 2009): B16–19.

16. As quoted in Wilson, "Is Having More Than Two Children an Unspoken Taboo?" B18.

TEXTBOX 4.1

1. Carol S. Hollenshead, Beth Sullivan, and Gilia C. Smith, "Work/Family Policies in Higher Education: Survey Data and Case Studies of Policy Implementation," *New Directions for Higher Education* 2005, no. 130 (Summer 2005): 41–65.

2. Saranna Thornton, "Where—Not When—Should You Have a Baby?" *Chronicle of Higher Education* 51, no. 7 (October 8, 2004): B12.

3. Kelly Ward and Lisa Wolf-Wendel, "Fear Factor: How Safe Is It to Make Time for Family?" *Academe* 90, no. 6 (November–December 2004): 28–31; Kelly Ward and Lisa Wolf-Wendel, "Work and Family Perspectives from Research University Faculty," *New Directions for Higher Education* 130 (Summer 2005): 67–80.

4. Mary Ann Mason, Marc Goulden, and Karie Frasch, "Why Graduate Students Reject the Fast Track," *Academe* 95, no. 1 (January–February 2009): 11–16.

CHAPTER 5

1. AAUP figures cited in Peter Conn, "We Need to Acknowledge the Realities of Employment in the Humanities," *Chronicle of Higher Education* 56, no. 30 (April 4, 2010): B6.

2. Cited at www.beyondacademe.com/.

3. Spalter-Roth and Kennelly, "The Best Time to Have a Baby."

4. Lisa Wolf-Wendel and Kelly Ward, "Academic Life and Motherhood: Variations by Institutional Type," *Higher Education* 52, no. 3 (October 2006): 487–521.

5. Mary Ann Mason and Marc Goulden, "Do Babies Matter (Part II)? Closing the Baby Gap," *Academe* 90, no. 6 (November–December 2004): 10–15.

6. Hollenshead, Sullivan, and Smith, "Work/Family Policies in Higher Education."

7. The "Dependent Care Fund for Short-term Professional Travel (DCF)" is described on the Harvard senior vice provost's website, at www.faculty.harvard.edu/ work-life-benefits-and-perks/child-care/dependent-care-fund.

8. Wolf-Wendel and Ward, "Academic Life and Motherhood."

9. Wolf-Wendel and Ward, "Academic Life and Motherhood."

10. Mary Ann Mason, "Graduate Students: The Underserved Minority" (paper delivered at the meetings of the Graduate School Council, December 9, 2006), available at www.cgsnet.org/portals/0/pdf/mtg_am06Mason.pdf.

11. Wolf-Wendel and Ward, "Academic Life and Motherhood," 501.

12. Wolf-Wendel and Ward, "Academic Life and Motherhood," 504.

13. Howard Greene and Matthew Greene, *Greenes' Guides to Educational Planning: The Hidden Ivies: Thirty Colleges of Excellence* (New York: HarperCollins, 2000).

14. Daniel Taub, "The Liberal Arts College as a Home for Research," *Chronicle of Higher Education* 54, no. 37 (May 23, 2008): A31.

15. Kristen Ghodsee, "A Research Career at a Liberal Arts College," *Chronicle of Higher Education* 54, no. 33 (April 2008): C1–4.

16. Wolf-Wendel and Ward, "Academic Life and Motherhood," 510.

17. "The Disposable Academic: Why Doing a PhD is Often a Waste of Time," *Economist* 397, no. 8713 (December 18–31, 2010): 156–58.

TEXTBOX 5.1

1. Conway, "One Approach to Balancing Work and Family."

2. Nicholas H. Wolfinger, Mary Ann Mason, and Marc Goulden, "Staying in the Game: Gender, Family Formation and Alternative Trajectories in the Academic Life Course," *Social Forces* 87, no. 3 (March 2009): 1591–1621.

3. Wolfinger, Mason, and Goulden, "Staying in the Game," 1605.

4. James Monks, "Public versus Private University Presidents Pay Levels and Structure" (Working Paper 58, Cornell Higher Education Research Institute), at digitalcommons.ilr.cornell.edu/cheri/21, as cited in Wolfinger, Mason, and Goulden, "Staying in the Game," 1595.

CHAPTER 6

1. Liran Einav and Leeat Yariv, "What's in a Surname? The Effects of Surname Initials on Academic Success," *Journal of Economic Perspectives* 20, no. 1 (Winter 2006): 175–88.

2. William Germano, *Getting It Published: A Guide for Scholars and Anyone Else Serious about Serious Books* (Chicago: University of Chicago Press, 2001).

3. Hamermesh, "An Old Male Economist's Advice to Young Female Economists," 12.

4. As quoted in Wilson, "Is Having More Than Two Children an Unspoken Taboo?" B18.

5. Michael Piette and Kevin Ross, "A Study of the Publication of Scholarly Output in Economics Journals," *Eastern Economic Journal* 18, no. 4 (Fall 1992): 429–36.

6. Michèle Lamont, *How Professors Think: Inside the Curious World of Academic Judgment* (Cambridge, MA: Harvard University Press, 2009).

7. Pat Phelps, "Collegiality Lessons," *Chronicle of Higher Education* 50, no. 47 (July 30, 2004): C3; Saranna Thornton, "When, Where, and Why to Schmooze," *Chronicle of Higher Education* 51, no. 4 (September 17, 2004): A47.

8. Hamermesh, "An Old Male Economist's Advice to Young Female Economists," 12.

TEXTBOX 6.1

1. Samantha Stainburn, "The Case of the Vanishing Full-Time Professor," *New York Times*, December 30, 2009, at www.nytimes.com/2010/01/03/education/edlife/03strategy-t.html.

2. Gerardo Marti, "From Adjunct to Assistant Professor," *Chronicle of Higher Education*, April 4, 2007, at chronicle.com/article/From-Adjunct-to-Assistant/46463/.

3. Martin J. Finkelstein and Jack H. Schuster, *The American Faculty: The Restructuring of Academic Work and Careers* (Baltimore: Johns Hopkins University Press, 2008).

CHAPTER 7

1. If you are at an institution of this kind, there is usually a minimum standard of quality teaching that you need to uphold. Figure out what it is, do a bit more than the minimum, and save the guilt until after tenure. Certainly you do have to show up for class most of the time. If there is high probability that you will not get tenure, be aware that when you go looking for the next academic job they may want to see your student opinion forms.

2. R. D. Abbott and others, "Satisfaction with Processes of Collecting Student Opinions about Instruction: The Student Perspective," *Journal of Educational Psychology* 82, no. 2 (June 1990): 201–6; H. W. Marsh and L. A. Roche, "Making Students' Evaluations of Teaching Effectiveness Effective," *American Psychologist* 52, no. 11 (November 1997): 1187–97; W. J. McKeachie, "Student Ratings: The Validity of Use," *American Psychologist* 52, no. 11 (1997): 1218–25; J. F. Newport, "Rating Teaching in the USA: Probing the Qualifications of Student Raters and Novice Teachers," *Assessment and Evaluation in Higher Education* 21, no. 1 (1996): 17–21.

3. Gabriela Montell, "Do Good Looks Equal Good Evaluations?" *Chronicle of Higher Education's Career Network*, October 15, 2003, at chronicle.com/article/Do-Good-Looks-Equal-Good/45187/.

4. Donald H. Naftulin, John E. Ware, Jr., and Frank A. Donnelly, "The Doctor Fox Lecture: A Paradigm of Educational Seduction," *Journal of Medical Education* 48, no. 7 (July 1973): 630–35; R. Williams and J. Ware, "Validity of Student Ratings of Instruction under Different Incentive Conditions: A Further Study of the Dr. Fox Effect," *Journal of Educational Psychology* 68, no. 1 (February 1976): 48–56.

5. Meghan Millea and Paul W. Grimes, "Grade Expectations and Student Evaluation of Teaching," *College Student Journal* 36, no. 4 (December 2002): 582–90.

6. See, for instance, Rosanne M. Cordell and others, eds., *Quick Hits for New Faculty: Successful Strategies by Award-Winning Teachers* (Bloomington: Indiana University Press, 2004); and Ken Bain, *What the Best College Teachers Do* (Cambridge, MA: Harvard University Press, 2004).

7. Terra McKinnish, "A Survival Guide to Having Children While on Tenure Track," *Newsletter of the Committee on the Status of Women in the Economics Profession*, Spring–Summer 2007, 11.

8. Hamermesh, "An Old Male Economist's Advice to Young Female Economists," 12.

TEXTBOX 7.1
1. Kristen Ghodsee, "Single Parenting in the Field," *Anthropology News* 50, no. 7 (October 2009): 3–4.

TEXTBOX 7.2
1. Saranna Thornton, "Extended Tenure Clock Policies: Theory . . . and Practice," *Newsletter of the Committee on the Status of Women in the Economics Profession*, Winter 2005, 13–15.

Suggested Reading

In addition to the articles, books, research papers, and websites listed in the endnotes, here is a selection of books that might be useful for the beginning academic. Although there are many books out there, these are a handful that we have found useful, which provide advice on a wide variety of academic issues.

Bain, Ken. *What the Best College Teachers Do.* Cambridge, MA: Harvard University Press, 2004.

Buller, Jeffrey. *The Essential College Professor: A Practical Guide to an Academic Career.* San Francisco: Jossey-Bass, 2009.

Cahn, Steven. *From Student to Scholar: A Candid Guide to Becoming a Professor.* New York: Columbia University Press, 2008.

Cooper, Lorri, and Bryan Booth. *The Adjunct Faculty Handbook.* 2nd ed. New York: Sage, 2010.

Deneef, A. Leigh, and Craufurd D. Goodwin, eds. *The Academic's Handbook.* 3rd ed. Durham, NC: Duke University Press, 2006.

Derricourt, Robin. *An Author's Guide to Scholarly Publishing.* Princeton, NJ: Princeton University Press, 1996.

Evans, Elrena, and Caroline Grant, eds. *Mama, PhD: Women Write about Motherhood and Academic Life.* Piscataway, NJ: Rutgers University Press, 2008.

Germano, William. *Getting It Published: A Guide for Scholars and Anyone Else Serious about Serious Books.* Chicago: University of Chicago Press, 2001.

Gray, Paul, and David Drew. *What They Didn't Teach You in Graduate School: 199 Helpful Hints for Success in Your Academic Career.* New York: Stylus, 2008.

Johnson, W. Brad, and Carol A. Mullen. *Write to the Top: How to Become a Prolific Academic.* New York: Palgrave Macmillan, 2007.

Lamont, Michele. *How Professors Think: Inside the Curious World of Academic Judgment.* Cambridge, MA: Harvard University Press, 2009.

Luey, Beth. *Handbook for Academic Authors.* 4th ed. New York: Cambridge University Press, 2002.

Lyins, Richard, Marcella Kysilka, and George Pawlas. *The Adjunct Professor's Guide to Success: Surviving and Thriving in the College Classroom.* New York: Allyn and Bacon, 1998.

Marotte, Mary, Paige Reynolds, and Ralph Savarese, eds. *Papa, PhD: Essays on Fatherhood by Men in the Academy.* Piscataway, NJ: Rutgers University Press, 2010.

Mason, Mary Ann, and Eve Mason Ekman. *Mothers on the Fast Track: How a New Generation Can Balance Family and Careers.* New York: Oxford University Press, 2008.

Monosson, Emily. *Motherhood, the Elephant in the Laboratory: Women Scientists Speak Out.* New York: ILR Press, 2010.

Silvia, Paul. *How to Write a Lot: A Practical Guide to Productive Academic Writing.* Washington, DC: American Psychological Association, 2007.

Toth, Emily. *Ms. Mentor's Impeccable Advice for Women in Academia.* Philadelphia: University of Pennsylvania Press, 1997.

Toth, Emily. *Ms. Mentor's New and Ever More Impeccable Advice for Women and Men in Academia.* Philadelphia: University of Pennsylvania Press, 2008.

Vick, Julia, and Jennifer Furlong. *The Academic Job Search Handbook.* 4th ed. Philadelphia: University of Pennsylvania Press, 2008.

Zanna, Mark P., and John M. Darley. *The Compleat Academic: A Career Guide.* Washington, DC: American Psychological Association, 2003.

Index

2-2 load, of teaching, 23, 89

AAU. *See* Association of American Universities
AAUP. *See* American Association of University Professors
academia: alternative pathways in, 29, 107–9; difficulties of, 182–83; feminization of, 28; myths on motherhood and, 23–40; as pyramid, 86
Academia.edu, 125, 127
academic advising. *See* advising
academic careers: deciding on, 41–61; teaching during, 28–29, 43, 48, 51
"Academic Life and Motherhood: Variations by Institutional Type" (Wolf-Wendel and Ward), 92–93, 94, 95, 103
academic profession, 17, 28–29; service to, 167–69
Academus superstarus, 5

"Accept, Avoid, Resist: How Faculty Members Respond to Bias against Caregiving . . . and How Departments Can Help" (Colbeck and Drago), 197n5
adjunct faculty positions, 28, 87, 105–7, 121–22
administrative jobs, 177–78
admissions policies, 97, 179; graduate, 90, 165–66
adoption, 64, 73, 77–81, 145; international, 78
advising: on dissertations, 83–84; graduate students, 100–101; undergraduate students, 99, 101, 165–66
advocacy, for women, 6, 53, 79, 175
alternative career paths, 57–61
alternative pathways, in academia, 29, 107–9
American Association of University Professors (AAUP), 53, 86

American Council of Learned Societies, 10

American Economist Association, 58

The American Faculty (Finkelstein and Schuster), 122–23

American Historical Association, 86

American Statistical Association, 9

Amherst College, 97

Armenti, Carmen, 67, 197n5

artificial insemination, 72, 78

assessing assignments, 138

"Assessing the Silent Revolution: How Changing Demographics Are Reshaping the Academic Profession" (Finkelstein and Schuster), 28–29

assets, portable, 112, 135, 165–67

assignments, 137–39, 162; assessing, 138; designing, 84, 138

assistants, graduate students as, 90, 98, 121, 135

associate's colleges, 102–3

Association of American Universities (AAU), 89, 187–89

Athey, Susan, 58

au pairs, 38

authorship, sole, 115

auto-response vacation messages, 120

baccalaureate colleges, 88, 97–102

Bates College, 97

being-smart/working-hard myth, 25–26

Bennetts, Leslie, 57

Berkeley Parents Network, 73–74

beyondacademe.com, 108

blogs, 6, 138, 175

books: chapters of, 94, 102, 114, 146; contracts for, 113; first-year, 165; reviews of, 94, 115, 168; trade, 175

Bowdoin College, 9, 17–18, 60, 97

breastfeeding, 8, 31, 33, 42, 47, 78, 148, 184

Brown University, 89

caesarean section, 31

capitalist-driven colleges/college systems, 29

Carey, Ernestine Gilbreth, 31–32

Carleton College, 97

Carnegie Classification System, 93

Carnegie Foundation for the Advancement of Teaching, 87

Census Bureau (U.S.), 19, 108

Center for the Education of Women, 79

challenges, personal, 51–52, 183

chapters, of books, 94, 102, 114, 146

Cheaper by the Dozen (Gilbreth and Carey), 31–32

childbearing: average age of first, 50; physiologically optimal years for, 4; tenure and, 66–74, 158

child care: child-care-is-lower-quality-than-mother-care myth, 32–38; economics of, 34; quality of, 32–33, 37, 85, 184; research on, 35–36; university centers for, 38

"Child Care Quality: Does It Matter and Does It Need to Be Improved?" (Vandell and Wolfe), 36

childlessness *v.* opting out of labor market, 4–9

childless women, 42, 65, 106

children: childlessness *v.* opting out of labor market, 4–9; conversations about, 65, 111; conversations with, 171, 178–79; having, during graduate school, 67, 69–70, 74, 85; how many to have, 76–82; time with, 148–50, 179–80; travel with, 151–54; wanting v. not wanting, 65–76, 183

Citeulike.org, 127

class size, 135, 177

co-authorship, 20, 114, 116–17, 173

Colbeck, Carol, 197n5

Colby College, 97

collaborators, 19, 84, 129, 160

colleagues: in graduate school, 84; junior, 81, 120, 126; male, 5, 13–14, 39; senior, 126–29, 131–34, 141–43; women, 5, 39, 111

colleges: associate's/community colleges, 102–3; baccalaureate/liberal arts colleges, 88, 97–102; capitalist-driven, 29

college tuition programs, 176

collegiality, 131–32

"Collegiality Lessons" (Phelps), 130

colloquia, 84, 132, 165

Columbia University, 89, 91

"Combining Childbearing with a Career" (Ingram), 69

Committee for the Status of Women in the Economics Profession (CSWEP), 16

committees: grant-review, 128, 168; meetings of, 23, 89, 119, 159, 166; on tenure, 81, 118, 128–29, 136, 159, 164, 166

community colleges, 102–3

commuter relationships, 54, 72

competition, in job market, 28, 87, 113

comprehensive universities, 93–97

conferences, professional, 19, 94, 102, 126

consensus, 164

consequences, of choices, 61

conversations: about children, 65, 111; with children, 171, 178–79

Conway, Karen, 76, 105

Cordell, Rosanne M., 137

Cornell University, 89

Cost, Quality and Child Outcomes in Child Care Centers Study, 36

course opinion forms, 163

course revisions, 161–63

Critique of Pure Reason (Kant), 4

CSWEP. See Committee for the Status of Women in the Economics Profession

curriculum-review boards, 141

Dartmouth College, 89

day care centers, 32, 92, 149–50

deadlines, 19, 44, 84, 120, 133

deciding: on academic careers, 41–61; on motherhood, 63–82

delaying motherhood, 55, 63

designing assignments, 84, 138

difficulties, of academia, 182–83

disabled persons, status of, 165

dissertations: advisers on, 83–84; filing, 85–86; finishing, 64, 68–69, 83, 122; publishing, 46–47, 113, 117

distance courses, 122, 152

"divide and conquer" strategy, of parenting, 77

dossiers: for promotions, 169, 172, 174; for tenure, 81, 137, 142–48

double-blind reviews, 56, 114

Douglas, Susan, 33

Drago, Robert, 197n5

"Dr. Fox Effect," 136–37

Duke University, 89

Econometric Society, 116

economics: of child care, 34; profession, 16

editing journals, 84, 168–69

editorial boards, 168

"The Effect of Children on Women's Wages" (Waldfogel), 42

Eigenfactor, 118

Einav, Liran, 116

email, 85, 100, 119–20; .pdf attachments in, 126; surveys, 181–82

emergency leave, 80

employment, and PhDs, 86–87

encyclopedia entries, 114–15, 146–47

ER (television program), 50

ethnography, 160

evaluations: self-evaluations, 138, 142–46, 173; of teaching, 94, 99, 135–39, 163

Evans, Elrena, 6–7, 58

exams, designing, 84

"Executive Women and the Myth of Having It All" (Hewlett), 4–5

expectations: gendered, 99; of students, 84

expressiveness, 137

"Extended Tenure Clock Policies: Theory . . . and Practice" (Thornton), 79, 130, 145

external reviewers, 128–29, 135, 142–43, 145, 173

Facebook, 132

faculty: adjunct positions, 28, 87, 105–7, 121–22; handbooks for, 78, 80, 88, 96; poaching of, 175; service commitments of, 23, 54, 94, 134, 169; websites of, 124, 127; work week of, 23–24

family: after full professorship, 178–80; after tenure, 169–70; before tenure, 148–56; family-friendly policies, 79–81; pictures of, 133–34, 170; values, 34; work-family balance issues, 6–10, 14, 88, 184

Family and Medical Leave Act (FMLA), 79, 81

fear factor, 80

"Fear Factor: How Safe Is It to Make Time for Family?" (Ward and Wolf-Wendel), 80

fellowships, 90

The Feminine Mistake (Bennetts), 57

feminism, 30, 33, 39, 42; second-wave, 194n11

"Feminism, Capitalism and the Cunning of History" (Fraser), 30

feminization, of academia, 28

fieldwork, 69, 72, 144, 150, 152–53

Finkelstein, Martin J., 28–29, 122–23

firm-specific investment, 165–66

first-year books, 165

flexible scheduling, 58, 79, 155, 180

flex time, 25

FMLA. *See* Family and Medical Leave Act

Ford Foundation, 9

Fraser, Nancy, 30

Friedan, Betty, 42

"From Adjunct to Assistant Professor" (Marti), 122

Fukuyama, Francis, 113

full professorship, promotion to, 171–80; criteria for, 173–74; family after, 178–80; job-changing after, 175–77; motivation for, 171–72; research after, 174–76; schedule for, 172–73 funding, for research, 26, 89, 100–101, 159–60; internal, 127–28

gendered expectations, 99
gender equity, 14, 163
gender wage gap, 42
general audiences, 160, 174
general human capital, 165
genres, 160
geographic preferences, 89, 105
Germano, William, 116
gesticulation, 137
Getcited.org, 127
Getting It Published (Germano), 116
Giger, Maryellen, 120
The Girlfriends' Guide to Pregnancy (Iovine), 196n10
glass ceiling, 13–14
"The Glass Ceiling and the Maternal Wall in Academia" (Williams), 13, 194n2
goals, personal, 50–51
Goulden, Marc, 14–15, 106
grades, 27
grading, 90, 103; dislike of, 138, 159, 162; teaching and, 136; time spent on, 20, 84, 139
graduate admissions, 90, 165–66
graduate school, 83–109; colleagues in, 84; having children during, 67, 69–70, 74, 85; job market and, 86–89; teaching during, 84–85
graduate students: advising, 100–101; as assistants, 90, 98, 121, 135
Grant, Caroline, 6–7, 58
grant-review committees, 128, 168
grants, 124, 150; national, 26; for summer support, 178; winning, 59,

97–98; writing, 90–91, 104, 114, 127–29
Greene, Howard, 97
Greene, Matthew, 97
Grey's Anatomy (television program), 50
group work, 162

Hamermesh, Daniel, 26, 117, 132, 139
Hamilton College, 97
handbooks, for faculty, 78, 80, 88, 96
Harvard University, 10, 60, 63, 65, 91–92
Haverford College, 97
health insurance, 68–69, 78, 85, 106, 158
Herr, Jane, 63
Hewlett, Sylvia Ann, 4–5, 42
The Hidden Ivies (Greene and Greene), 97
high mobility, 53–54
high school, teaching at, 107–9
The Hobbit (Tolkien), 138
Hollenshead, Carol S., 79, 88
homeschooling, 152
hormonal injections, 31, 66
hospital fantasies, 111–12
hotel-room interviews, 170
housecleaning, 154
"housewife" designation, 41–42
How Professors Think (Lamont), 128
human capital, general, 165–66
human-resource issues, in China, 19
human-subjects research, 166

immune system development, 33
independent research, 48, 117–18
independent scholars, 124
Indiana University, 29
infertility, 5, 19, 65, 183
Ingram, Beth, 69

instinctual behavior, 32

Institute for Advanced Study, 10, 31, 65, 150

Institute for Population Research, 150

institutional affiliation, 124

institutional changes, 6, 53, 79, 185

institutional culture, 39, 82, 131–32

institutional-research boards, 166

interim deadlines, 84

internal funding, for research, 127–28

international adoption, 78

Internet, 152

interviews: in hotel room, 170; on-campus, 1–3

investments: firm-specific, 165–66; general human capital, 165–66

Iovine, Vicki, 196n10

"Is Having More Than Two Children an Unspoken Taboo?" (Wilson), 77

IVF treatments, 31

Ivy League schools, 89, 91, 133

job-changing, after full professorship, 175–77

job market, 5, 53, 83–87; competition in, 28, 87, 113; graduate school and, 86–89

John Bates Clark Medal in Economics, 58

journals: editing, 84, 168–69; peer-reviewed, 7, 46, 96, 114, 118; refereeing for, 115; writing articles for, 46, 57, 85, 115–16, 126

junior colleagues, 81, 120, 126

Kant, Immanuel, 4

lab schools, 92

ladder-rank faculty, 15

Lamont, Michèle, 128

Leave It to Beaver (television program), 42

lecture series, 168

lesbian couples, 78

"Let's Just Get Rid of Tenure (Including Mine)" (Levitt), 113

letters of recommendation, 23–24, 123–24, 140

Levitt, Steven, 113

liberal-academics-make-exceptions myth, 38–39

liberal arts colleges, 88, 97–102

listservs, for pedagogy, 138

Little Ivies, 97

long hours, 55

Louis XIV (king), 26

male colleagues, 5, 13–14, 39

Mama, PhD (Evans and Grant), 6–7, 58

"Managing to Have Children on the Tenure Track: A Qualitative Study" (Wolf-Wendel and Ward), 68

market-driven universities, 29

Marotte, Mary, 7

Marti, Gerardo, 122

Mason, Mary Ann, 14–15, 24, 65, 68, 81, 93, 105, 106; Berkeley Parents Network and, 73–74

Massachusetts Institute of Technology (MIT), 89, 105

mastitis, 31

maternal wall, 14

maternity leave, 18, 39, 41, 47, 78

Max Planck Institute for Demographic Research, 160

"May Babies and Posttenure Babies" (Armenti), 67, 197n5

MBA degrees, 63
McKinnish, Terra, 138–39
medical interventions, 4, 66
mentoring, 59, 101, 132, 175
meritocratic principles, 25–26, 56, 60
Michaels, Meredith, 33
micromanaging, 164–65
Middlebury College, 97, 178
midterms, 27, 94
minorities, status of, 165
MIT. *See* Massachusetts Institute of
    Technology
mobility, high, 53–54
Modern Language Association (MLA),
    46
mommyism, 14
The Mommy Myth (Douglas and
    Michaels), 33
Mommy Wars, 42
Monks, James, 106
Monosson, Emily, 6–7
more-time-with-kids myth, 23–25
morning sickness, 46, 68
"mother guilt," 33
motherhood: academia and, myths on,
    23–40; deciding on, 63–82; delaying,
    55, 63; motherhood-is-instinctual
    myth, 32; wage gap of, 42
*Motherhood, the Elephant in the
    Laboratory: Women Scientists Speak
    Out* (Monosson), 6–7
motivations, 47–50
movement, about the classroom, 137
myths, on motherhood and academia,
    23–40; being smart/working hard,
    25–26; child care is lower quality
    than mother care, 32–38; liberal
    academics make exceptions,

38–39; more time with kids, 23–25;
    motherhood is instinctual, 32; no
    sexism, 27–30; pregnancy will be
    easy, 30–32; senior women are allies,
    39–40; students are like you, 27

nannies, 38
National Endowment for the
    Humanities Summer Stipends, 47
national grants, 26
National Institute of Child Health and
    Human Development (NICHD),
    35–36
National Institute of Health (NIH), 100
National Science Foundation, 9–10,
    160
National Study of Postsecondary
    Faculty, 98
negotiating processes, 176
networking, 25–26, 184; old boys'
    network, 53, 126; tenure and, 126–34
newsletters, 147, 182
New York University, 89
NICHD. *See* National Institute of Child
    Health and Human Development
NIH. *See* National Institute of Health
no-guilt parenting, 149–50
no-sexism myth, 27–30

Oberlin College, 97
offprints, 26, 126, 184
old boys' network, 53, 126
"An Old Male Economist's Advice
    to Young Female Economists"
    (Hamermesh), 26, 117, 132, 139
on-campus interviews, 1–3
"One Approach to Balancing Work and
    Life" (Conway), 105

opting out, of labor market, 3–4;
    childlessness *v.*, 4–9
O'Reilly, Andrea, 77
original scholarship, 115
outlining, 119
outsourcing, 8, 184

paid parental leave, 78–79, 88–89, 106,
    175, 184
panels, 84
Papa, PhD (Marotte, Reynolds, and
    Savarese), 7
parental leave, 30–31, 68, 78–81, 96–97,
    145; paid, 78–79, 88–89, 106, 175, 184
parenthood: single, 64, 71, 77; tenure
    and, 13–14, 111–12
parenting: "divide and conquer" strategy
    of, 77; no-guilt, 149–50; teenagers,
    11, 76, 178–79
part-time positions, 105–7
.pdf attachments, in email, 126
pedagogy, 37, 144, 161–63; listservs for,
    138
peer-reviewed journals, 7, 46, 96, 114,
    118
Peking University, 150
*Perfect Madness: Motherhood in the Age
    of Anxiety* (Werner), 33
personal challenges, 51–52
personal goals, 50–51
PhDs: average age for completing, 63;
    employment and, 86–87; excess
    supply of, 58; percentage earned by
    women, 3, 28; ratio of tenure-track
    jobs to, 28
Phelps, Pat, 130
physiologically optimal years, for
    childbearing, 4

pictures, of family, 133–34, 170
plagiarism, 162
planning, 16
poaching, of faculty, 175
Pomona College, 97
portable assets, 112, 135, 165–67
postdoctoral fellowships, 4, 45, 53,
    103–7, 121
post-partum depression, 31
Poverty Institute of the University of
    Wisconsin, 9
pregnancy, 8, 18–19, 67–72; pregnancy-
    will-be-easy myth, 30–32
presses, university, 113, 115–17, 131,
    143, 172
Princeton University, 31, 60, 65, 89, 91
problem sets, 162
professional conferences, 19, 94, 102, 126
professional societies, 94, 168
professors, stereotypes of, 136
Professorus breadwinnerus, 5
Professorus momus, 5–6, 10
promotions: dossiers for, 169, 172,
    174; to full professor, 171–80;
    promotions-and-tenure committees,
    166
publications, 98, 108, 113; quantity *v.*
    quality of, 115
"Public *versus* Private University
    Presidents Pay Levels and Structure"
    (Monks), 106
"publish or perish" mentality, 88–89
pyramid, academia as, 86

quantity *v.* quality, of publications, 115
questionnaires, 181
Quick Hits for New Faculty (Cordell),
    137

Radcliffe Institute for Advanced Study, 10, 65
raises, 55, 172–73
readings, assigning, 85
Reed College, 97
refereed works, 98
refereeing, for journals, 115
regional comprehensive universities, 93
regional undergraduate students, 93
rejection, 49, 56–57, 91, 114–15, 117
research: after full professorship, 174–76; after tenure, 159–61; before tenure, 112–26; on child care, 35–36; commitments, 90–94; funding for, 26, 89, 100–101, 127–28, 159–60; independent, 48, 117–18; institutional-research boards, 166; leaves for, 19, 81, 184; productivity in, 20, 67, 89, 91, 94; semesters for, 157; support for, 60, 100, 157; teaching *v.*, 135–36; universities, 89–93
ResearcherID.org, 127
Research I universities, 44, 48, 89, 91, 94, 104
Research II and III universities, 87, 93
retrospective letters, 136
reviewers, 113–15, 127–29. *See also* external reviewers
reviews, of books, 94, 115, 168
Reynolds, Paige, 7
Rockefeller Foundation, 9
role models, 73, 87, 108, 183
Rowling, J. K., 143
Russell Sage Foundation, 9

sabbaticals, 58–60, 101, 121–22, 176
sacrifices, 52–57, 60, 183

salaries, 55, 85, 105, 122, 177
San Francisco State University (SFSU), 122
SAT tests, 179
Savarese, Ralph, 7
saying "no," 125, 141, 154, 167, 184
scholarly works, 98
scholarship, original, 115
school readiness, 35
Schuster, Jack H., 28–29, 122–23
Scimago, 118
searchmothers.com, 77
second-wave feminism, 194n11
secularization, 163
self-evaluations, 138, 142–46, 173
self-promotion, 126
senior colleagues, 126–29, 131–34, 141–43
senior seminars, 161
senior-women-are-allies myth, 39–40
service, 26, 51, 88–90; to academic profession, 167–69; after tenure, 163–67; before tenure, 141–48; faculty commitments of, 23, 54, 94, 134, 169
sex discrimination, 7, 53
sexism, 14, 27–30, 60
SFSU. *See* San Francisco State University
sick leave, 75, 106
silent revolution, 28, 121
single-blind reviews, 56
single parenthood, 64, 71, 77
Smith College, 97
Smith, Gilia C., 79, 88
socialization, of children, 33
socializing, 130–31, 133
social media, 126, 130, 132
sole authorship, 115
Spousus supportus, 5, 55

Stack, Steven, 67

Stanford University, 89

starting salaries, 55

statistical work, 144

"stay-at-home mom" designation, 41–42

"Staying in the Game: Gender,
   Family Formation and Alternative
   Trajectories in the Academic Life
   Course" (Wolfinger, Mason, and
   Goulden), 106

stereotypes: of professors, 136; of
   women, 13; of working conditions,
   87–88, 101

stress, 19, 55, 136, 169, 171

striving comprehensive universities, 93

student judiciary boards, 167

students, 60; expectations of, 84;
   students-are-like-you myth,
   27. *See also* graduate students;
   undergraduate students

Sullivan, Beth, 79, 88

summer break, 75, 128, 167

summer support grants, 178

Survey of Doctorate Recipients, 14–15

surveys, by email, 181–82

"A Survival Guide to Having
   Children While on Tenure Track"
   (McKinnish), 138–39

Swarthmore College, 97

syllabi, 90, 136–37, 165, 182

symposia: attending, 184; organizing,
   160, 168

talks, giving, 26, 91, 127–28, 165, 171

Taub, Daniel, 98

teaching: 2-2 load, 23, 89; after tenure,
   161–63; before tenure, 135–41, 174,
201n1; during academic career,
   28–29, 43, 48, 51; during graduate
   school, 84–85; evaluations, 94,
   99, 135–39, 163; grading and,
   136; at high school, 107–9; loads,
   93–94, 97, 135; research *v.*, 135–36;
   undergraduate students, 27, 90, 97,
   137; videotaping of, 137

teenagers: au pairs, 38; parenting, 11, 76,
   178–79

tenure, 8, 11; average age for achieving,
   63; childbearing and, 66–74, 158;
   clock-stopping leaves from, 39, 78–
   79, 145, 175; committees on, 81, 118,
   128–29, 136, 159, 164, 166; dossiers
   for, 81, 137, 142–48; early years after,
   157–70; family after, 169–70; family
   before, 148–56; meeting standards of,
   38–39, 88, 91–96, 109; networking
   and, 126–34; parenthood and, 13–14,
   111–12; promotions-and-tenure
   committees, 166; ratio of tenure-
   track jobs to PhDs, 28; research after,
   159–61; research before, 112–26;
   service after, 163–67; service before,
   141–48; teaching after, 161–63;
   teaching before, 135–41, 174, 201n1;
   women and, 3–4, 14–15

Thompson's Journal Citation Reports,
   118

Thornton, Saranna, 79, 130, 145

time management, 118–19, 159, 181;
   grading and, 20, 84, 139; more-time-
   with-kids myth, 23–25; time with
   children, 148–50, 179–80

Tolkien, J. R. R., 138

trade books, 175

travel: allowances for, 177; with children, 151–54
Trinity College, 97
tutors, 151–52, 179

übermoms, 5
undergraduate students: advising, 99, 101, 165–66; regional, 93; teaching, 27, 90, 97, 137
undesirable locations, 54
"the unforgiving decade," 4
university child care centers, 38
University of California, Berkeley, 9, 73, 89, 105, 122
University of California, Los Angeles, 89
University of California system, 14, 94
University of Chicago, 89, 120
University of Iowa, 69
University of Michigan, 9, 16–17, 79, 89
University of New Hampshire, 76, 105
University of Pennsylvania, 89
University of Wisconsin, 9
university presses, 113, 115–17, 131, 143, 172

vaginal delivery, 31
values, family, 34
Vandell, Deborah Lowe, 36
videotaping, of teaching, 137
visibility, 25–26
voice modulation, 137
volunteering, 141, 155, 170

wage gaps, 42
Waldfogel, Jane, 42
wanting v. not wanting children, 65–76, 183

Ward, Kelly, 68, 80, 92–93, 94, 95, 103
websites, of faculty, 124, 127
web surfing, 85, 120
Wellesley College, 97
Werner, Judith, 33
Wesleyan colleges, 97
W. E. Upjohn Institute for Employment Research, 9
"What's in a Surname? The Effects of Surname Initials on Academic Success" (Einav and Yariv), 116
"Why We Should Get Rid of Tenure" (Fukuyama), 113
Williams College, 97
Williams, Joan C., 13, 194n2
Wilson, Robin, 77
Wolfe, Barbara, 36
Wolfinger, Nicholas H., 106
Wolfram, Catherine, 63
Wolf-Wendel, Lisa, 68, 80, 92–93, 94, 95, 103
women: advocacy for, 6, 53, 79, 175; childless, 42, 65, 106; colleagues, 5, 39, 111; percentage of PhDs earned by, 3, 28; senior-women-are-allies myth, 39–40; stereotypes of, 13; tenure and, 3–4, 14–15
Woodrow Wilson International Center for Scholars, 10
"Work Environment and 'Opt-Out' Rates at Motherhood across High-Education Career Paths" (Herr and Wolfram), 63
work-family balance issues, 6–10, 14, 88, 184
"Work/Family Policies in Higher Education: Survey Data and Case

Studies of Policy Implementation"
(Hollenshead, Sullivan, and Smith),
79, 88
working conditions, 28, 102; stereotypes
of, 87–88, 101

works in progress, 147
work week, of faculty, 23–24

Yale University, 60, 89, 91
Yariv, Leeat, 116

About the Authors

Rachel Connelly is the Bion R. Cram Professor of Economics at Bowdoin College. She has published numerous articles on the effect of broad demographic trends on the labor market and human capital decision making and on the economics of child care with articles appearing in the *China Journal, Demography, Econometrica, Economic Development and Cultural Change, Feminist Economics, Industrial Relations, Journal of Human Resources, Journal of Labor Economics, Review of Economics and Statistics, Review of Economics of the Household,* and the *Southern Economics Journal,* among others. She is the author of *Kids at Work: The Economics of Employer Sponsored On-Site Child Care,* with Deborah DeGraff and Rachel Willis (2004) and *Time Use of Mothers in the United States at the Beginning of the 21st Century,* with Jean Kimmel (2010). Her research has been funded with grants from, among others, NSF, the ILO, the W. E. Upjohn Institute for Employment Research, the Joint Center for Poverty Research, the Ford Foundation, the Russell Sage Foundation and Rockefeller foundation. Her newest projects include a study of American mothers' time use with Jean Kimmel, settlement of women migrants in urban China with Ken Roberts and Zheng Zhenzhen, and changes in women's labor force participation in China with Margaret Maurer-Fazio and Lan Chen. Rachel lives in an old farm house in Brunswick, Maine, which is full of toys, too many books, and the constant chaos of her husband's building projects. She is the mother to four sons ranging in age from fourteen to twenty-four years, and is enjoying the new role of mother-in-law to a current graduate student in marine biology.

Kristen Ghodsee is the John S. Osterweis Associate Professor in Gender and Women's Studies at Bowdoin College. She is the author of *The Red Riviera: Gender, Tourism and Postsocialism on the Black Sea* (2005), *Muslim Lives in Eastern Europe: Gender, Ethnicity and the Transformation of Islam in Postsocialist Bulgaria* (2009), *Lost In Transition: Ethnographies of Everyday Life After Socialism* (2011), and numerous articles on gender, civil society and Eastern Europe. She is the winner of national fellowships from NSF, Fulbright, NCEEER, IREX, and ACLS, as well as the recipient of residential research fellowships at the Woodrow Wilson International Center for Scholars in Washington, DC, the Institute for Advanced Study in Princeton, and the Radcliffe Institute for Advanced Study at Harvard University. Her current research focuses on re-examining the importance of communist women's organizations to the development of the international feminist movement. Kristen and her ever-adventurous daughter, Kristiana, have lived an itinerant existence worthy only of Romani wanderers and Central Asian nomads. Over the last six years, they have settled variously in Brunswick and Falmouth, Maine; Washington, DC; Princeton, New Jersey; Cambridge, Massachusetts; Rostock, Germany; and Sofia, Bulgaria. Although "home" is an ephemeral place, at the very minimum it has always contained a collection of tweed skirt suits, Greek alabaster statues of the Olympian gods, Wonder Woman comic books, and hundreds of Playmobil figurines.